ACCLAIM FOR *SHADOW SISTER*

"*Shadow Sister* plunges readers into the worlds of two very different sisters: Jenna, who ran away from home to escape her past, and Sarah, who stayed home and forgot who she really was. Jones skillfully handles the juxtaposed settings and the sisters' divergent viewpoints to illustrate the way God pulls family back together...even if sometimes it must first be pulled apart." ~ Heather Day Gilbert, Grace-Award winner and best-selling author of *God's Daughter*

"With lyrical prose and a complex cast of characters, *Shadow Sister* tenderly reminds the reader there is hope in the midst of our brokenness. Bravo to Katherine Scott Jones for crafting a beautiful and bittersweet story about letting go of the past and embracing what lies ahead." ~ Heidi McCahan, author of *Unraveled* and *Covering Home*

"A twisting tale of love and betrayal that ends in new beginnings. *Shadow Sister* does not disappoint, satisfying not only the intellect, but the soul as well. Delving deep into issues that cripple families and developing countries, Jones pours God's grace into the nooks and crannies, and then wraps it up in a blanket of forgiveness that warms the reader's heart." ~ Paula Scott, author of *The Mother Keeper*

"A beautiful story of family, love, and hope, *Shadow Sister* is a refreshing story of one woman's journey through loss and heartache to redemption. Jones's ability to create real characters and places will leave you wishing you could roam the streets of Bolivia. It will also open your heart to the marginalized and those serving them. I was left inspired and encouraged. I definitely recommend this book!" ~ Jamie Lapeyrolerie, INSPY Awards advisory-board member

PRAISE FOR *HER MEMORY OF MUSIC*

"*Her Memory of Music* is a nuanced page-turner. In this novel, Jones delivers compelling characters and a story that's hard to put down. She deftly explores complex emotions intertwined with life's dark moments and disappointments." ~ Lisa McKay, Christy-award-nominated author of *My Hands Came Away Red*

"*Her Memory of Music* is so fine-tuned, it reads more like a veteran novelist's tome than a debut. Heavy topics are addressed with a nimble hand, propelling the story's momentum to a riveting climax." ~ Jolina Petersheim, bestselling author of *The Outcast*

"From a fresh, new voice, *Her Memory of Music* has all the elements of a lovely read. Jones weaves a captivating story." ~ Sherri Sand, author of *Leave It to Chance*

"*Her Memory of Music* has so much to love—a charming island setting, a gifted musician, a child at risk, gentle romance and parallel mysteries. It is a grace-filled and entertaining read." ~ Rachel Phifer, author of *The Language of Sparrows*

"In her remarkable debut novel, Katherine Scott Jones captures our universal ache for wholeness." ~ Kim Galgano, speaker, life coach, and author of *The Chance to Choose*

shadow sister

KATHERINE SCOTT JONES

shadow sister

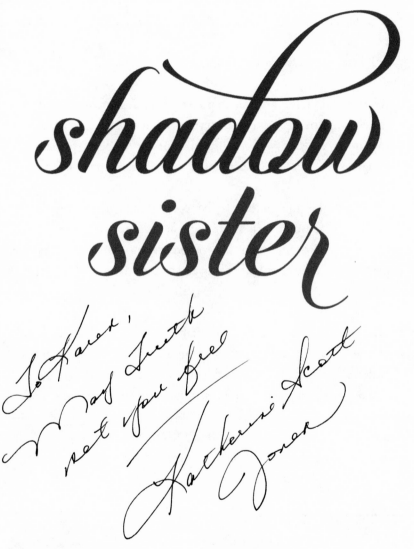

To Karen,
May Truth
set you free

Katherine Scott
Jones

KATHERINE SCOTT JONES

REDEMPTION PRESS

Scripture taken from the HOLY BIBLE, NEW INERNATIONAL VERSION Copyright© 1973, 1978, 1984 International Bible Society. Used by permission of Zondervan Bible Publishers.

ISBN: 978-1-68314-161-7
        978-1-68314-162-4 ePub
        978-1-68314-163-1 Mobi
Cover design: © Jenny Zemanek, Seedlings Design Studio
Library of Congress Catalog Card Number: 2018936377

For those who give their lives
as the hands and feet of Jesus,
whose real stories inspired mine.

"Then you will know the truth,
and the truth will set you free."
~ Jesus, the Gospel of John

PROLOGUE

JENNA
Cortadera, Bolivia
Present day

"Jenna—" Jonas stands from the scuffed table in the smoky hotel restaurant. "Baby, it's time."

At his quiet announcement, I close my journal, cap my pen, and rise. Reaching for the *serape* sling hanging from the back of my chair, I fumble twice before managing to tuck the book and pen inside its folds.

"You okay?" His hand on my waist reaches warmth through my thin blouse.

"Fine." In truth, now the moment has come, my heart races like the trilling notes of a zampona pan-flute. But I meet my husband's espresso-brown gaze, allowing his peace to steady me. Come what may, for better or worse, I'm doing the right thing at last.

No more secrets.

I call to Miski, the golden puppy that's been dozing beneath my chair while I've been sketching and, before that, sharing a feast of fried-egg sandwiches and spiced api with Jonas. Our last meal together for some time. As we leave the hotel restaurant, the sinking September sun casts long, lazy shadows across the cobbled village square. Something tugs on my wrist and I see that a charm from my silver bracelet has snagged on my skirt. "Hold on a sec." I pause in the shade of the porch to untangle it.

"Jenna! Jenn-na!" Dolores, one of the ladies from our women's co-op, hastens toward us in a swirl of red skirt and petticoats.

I tug my bracelet free as Jonas, smiling, takes my bag and hooks it over his shoulder. "I'll ask the driver to wait five minutes," he says.

Smiling back, I quash my private anxieties, then raise a hand to greet Dolores as Miski plops himself across my sandaled foot with a soft, puppy grunt.

"I am glad to see you," Dolores says in Spanish, but then her yellowed smile fades. "I am worried about Matilde." Her youngest daughter soon expects the arrival of her seventh child.

"Is she feeling worse?" I ask, also in Spanish.

"*Así-así*. She is getting very fat. Around the ankles, no? And so tired all the time. Some days, she doesn't make it out of bed until halfway through the morning. This pregnancy, it has not been like the others. But of course, a boy will make them all happy. After six girls, her luck must change, no?" Dolores says all this lightly but a pucker creases her broad brow.

I bite my lip. After little Nora's birth eleven months ago, I carefully explained to Matilde how she could minimize the chance of another baby too soon. But I had the sense even then that Matilde wouldn't listen. She wants so much to make Sixto happy.

Her choice means she hardly gathered strength after Nora's birth before she was pregnant again. Even more troubling, the last time I saw her, she showed continuing signs of anemia and possibly pre-eclampsia. With the nearest hospital four hours away, I dread any kind of complication. *Please, God. Please let Matilde be all right.* I don't think I could stand anything happening to Matilde, the closest thing I have to a best friend in Magdalena.

"Try not to worry." I touch Dolores's arm. "I'll look in on her as soon as I get back. If we need to run some tests, we will." I make a mental note to ask Abby's advice, maybe even call her from Santa Cruz.

But Dolores shakes her head, her thick black braid bouncing on her shoulder. "Is more than that. It's Sixto. He is complaining now because Matilde is gone from the house so much."

I frown. "But Matilde wants to come to class, wants to learn to read. Not only for her sake but for her girls'." And I would encourage her in any way I could. Matilde has so much to offer the community, her agile mind one of the joys of my life. "Would it help if Jonas talked to Sixto?"

Dolores shrugs. "Perhaps. But it might be better for you to talk to Matilde. Maybe you will see her tomorrow?"

"Not tomorrow. I'm on my way home to the States to see my family. I won't be back for a couple of weeks, but Jonas will return to Magdalena tomorrow. I'll ask him to talk to Sixto—and have him check on Matilde's symptoms, too."

Dolores glances toward Jonas, now standing beside the microbus chatting with a man in a dusty black hat. Miski chooses that moment to leave me and gallop across the square, prancing over the man's thick boots before Jonas scoops him into his arms. The other man chuckles, showing crowded, yellow teeth.

Dolores narrows her eyes. "You are going with that man? He is your driver?"

"I guess so. Why?" I study the man. His complexion is coppery-brown, his hairline low, barely an inch or two above coarse, salt-and-pepper eyebrows.

"I know him." Dolores frowns. "He drives too fast; he is not reliable."

I hide a smile. Most drivers in Bolivia have this reputation. "I'm sure he's fine or the bus company would not hire him." I glance again toward the microbus. Jonas has moved to its front fender, Miski tucked like an American football into the crook of one muscled arm. The fading sun burnishes Jonas's beautiful coffee-colored skin as he bows his head, his big hand splayed on the vehicle's rust-splotched hood. "There, see? Jonas is asking God to send His angels to guard us. He is with us."

Dolores sucks in a sharp breath, and by the brows drawn over the kind, black eyes, I sense an argument brewing. But then the older woman's shoulders slump. She seems to realize she can't win an argument against the power of God's angels. "*Bueno.*" Sounding more defeated than reassured. "Then I too will pray."

"*Gracias.*" I catch Jonas's eye as he twirls a finger in the air: *Wrap it up.* I give him a nod, then impulsively lean in to hug Dolores. After a brief hesitation, Dolores hugs me back, tolerant of my American ways. My heart lifts as I breathe in her honest smell of good perspiration and chicken grease. "Tell Matilde I'll see her as soon as I get back. And try not to worry. Both of you."

Dolores nods and pats my shoulder gently. "*Vaya con Dios,*" she murmurs. Go with God.

Jonas climbs into the bus behind me. I ignore the faded stink of sweat, animal musk, and spoiled beer, and lead the way to the very back, where Jonas and I might enjoy a small measure of privacy.

The microbus holds only twelve other passengers. Minutes later, we are crammed in and underway. Turning to peer out the rear window, I wave to Dolores. The woman remains motionless, staring after us until we disappear from sight.

The sun continues its descent behind the Andean foothills, washing the verdant fields in rose and tangerine light. Jonas drapes his arm across the back of my seat, and I lean into him, cradling Miski. The puppy, lulled by the rocking of the vehicle and the security of my lap, falls asleep, twitching occasionally.

I reach into my *aguayo* for my leather-bound journal and turn to the page I was working on, wanting to finish while there is still light. As I balance the book on top of the dozing dog, several slim envelopes slip from its pages and flutter to the floor. I lunge for them, the sudden motion causing Miski to open one brown eye, but Jonas's long arm reaches the envelopes first.

His ebony eyebrows draw together as he recognizes what he holds. "You said you would burn these."

The accusation in his tone makes my toes curl. "I just thought … maybe when I'm home, I can figure out who sent them."

"Knowing won't change anything." And before I can react, he tosses them through the open window.

"Jonas!"

"You're obsessing again after you promised not to."

"But don't you want to know?"

"I don't want to give him the satisfaction of knowing he affected you. Only a coward would pull such a stunt. He's not worth your time."

"It could be a *she*."

"Jenna—"

"Okay! Okay, I know."

"Do you? Baby." His voice gentles as he sandwiches my hand between his. "You've got to stop this. You're going to tell Sarah the truth. After that, whatever this spineless wretch is threatening will have no hold on you. You understand? No hold at all. You'll be free."

I cringe at my husband's words, unable to share his anger. I am actually weirdly relieved at being forced to come clean. I deserve this.

What's happening to me, as wrong and twisted as it seems to Jonas, is justice. He knows the truth now and by God's grace loves me still. But when I tell Sarah … I tremble to think of her reaction.

The notes. They haunt me. The first accusation arrived in my Cortadera post office box a month earlier. The other three awaited me last week. My name and address were typed on the plain white envelopes. No return address. Each bearing the postmark of a different Washington town. The last one contained a demand.

I dissolved into a heap right there in the village square, such a wreck I couldn't even ride my motorbike home. Poor Jonas had to all but carry me back to Magdalena, where I confessed everything.

Well, not everything. Sarah deserves to be the first to know the last chapter of my story. But Jonas knows everything else, all the parts that matter.

I think I hesitated to go to Jonas with the first note because I couldn't imagine who wrote the hateful threats. Partly because I can think of no one who would be so vicious, but mostly because no one knows. *No one.* It is impossible. So a small part of me kept hoping it was some kind of perverse joke.

Now Jonas glances at my open journal. "You're still working on your plans?"

I follow his gaze, glad to talk about something else. On the page are rough sketches, thumbnails outlining several murals I hope will someday grace a new literacy center in Cortadera. "I thought I'd show Sarah my ideas while I'm home. See if she'll consider coming to paint them for me."

"But she stopped painting, didn't she? After her … after the accident."

"Yes, but I keep hoping a project like this might convince her to start again." I trace my fingers over what I've drawn. Mine are only crude sketches, but in my sister's hands, they will become master-pieces. And then …

In my heart of hearts lives a prayer I barely dare whisper even to myself. If Sarah paints these murals, I'll see it as a sign. A sign that she has really, truly forgiven me.

Jonas's talk of the literacy center reminds me of my conversation with Dolores. "By the way, can you check in on Matilde while I'm gone? We may need to run some tests. And keep an eye on Sixto. Dolores told me he's giving Matilde grief again over coming to my classes."

"Did she also tell you they can't use their well anymore?"

His faintly derisive tone puzzles me. What isn't he saying? Then I straighten. "Did someone damage their hand pump?"

"The handle and head assembly didn't just walk off by them-selves."

Without a handle and head assembly, a pump is useless. "Why didn't you tell me earlier?"

"You had enough on your mind."

Sixto. Impatience tightens a cord inside me. Why can't he see that easy access to clean water makes life better not only for his wife but for the whole family? This isn't about just Matilde.

"No, Dolores didn't tell me that. Neither did Matilde. She doesn't like me thinking badly about her husband. So, what can we do?"

Jonas leans his head back, rubs his forehead. "I could use some help repairing our solar panel. I'll ask Sixto to lend me a hand. Give us a chance to talk without coming across like I'm preaching."

I nod, knowing it's the best he can do. Change comes so pain-fully slowly down here, even good change, which is often met with suspicion simply because it's different. And not just in the lives of the women. Jonas faces similar challenges getting the men in the agricultural co-op to buy into his ideas for new crops or genetically-engineered seeds.

Fingering the silver charms of my bracelet like beads on a rosary, I think of everyone's hope that Matilde will give birth to a boy. *Please God, let it be a boy.* It's a frivolous prayer, but I'm unable to help the hope that the addition of a boy to the family will distract Sixto from his simmering resentment over his wife's determination to make a better life for herself and their girls.

The constant jarring makes it impossible to add to my sketches, so I close my journal as the sun slides behind the horizon, leaving a rolling landscape illuminated only by the light of a full moon. We are climbing into the foothills now. Nestling against Jonas, I savor the solid strength of him. Three years of digging wells and hauling stone have given my husband a physique Hugh Jackman would envy. "I'll miss you."

He presses a kiss into my hair. "Don't stay away too long."

"I won't. I have to be back for Matilde's baby, remember?" The bus jerks as our driver avoids one of a thousand potholes that mark the narrow, winding road. The motion jolts me against Jonas, but then our progress smooths and I close my eyes.

Suddenly I'm awakened by a violent lurch. I struggle upright. "Where are we?"

"Been descending a while." Jonas raises his voice against the shriek of brakes as the bus resists the pull of the steep switchback. "I'd say we're still a couple of hours from Santa Cruz, but I'm not sure. Can't see much out there."

The tension in his voice causes an anxious tingling to spread across my skin. I attempt to see past the other passengers to the road ahead, illuminated only by the headlights. "He's going awfully fast, isn't he?" Miski, oblivious, snores softly in my lap.

Jonas tries to smile, squeezes my hand. "Faster than I would like, but he knows these roads better than we do."

A frisson of fear shoots down my spine as I hear the echo of my conversation with Dolores. "Should we ask him to stop? Take a break?"

"It's fine. Go back to sleep if you can. We'll be there soon."

I know I won't sleep now, but so that Jonas won't worry, I rest my head once more on his shoulder and cup Miski's soft little rump in my palm, trying to draw from the puppy's trusting calm. We are traveling a series of switchbacks to get through an Andean pass. With every turn, the motion throws us sideways.

A fresh lick of apprehension brings perspiration to the surface of my skin. Inside the bus, the air goes thick and heavy. For the first time, I notice the absolute silence of the other passengers. *Please, God, keep us safe. Please, God, oh, please.* My prayer becomes a mantra.

We ride for another ten minutes in tense silence. After cresting another small summit, a new descent begins. The rhythmic squawk of brakes at every turn punctuates the dead quiet. I begin to relax. The driver has slowed. We've made it past the worst. I turn to say so to Jonas when a shout opens up the night.

For one split-second, I feel a curious thrill of weightlessness as we hurtle off the road into blackness. A terrifying crunch, the bus landing nose first. Momentum pitching us tail over head. Down the mountain. Glass shatters. Bodies tangle. I am propelled though cold mountain air.

And then—I'm not. I open my eyes, sensing the passage of time. How much time? I feel oddly weighted, as if I've been lying still for hours, but perhaps it has been only seconds. I am on my back. Pain rips up my spine. A silent scream fills my head as I try to writhe away from the searing agony. Why won't my body respond to my brain?

I become aware of other noises in the dark. A distant scream. A moan, then a liquid gurgle. Jonas? I will my hand to reach for him but nothing happens. I cannot move.

Cannot move? *Oh God … Oh God!*

Panic bubbles. I struggle to draw breath. *Oh God, where's Jonas?* My lips part to call his name. *Jonas, come to me!* But all that emerges is an animal groan.

Then another sound, not far away. The soft whimper of a puppy. Miski. Miski is hurt. *Oh, sweetie, you need your mama. Come here to me, Miski. Come to me!* My eyes fill with tears that slide into my hair.

I hear my name. Jonas, a wire of panic threading his voice. And then—*oh, thank you, Jesus!*—there he is, hovering over me, blocking the glare of the moon. Oh, beloved face! Looking so worried! Blood seeps from a gash on his forehead, his eyelashes are wet with it. From the way he holds his arm, I know he is hurt. But why does he look so worried? He need not be worried, not now that he has found me.

In another moment, I'll sit up, take Jonas's hand. Together, we'll find Miski. Then we'll help all the others who are hurt. Just as soon as I catch my breath …

Jonas curls over me, presses his mouth to mine. He blows out a puff of air, my chest rising as his warm breath fills me, strangely comforting. Intimate. And then—oh merciful God!—the pain disappears. Like that, gone. *Oh Jesus, You are so good.* I sense His presence as surely as if He is sitting on the scabby ground beside me. I feel bathed in warmth. He is near. So near! I've known His presence often here in this land, want others to know it too. These people who love stories so.

What a story I'll have to tell them now.

CHAPTER 1

SARAH
Selah, Washington
Present day

S he can't breathe.

Weight, cold and black, crushes her chest, only moments after a terrible roar rent the thin mountain air, drowning terrified shouts. Now silence reigns. And pain. In the chaotic tumble of snow and debris, she had the presence of mind to let go of her ski poles and wrap her arms around her head. But the tiny pocket of oxygen she created quickly becomes toxic, filling with her own expended breath. Every limb screams. She longs to cry out. To find TJ. She wills her legs to move. An unseen grip holds her fast.

Something wet slides across her cheek.

Sarah jerks upright, gasping. She stares blindly into the darkness of her bedroom, disoriented, until she recognizes the jagged rasps tearing into the silence as her own gulps for air. *Breathe, Sarah. Just breathe. Dear Jesus, help …*

She struggles onto an elbow, instinctively reaching for the gold cross at her neck, twisting its chain as she practices the breathing technique they taught her in rehab. Slow and rhythmic. Gradually, her pulse slows, her panic ebbs. Relief and anguish rush to fill the void. She's thankful to be alive but crushed all over again to find TJ gone, leaving her alone, no one but herself to blame.

She blinks and sees the faint outline of her chocolate lab's head at the edge of her bed, his warm muzzle only inches from her face. Her thrashing about must have worried him. "Cork?" she manages, freeing her legs from the tangled sheet. He pants softly, amber eyes boring into hers. "I'm fine, fella, just one of my dreams. Go back to bed." She points to his overstuffed cushion on the floor, and when he doesn't budge, repeats, "Cork, bed."

He whines and backs toward the door. Still wrapped in the shroud of her nightmare, she doesn't move until he whines again, adding a low growl for emphasis.

"You need to go out?" Her left knee aches as her toes touch the floor, an everyday reminder that her dream is not just a dream. The floorboards cool her feet as she crosses the room. No sooner has she opened the door a crack than Cork shoots past her. But he doesn't head for the wide, banistered staircase. Instead, he darts toward Jenna's old room, paws at the closed door.

Weird. It's like he knows Jenna is coming home tomorrow. Then it dawns on her: *she's already here.*

Of course. How like Jenna to take a different flight, hire a cab from the airport, and sneak home earlier than expected. To catch them all unawares.

A spark of mischief she's not felt in years ripples through Sarah as she contemplates this chance to foil her sister's surprise. Cork looks back at her, cocking his head, imploring her to hurry. Quietly, so as not to alert Jenna, she opens the door. Cork brushes hard against her bad knee as he darts past, making her grab the doorjamb for support.

Holding her breath, she waits, imagining Jenna relaxed in sleep, anticipating her shout as Cork pounces.

But her expectation is met by silence.

She pushes wide the door. Moonlight slants across Jenna's empty bed, its green and violet pinwheel quilt smooth and neat.

Swallowing disappointment, Sarah scans the room for any sign of Jenna's presence. Nothing. Her belongings remain just as she left them years before, from the pillows lined up on the window seat to the rows of thick, non-fiction titles marching across the shelves. As Sarah crosses the threshold, a draft brushes her bare arms, strangely warm given the window opened to the cool, September night.

Cork runs a tight circle and leaps onto the bed. "Cork!" she hisses, not wanting to wake Dad, who sleeps across the hall. "Get down." In the Lanning house, dogs on beds are strictly *verboten*, although Sarah has long suspected Jenna breaks this rule. Cork ignores her command, so she snaps her fingers and tries again. "Down!"

He paws the quilt and whimpers.

A mental picture of Nana's shredded heirloom flashes before Sarah as she hooks her finger inside Cork's collar and tugs.

He stiffens his limbs, digging in.

She lets go and glares at him. "What is *wrong* with you?"

She leans down and tries scooping him into her arms, but he drops to the bed, a limp, dead-weight she's unable to shift. She straightens and lifts the edge of the quilt to drag it off the bed, beast and all. Cork's lips flutter over bared teeth, a low growl erupting inside his chest.

What the heck? She stumbles backward, staring at the dog until he ducks his head and whines. Relieved, she approaches again and strokes his fur, but when she reaches for his collar, he whips his head and shows his teeth.

Sarah backs to the window and narrows her eyes at him, rubbing her arms against the chill flooding the room. She turns and lowers the sash several inches.

In Silverwood's fields beyond the courtyard, the full moon illuminates rows of chardonnay vines in opulent display. Beyond them stand the syrah vines, then the cabernet, all heavy with ripe fruit. It won't be long now, a month at the most, until they start moving their people through those acres, divesting them of their treasure.

The silvery light slanting through Jenna's window captures an object on top of the bookshelves in a muted glow: a carved mahogany box the size of a bread loaf.

She remembers this box well. A fiercely guarded gift from Dad to Jenna on her tenth birthday. It features clusters of grapes carved into all four sides and the Lanning family crest on top. Its lock opens with a tiny, old-fashioned key, whose hiding place Sarah has never found.

She picks up the box. Something inside slides and rattles. Out of habit she tries the lid, but as usual, it holds fast. The box leaves a waxy residue on her fingertips. The whole room smells of orange peel and furniture polish, evidence that Ana has been in here, preparing the room for Jenna's arrival.

The prodigal daughter returning home.

To the equally proverbial delighted father.

Her insides lurch, signaling the familiar internal tug-of-war that begins whenever she considers the uneven tripod that remains of their family. Dad. Jenna. Herself.

Somehow, whenever Jenna is around, Sarah ends up the short leg.

What reason does she have to believe this time will be any different? Since Jenna called last week to request a plane ticket home, Dad's been over the moon at the thought of seeing his beloved daughter again. Though Jenna didn't give any hint of her long-term plans, he's already asked Sarah to include her in the upcoming Harvest Festival. He could hardly stop smiling in anticipation.

A qualm settles in Sarah's stomach as she wonders again why her sister is breaking her self-imposed exile—and what it might mean for her. Will this be when she knows at last that Jenna has forgiven her? She presses a hand over her heart, as if to relieve the ache that throbs beneath her skin whenever she thinks about Jenna's leaving. Will the sting of rejection ever fade?

A breeze ruffles the sheer drapes framing the window, drawing her attention once more to the vines awaiting harvest. When Mom was alive, she liked to say that each bottle of every vintage had its own unique character. The amount of sun and rain in any particular season gave grapes an indefinable quality, a *goût de terroir*, the taste of the land. No other grapes in the world tasted the same, and thus, no wine did either.

She also said the best wines, like the truest, noblest characters, were produced under stress. Pamper a vine and you'd get a soft grape: flabby, without the necessary acid to form the backbone found in the best wines. On the other hand, too much deprivation led to death. But the right amount of drought, when the vine had to cast its roots down … down … summoning all its strength and will to survive—those vines were capable of creating a wine able to hold its own among the finest in the world.

Sarah sighs, her heart squeezing again. Probably a good thing Mom didn't live to see what happened between her and Jenna. How the cord of family loyalty that bound them from childhood began to fray soon after Mom died. Then snapped completely when Jenna left the vineyard for Bolivia six years ago, an absence broken only once, two years later. Mom would have grieved to know they'd hardly spoken in all that time.

It doesn't have to be this way. Not anymore.

The voice sounds only inside her head, yet it's clearly Jenna's. The *old* Jenna. The before-Mom-died Jenna, her timbre wry and husky, as if every word verged on a good laugh. So vivid that the hairs on Sarah's neck tingle and she turns to see if her first assumption was correct and Jenna has made it home after all.

"Jen?" She whispers the name aloud, but all she hears is the pounding of blood in her ears. Jenna isn't here, but in a jiu-jitsu move so like her sister, Sarah's apprehension flips into anticipation. Hope swells inside her chest.

This visit will be different, she can feel it. She may not be able to bring TJ back and undo the harm she caused, but she can at least repair what's broken between her and her sister. Can't she? *Yes.*

She replaces Jenna's box on the shelf and turns to look at the dog. Cork stares back from the bed, unblinking. Jenna's bedside clock reads 2:42. In a few hours, she'll have to be up for another long day, and she's too drained to fight with her unaccountably feral dog. His immobility forces her decision. Nana's quilt will have to take its chances.

Back in her room, Sarah pulls the covers to her chin and closes her eyes.

Downstairs, the phone rings.

$\mathscr{C}$HAPTER 2

Two rings. Three.
Jenna.

Propelled by inexplicable dread, Sarah swings from the bed and hastens toward the stairs. There is no light, no sound from Dad's room as she passes his door. And then, just as she touches the glossy banister, the ringing stops. Too soon for the call to have rolled to voicemail. Sarah freezes, listening into the silence, her ears reaching for a familiar voice. Their landline has only three extensions: in her downstairs office, in Dad's office, and in Vina and Tomaso's bedroom behind the kitchen.

Only the rhythmic work of Mom's grandfather clock sounds in the foyer below, counting off the seconds. Relief sighs between Sarah's lips. Wrong number? *Must be*, she breathes, her heart rate slowing as she finds her way back to bed.

But wakefulness lingers and sleep doesn't claim her until dawn touches the sky.

"I've heard their winemaker is absolutely incredible."

The comment catches the corner of Sarah's ear, pulling her from sleep-deprived malaise. She's clearing a table in the dining room following the lunch rush and slows down to shamelessly eavesdrop on two women finishing salads at a nearby table.

"They say he's something of a prodigy," her companion adds. "He's not even thirty."

The pair look like they might be mother and daughter, both carefully blond, flashing trendy boots and designer bags. Coasties from Seattle, probably. Day-tripping into wine country.

The younger one continues. "The article said he's the reason Silverwood's won all their awards lately. His red blends put them on the map."

They're speaking of Shane. Sarah wonders which article the woman read. Both *The Seattle Times* and *Washington Wine* magazine have recently sent out reporters. She smiles as she picks up the tray of soiled dishes. Perhaps she'll pass along this conversation next time she sees him. He'd certainly love to hear it. Then again, maybe she won't. Dad keeps his ego plenty well stoked as it is.

On her return from the kitchen, she pauses at the console in the foyer and turns down the jazz piped into the dining area. The salad ladies are the last of the noontime crowd. At half past two, it's unlikely the restaurant will be getting many more for lunch.

Vina works near the enormous stone fireplace, angling her wide hips between the polished bistro tables as she straightens silverware and refreshes candles for the dinner hour. She and Tomaso have worked for Dad from the time Sarah and Jenna were toddlers—Tomaso as their field manager, Vina as housekeeper and catering manager.

When Vina catches her eye, Sarah crosses the room to join her.

"Have you had a chance to look over the Festival menu?" Vina removes two spent candles from a table and replaces them with fresh ones.

"Haven't been at my desk today, but I'll get there as soon as we finish here." A busload of tourists had pulled into the drive at ten o'clock and another right before lunch. The steady stream of customers kept all hands on deck at both the tasting counter and in the dining room until now. "I'll take a look and run it by Dad for final approval. Is there something in particular you wanted to know?"

"The sweet potato gnocchi. Your father added that last night but didn't say whether he wanted chardonnay or pinot gris for the pairing."

Sweet potato gnocchi in sherry cream sauce with sage. Jenna's favorite, no doubt ordered by Dad in honor of her homecoming. Despite Sarah's earlier optimism, something unpleasant scrapes along her sternum. Has Dad ever included *her* favorites on a Festival menu? Then she scolds herself. She's not the daughter who hasn't been home in four years. "I suspect he'll want the chard," she says, "but I'll ask."

"*Bueno.*"

Warmth kisses Sarah's spirit as Vina's kind glance grazes her face. Vina understands Sarah's ambivalence regarding Jenna's return and doesn't think any the less of her for it.

"*¿Y la música?*"

"*Uno más en la mañana,*" Sarah replies, lapsing into the familiar tongue. Another jazz combo is coming tomorrow to audition for Festival weekend, though Sarah is fairly certain the one she heard yesterday will get the gig. "After that, I think we're set."

Cork wanders in from the patio, where he's been sunning himself on the warm pavers. When Sarah awakened this morning after oversleeping her alarm, she found someone had let him out of Jenna's room. Dad, most likely, probably wondering how Cork got trapped inside. She'd poked her head around Jenna's door, relieved to find Nana's quilt none the worse for wear. All day Cork has behaved as if nothing happened in the wee hours, barking at busses and greeting visitors with his usual tail-waving aplomb.

He pads over. As she bends to stroke his silky ears, she remembers what she meant to ask Vina. "Did that wrong number this morning awaken you and Tomaso?"

"Wrong number?" Vina's lined brow furrows. "When?"

"Super early, three-ish? You didn't hear it?"

She shakes her head, smiles wryly. "Not that I would, above Tomaso's snores. I'm sorry it woke you."

"It didn't. This fella already had me awake." She gives Cork's ear a tug. "I was glad it was a wrong number, actually. I thought it might have been about Jenna."

"Why would you think that?"

She shrugged, recalling the dread that drove her from her bed. "Just a feeling."

"I guess the phone ringing at three in the morning always makes us imagine the worst."

"I suppose so." Through the window, Sarah watches a red VW pull into the circular drive. "Customer. I'll take care of it." She starts toward the foyer to greet the newcomer.

A woman in slim jeans and a yellow, gauzy blouse pushes through the heavy double doors, swiping off her shades as she enters. As their eyes meet, Sarah pulls up short. "Kellie?"

"Sarah, hi." She seems unsurprised to see her. She smiles and glides forward with a ready hug. "How long has it been, like a million years?"

Sarah squeezes her lightly and steps back, returning her smile. "You look great."

"So do you." Half-a-lifetime ago, they attended Central Washington University together. "And wow, this place is amazing." Kellie tucks her sunglasses into her short, black curls and glances around, taking in the maple-wood tasting counter, the half-brick walls and wine-red wainscoting, the dining room with its classic Italian decor. She gestures at the luminous mural gracing the wall above the tasting counter. "Is that your work?"

"No, it's my mom's." She points to the *trompe l'oiel* clusters of grapes painted on every beam and above every doorway to give the illusion of an arbor. "That too."

"They look so real." Kellie glances at the wash rag in Sarah's hand. "You work here now?"

"Work, eat, breathe. And sometimes sleep."

Kellie tips her head. "You ever make it to Italy?"

"Nope." Sarah drops the rag behind the hostess podium. "How about you?"

"I was hoping to go my senior year before I realized a degree in graphic arts would pay the bills better." Her gaze slides sideways to the narrow rack where Vina displays various homemade condiments and vine-related knick knacks for sale. She picks up a jar of Vina's syrah pepper jelly, glances at the label, cups the jar in both hands. "I heard about the accident, Sarah. I know it was a long time ago, but I'm really sorry. About TJ and ... what happened to you."

"Thanks." Not quite meeting Kellie's eye. Wondering, as always, how much outsiders know of the truth. TJ was Kellie's friend too. Does she realize his death was Sarah's fault?

Kellie replaces the jelly on the shelf. "Did you ever go back? To school, I mean?"

Sarah shakes her head.

"Why not?"

"I was in physical therapy for nearly six months. By the time I figured out how to walk again, I'd missed so much school that it didn't seem worth picking up where I'd left off."

"Must have been hard."

"It was." She shrugs. "But as you can see, there's always plenty to do around here, especially since Jenna left. I haven't been bored." She glances toward the counter. "I suppose you're here for a tasting? Or lunch? The kitchen closes in a few minutes, but I'm sure I could squeeze you in."

"I'm looking for Shane, actually. Shane Ferrell? He's expecting me."

"Shane is?"

"I bumped into him recently, and he mentioned you're looking for a new webmaster. I'm applying for the job."

"Oh." Shane hasn't mentioned opening a new position. Shouldn't he have talked it over with her and Dad? Sunnie wasn't leaving to get married for another four months. Then again, maybe he did discuss it with Dad, who seems to be counting on Shane for more and more these days.

The pause lengthens. "So," Kellie prompts. "Do you know where I'll find him?"

"I'd try his office." Sarah points across the courtyard to the small, stone building that is both his sleeping quarters and work space. "That one, just beyond the stables."

"Thanks." Kellie turns to go. "Good to see you again, Sarah. Maybe we'll be seeing more of each other. If things work out."

"Sure." She watches Kellie leave, tall and confident, her black heeled boots tapping in regular rhythm across the brick-paved courtyard. Sarah heads in the opposite direction, skirting a blue Miata on her way to the house and her own office, where a mound of work awaits her.

Kellie's words linger as Sarah passes from the molten September heat into the coolness of the indoors, adding to the niggling unease that's dogged her since Cork's early morning awakening. She doesn't usually waste time looking back, but today a gray cloud of regret descends. Maybe because Kellie's words tangle with her own thoughts. *Once upon a time, Sarah, you had dreams bigger than anyone's.*

And they didn't include dropping out of college to work at her father's vineyard.

CHAPTER 3

Kellie might be an unexpected trigger, but this time of year usually brought Sarah face-to-face with the ghost of her old dreams. Until she was twenty, harvest always coincided with a new school year, which she anticipated as greatly as she did grape harvest. But six years have passed since she last returned to school in September.

Time to get over it.

Years ago, she determined to launch herself into the art world, as Mom had. And like Mom, she would start in Europe. Sarah's ambitions seemed more achievable with every passing year. Her paintings began placing at national art competitions, even winning a few local commissions. But could a girl from Selah, Washington, really compete with trained artists from New York and Paris and Rome? Mom always said, "Start where you are," adding that dreams were limited only by the scope of imagination. After Mom died, Sarah's living out that dream seemed the best way to honor her memory.

On her way to her office, Sarah glances into the living room. A framed family portrait graces the space above the fireplace mantel. She's looked at it without really seeing it almost every day for the last twenty years. Mom painted it from a photo taken on their family's last trip to Provence. In it, Dad stands beside Mom, at the time barely older than Sarah is now. Tucked against her sides are two small girls, one with hair like molten honey, the other's the shade of autumn leaves. The lively glint in Mom's eyes belies the serene Mona Lisa smile on her lips.

The day stands out vividly in Sarah's memory. Mom had made a picnic dinner, and the sun cast long shadows across the lavender fields surrounding the vineyard where they stayed. She and Jenna chased each other while their parents chatted and sipped wine over a meal of rustic bread, brie, and fresh strawberries.

Then Sarah tripped over an exposed root.

"Mama, Sarah got hurt." Jenna, her little girl voice piping and worried.

"And you brought her to me, good girl. Good big sister, looking out for baby girl. Come here, Sarah-love, let Mama kiss away the hurt."

Jenna, pride and worry mingling on her small, oval face, holding Sarah's hand, Mom washing and salving her stinging knee.

"That's my girl." Dad crouching beside them both, touching Jenna's auburn tresses. "Looking out for your sister. Blood is blood, right? Yours is hers, and hers is yours."

Mama glancing up. "Harrison, really. It's just a scratch."

"And thank God for that. But it doesn't hurt to be reminded of what matters." Dad pulling Jenna to him, embracing her. "My girls should know they're Lannings to the core."

Sarah moves into the north wing, where she and Dad have their offices. Behind his closed door, she hears the murmur of male voices—his and Beck Lawson's, their attorney. It dawns on her: it's Beck's Miata parked in their circular drive. He usually postpones official visits until after harvest, when it's not so crazy-busy. But of course Beck is much more than their family attorney. Though a decade older than Dad, the two men are good friends. He's always been more like a favorite uncle to her and Jenna.

And, she recalls, he hasn't yet told her the name of his plus-one for the Festival.

She taps on the door. The voices stop. She is about to try the door when it opens. Beck's lean frame blocks her view of the room. She smiles. "Just the man I wanted to see. You never did tell me who you're bringing this weekend."

He doesn't answer, doesn't smile.

Her own wavers. "Beck?"

He steps into the hallway, shutting the door behind him. "Sarah." His face grows mottled. His hazel eyes, already red-rimmed, take on a strange sheen.

"What's wrong?" Her heart starts to pound. "Tell me."

"I'm afraid we have some bad news." He swallows. "Terrible news."

"It's Jenna, isn't it?"

His eyes tell the truth.

Dear Jesus. "Something bad has happened." Her mouth cracks with sudden dryness. "Is she hurt?"

Slowly, Beck shakes his head. "She's dead, Sarah." His face crumples. "Your sister is dead."

Sarah's world tilts as the words sink in and reverberate through her body. Jenna. Dead. *No. No, no, no, no.*

Beck catches her to him, the pulse at his neck thrumming wildly beneath her cheek. He wraps his arms around her. She presses into him, a sob catching in her throat.

She has no idea how long they stand like this. Everything feels locked into place: the knot she cannot swallow, her insides as hard and cold as ice, only her heart beating hotly at the center.

When she finally pulls back to look into Beck's suntanned face, she finds it pale. "It happened last night, didn't it?"

"Sometime before midnight, we think." His reddish-blond eyebrows draw together. "How did you know?"

"Someone called." Her scalp prickles.

"What?"

"The phone rang early this morning. It stopped before I could answer, but it was about Jenna, I know it was. I couldn't get downstairs quick enough to answer, so they hung up." If only she'd checked Caller ID. She thought to, but something held her back. A fear to be proven right? "I knew. I tried not to know, but deep down I did."

His chiseled features soften and he touches her cheek. "You two always did have that kind of connection."

It isn't true—hasn't been for many years—but she lets the comment go. "How—?"

"A bus accident. Others were killed too, many more injured." His fingers skim her cheek again. "I'm sorry to be the one to tell you."

Her eyes widen. "Dad," she whispers, moving toward the closed door of the study.

"Sarah." Beck grips her arm, stopping her. "Before you talk to your dad, there's something else you should know."

The door opens, and there is Shane, cell phone in hand. She draws back, shocked. Has he been with Dad the whole time? Did Dad tell Shane the news before telling *her*?

Her insides twist. It's one thing for Shane to be Dad's right-hand man in business matters, but this is *personal*. She pushes past Shane into her father's study, where he stands hunched against the fireplace, his back to the door. "Dad?"

His wide shoulders shudder before he turns and opens his arms. "Sarah."

She goes to him. Though she may never be his number-one, he's the only dad she has.

Dad repeats her name, his voice breaking. "We've lost her, Sarah. We've lost Jenna too."

"I know, Dad. I know." Tears rising, she presses her cheek against his chest hard enough for a button on his shirt pocket to embed in her skin.

His arms tighten around her. "And you have to bring her home."

She stills. "What?"

Behind her, Beck speaks. "Harrison, I didn't have the chance to tell her."

She turns, stares at Beck, a part of her brain registering that Shane has left the room. "Tell me what?"

Beck sighs. "Jenna left some instructions. In the event of her death."

"Instructions?"

"For you."

"Me?" For some unknown reason, her heart starts hammering.

"Jenna asked that you be the one to go to Bolivia to retrieve her belongings," Beck says. "To claim her—her remains. And scatter her ashes there."

"Though I still say that part's up for—"

"Harrison." Beck shakes his head, his expression pained. "Please."

Sarah can't take it in. "She asked for me?"

Beck nods. "She never mentioned this?"

"I—we've hardly spoken in the last six years. Are you sure?"

"She asked for you, and you alone." Beck passes a hand over his eyes.

Her head spins. It makes no sense. Why would Jenna do this? "When?"

"When did she leave her instructions?"

"No, when do I have to leave?"

"As soon as we can make arrangements."

She sits down, hard, on the cold, stone hearth.

"Harrison, you're not really going to let her do this." It's Shane, reappearing. He's perspiring slightly, his light-blue polo shirt sticking to his frame. "Even if you consider it, she certainly can't do it alone."

"Why shouldn't she?" Dad sinks into the chair behind his desk. "It's what her sister wanted."

Beck breaks in. "Perhaps this whole discussion should wait until—"

"It's not going to get any easier discussing it later." Shane cuts him off, color deepening his ruddy complexion. "Sarah is an inexperienced traveler grieving the loss of her sister. You haven't thought this through." Shane joins her at the hearth, pulling her limp hand into his. She has to resist pulling away. They've dated some, but this protectiveness seems a little out of line. "She'll be traveling the same roads Jenna was when she was killed. You'd be taking a terrible chance for no good reason."

"It's what Jenna wanted," Dad repeats.

Their words come to her, garbled and blurry, as if she's hearing them from underwater. She knows she should be comforted to have Shane rising to her defense. Instead, she feels diminished. Doesn't he think her capable? Her gaze fastens on a framed photograph on her father's desk, the one of their family from which Mom painted the portrait in the living room. *Blood is blood ...*

"Sarah?" Shane's hand tightens on hers. She realizes he's asked her a question.

She ignores him, looking at Beck. "Where is Jenna now?"

He looks startled. "Her body?"

"Yes."

"Still at the hospital, along with those who were injured. She was traveling with a companion who survived, though they say he's seriously injured."

Shane shifts and she meets his eyes. Something flickers in the depths of his gaze, there and gone too fast to name. As his features twist, she knows he's in genuine distress. *He's trying to be kind. To protect me.* She softens, squeezing his hand before letting go. "What if Shane went with me?"

Beck shakes his head. "Jenna specifically wanted you to go alone."

"Why?"

"I don't know."

"I already told you, it's ridiculous." Shane stands, and she has the sudden conviction they were arguing about this when she knocked on Dad's door. "Harrison, you must see that. You have to let me go, too."

Her father holds up a hand. "No, Shane, what we have to do is let Sarah go. Alone."

"But why?"

"Because Sarah is a Lanning." He rises from his desk, his gaze settling on her like a mantle. "And Lannings take care of their own."

CHAPTER 4

JENNA
Age 15
Selah, Washington

Music exploded from the mariachi band, blasting brassy tunes from the dais on the patio. Feeling especially pretty in the full-skirted, off-the-shoulder white dress that showed off my tan, I weaved my way among the scores of people who had turned out to celebrate my fifteenth birthday. Everyone was there: my friends from school, all the vineyard staff, even the migrant workers who had stayed over for the year. The cloth-draped gift table overflowed with wrapped packages. Grown-ups with glasses of wine in one hand and napkins of appetizers in the other wandered from the dining room to the patio, where TJ and Sarah were laughing over some shared joke as they lit lanterns against the deepening dusk.

Mom caught my eye and winked, knowing how much I enjoyed the attention. Vina had been the one to persuade Dad to throw me this *fiesta de quinceañera*. He normally didn't go for the whole His-panic-tradition thing, but she, and then Mom, had told him that throwing his daughter a Sweet Fifteen party and inviting the staff as guests would go a long way toward establishing good relationships.

At the tasting counter, beneath Mom's mural of Jesus at the wed-ding at Cana, Beck nursed a glass of chardonnay, alone. His wife, Susan, who'd been sick for as long I could remember, had died only three months ago. Now Beck visited the vineyard way more than he used to, sometimes simply to play poker and shoot the breeze with Dad over a bottle of wine.

Mom returned from the kitchen with a full platter of goodies, pausing to let me have first pick. I plucked a bacon-wrapped scallop from the tray and popped it into my mouth.

"Having fun?" Mom's caramel-colored eyes danced, knowing the answer.

I nodded, my mouth too full to speak.

"Enjoy the moment. It's yours." Tipping up on her toes—last summer I'd grown two inches taller than she—Mom kissed my cheek before gliding off. Swallowing my bite, I glanced toward Beck again and found his gaze following my mother's passage through the crowd. I frowned. I'd started noticing how often Beck hung around when Mom was nearby. Did Dad notice it too? Mom didn't seem to. She never paid more attention to Beck than she did anyone else who worked for Silverwood. Beck better be careful, I thought. Dad wouldn't like it if he got too friendly with Mom. Even if he did play poker with him.

Of course, Dad could handle himself and anyone else in his fam-ily who needed help. He prided himself on that.

I dismissed the thought and went to find my friends, who were hanging out on the far side of the patio where the soft-drinks table stood.

When the sun disappeared behind the Cascades, Dad bounded up to the dais and grabbed the mic to announce time for gifts. For the next hour, I opened package after package, the mound of discarded wrappings and ribbons growing beside me. Books, clothing, music, gift cards. Mom kept track of every item so I could write proper thank-you notes later.

Finally, the table was empty. "That's it?" Dad feigned dismay.

"That's it." I sighed, playing along because I knew he wasn't done yet.

"Hm. Not quite." And he drew from behind his back a long, slim package wrapped in lavender, my favorite color. "Happy birthday, Jenna-girl."

After carefully undoing the white bow, I slipped the paper off the box. Inside laid a slender silver chain graced with a single charm, gleaming in the lantern light. "Oh, Daddy!"

"Like it?"

"It's gorgeous."

"Let me put it on you." His big hands handled the tiny chain with surprising ease as he secured the bracelet around my wrist. The feather-light weight of the jewelry felt deliciously delicate against my skin. "Who's Daddy's number-one girl?" he murmured, for no one's ears but mine.

"I am."

"And what do Lannings do?"

"We take care of our own."

He kissed my cheek. "Don't ever forget it."

CHAPTER 5

SARAH
Selah, Washington
Present day

When she thinks back on it, Sarah remembers the details around Mom's death as if viewed through thick, warped glass. She remembers coming home from school that day to a house utterly silent except for Vina's quiet weeping, knowing by the way her scalp prickled that something was terribly wrong. She remembers her father's absence, Beck's unsteady but kind hand on her shoulder, Jenna's silence. The rest of it slips into nothingness. She doesn't remember how she slept through that first night or whether she did at all. She doesn't remember when her father came home from the hospital without Mom.

It was different after TJ died. With her own life tipped in such precarious balance, she didn't even know about his funeral until weeks after it happened. She lived in a kind of bubble, insulated from her grief. Until that bubble popped.

In the days after Jenna's death, though, she lives each hour in sharp relief. Every sound, scent, and sight launches an assault on her senses. The sun's glare pinches her eyes shut whenever she walks outside. A hawk's piercing scream scrapes her nerves. The grit of dust carried by the dry September breezes gathers on her tongue. When she was younger, her awareness of these details would have demanded expression, launching a painting spree. Now, every stabbing detail only serves to remind her that the world is an unfriendly place with Jenna eternally gone from it.

The evening before her flight to Bolivia, Sarah finds herself heading toward the stables at the edge of the courtyard. Mom designed the building after she married Dad. Until then, Lannings didn't keep horses. But Mom was an indefatigable equestrian. She would have slept on a horse if she could. She designed the stables to resemble an Old World carriage house, built of rough-hewn planks and stones. Though once home to half-a-dozen steeds, now only Sassy Britches, Mom's favorite, and Old Romeo, Tomaso's faithful mount, remain.

Stepping through the doorway, Sarah draws a lungful of hay-scented air, eyeing the tack draped on wall-pegs and the freshly swept cement floor. Double doors on either end stand open, allowing a fragrant draft of clean horse sweat and leather to flow through the structure.

Despite the passage of years, Mom's presence still lingers here, comforting Sarah.

Cork trots beside her, happy to be with her in this familiar place. She pauses at Romeo's stall to feed him an apple from a nearby barrel. Then she continues on to Sassy. The horse turns her sleek head as Sarah approaches, nickering when she holds out the fruit. The velvet fuzz of Sassy's lips brushes her palm as she claims the apple. She crunches it down, bits of core falling onto Sarah's boots. She gives

Sassy another apple for good measure before resting her forehead against the horse's. "Hey girl," she murmurs. They stand locked in this stance as Sarah empties her mind of everything that lies ahead.

Then Sassy bobs her head and Sarah opens her eyes, her gaze falling on an aluminum water bucket in the corner of the stall. Someone has whimsically plastered the receptacle with a Silverwood wine label featuring the Lanning family crest.

Lannings take care of their own. Those aren't the exact words knit into the crest's design, but they might as well be.

Sarah sinks down onto the baled hay piled outside Sassy's stall. *Lannings take care of their own.* She's heard it all her life. Family loyalty means everything to her father. When she and Jenna were kids, their parents took them on frequent trips to Europe, where they volunteered as laborers in Old World vineyards, absorbing every bit of wine-knowledge they could. At the tail end of one of these trips, they diverted to Scotland, where some of Dad's family still lived. There, he commissioned an artisan to design a new family crest. Woven into it are the Gaelic words for *family* and *loyalty* and *land.* The Lanning holy trinity, appearing on the label of every bottle Silverwood Cellars produces.

But apparently, family fealty stretches only so far. Because instead of taking care of Sarah after the accident that claimed TJ's life, Jenna chose to go away. Sarah endured alone those days when she didn't know how she could take another breath as guilt and grief overwhelmed her.

"There you are." Shane's voice slices through the silence, interrupting her thoughts. "No one knew where to find you."

Her heart gives an upward bound as he strides toward her, his square-shouldered form silhouetted by the mellow light shafting through the entrance. "I had to say goodbye to Sassy." Sarah's hardly seen Shane since she got the awful news. Though things feel unsettled between them, she's been too distracted to remedy it.

He draws alongside her and strokes Sassy's neck. "Sometimes I wonder why you and Harrison still keep these horses."

"Down to just two now." It's impossible not to touch Sassy. She is so beautiful, her coat golden and smooth, like melted sunshine. "We couldn't possibly send these away."

"I suppose not." He cocks his head. "How are you doing?"

"Okay." She tries not to think about the fact that by this time tomorrow, she will be halfway to Orlando to catch an even longer flight to La Paz. "A little nervous. I hope I haven't forgotten anything."

"It's not like you're going to darkest Africa. I'm sure they have stores." A corner of his wide mouth twitches. "Even in Bolivia."

"I'm sure they do." But that isn't what she means. She is thinking about the long list of to-dos she's leaving for him, Sunnie, Vina, and her assistant Ana, and hopes her instructions are clear. Harvest is the very worst time for her to leave.

The thought of unfinished business reminds her: "Did you ever talk to Kellie?"

"We touched base. She'll come out again next week for an interview."

"Okay, good." She's not sure, exactly, why she brought it up. An attempt to assert her own authority? Or maybe to put up a buffer, some kind of distance between them: she, the vintner's daughter; he, the hired hand. Despite dating him off and on for the last year, she finds their relationship anything but straightforward. She hadn't planned on seeing him tonight since he would deliver her to the airport tomorrow. His coming now has caught her off-guard.

A silence stretches between them. Then, unexpectedly, Shane chuckles. "You know, I can't help but think this is so like Jenna."

"What is?"

"This imperial summons. She could be like that, couldn't she?"

Sarah turns her head, searching his eyes in the waning light. "I forget sometimes that you knew her." Jenna dated him briefly her senior year of college. Sarah has a shadowy memory of her bringing him home one fall weekend. They apparently broke up soon after. "You never talk about her."

Shane keeps his gaze on Sassy, on the rhythmic strokes of his hand along her shoulder. "It was a long time ago."

"Not that long."

He shrugs. "I never felt like I knew her that well. She always kept a part of herself hidden, you know?"

She does know, much better than he. "Why do you suppose she sent for me? She must have had a reason."

"Maybe she knew it would be the last thing you'd want to do."

She shoots him a glance. "That makes her sound … mean."

"Well, it's true, isn't it?" She feels his eyes on her. "You don't really want to go."

"I wouldn't if I didn't have to." But she does have to. For Dad's sake, at the very least.

On one of the few occasions they've spoken in the last two weeks, Dad said, "I know her ashes must be scattered there, it's what she wanted. But her urn, at least, needs to be buried here, next to your mother. I don't think Jenna would deny me that much." The sorrow that weighted his voice pierced her heart afresh. Since news of Jenna's death, he's thrown himself into work, patrolling the vines for hours at a time, testing, sampling, and testing again, stopping only to sleep and occasionally eat. Although it triggers alarm bells in Sarah's brain, she knows eventually he will emerge from his way of mourning. She's seen him do it before.

Shane leans in so close she feels the soft puff of his breath across her cheek. "Sarah, what's to stop me from going with you? You know you don't want to do this alone."

"I have to."

"But why? I don't understand why you're so eager to do her bidding after the way she treated you."

Though she doesn't understand it either, she tries to explain the faint glimmer fluttering around the edge of her soul. "Jenna and I didn't have a falling out so much as we had a—a dying off. A fading out." It was one of those things she didn't realize until she looked back and saw that things hadn't been the same for a very long time. Years before the accident, which seemed merely the last straw. The waning of her relationship with Jenna began sometime after Mom died and continued throughout college, including Jenna's work-study semester in Bolivia her junior year. The rift seemed complete when she permanently left everyone and everything familiar for that country a year later. Apparently so eager to leave, she couldn't even wait to finish her journalism degree. "I wish I'd tried harder to make things right."

"You weren't the one who left, Sarah."

"But I didn't ask her to come back. And now, this wish of hers." Unbidden, she thinks of the locked wooden box on Jenna's bookshelf, its contents a secret. She realizes that's how she views this quest: as a locked box containing a mystery that cannot be discovered any other way. "I feel like she's trying to tell me something."

Something like fear flits across Shane's ruddy features, or maybe it's just doubt. "Even so, just say the word and I'm there with you. I don't care what Beck says."

She hesitates. A big part of her wants his company very badly. She hasn't been out of the country since she was a teenager, when she traveled with parents who took care of every detail. Since the accident, she's hardly been beyond county lines. She won't pretend the prospect of a solo international journey isn't a bit intimidating.

At the same time, there's something else, a flicker she dares to only whisper to herself: she wants to make Dad proud.

"Thank you," she says, "but I know Dad needs you here." Her palm glides over Sassy's velvety coat one last time before she pats the horse and turns to go. It's late and she'll have to rise early to accomplish all she has yet to do.

"Sarah." Shane catches her arm, his blue eyes pained. "Ever since we heard the news, I haven't been able to get you alone for three seconds."

"I know. It's been a crazy two weeks." With a thousand things to do. Applying for an expedited passport, finding a sub to teach her art class, rounds of vaccinations, packing, getting everything organized so the vineyard can carry on without her.

He clears his throat. "I realize this may not be the best timing, but—" He takes her hand, his fingers surprisingly smooth for a man who spends half his days outdoors. "This whole thing with Jenna has me thinking about how little time we really have in this life. How any of us could go at any moment, you know?"

She nods. Of course she knows. Even the losses she's already suffered can't dull the shock of death. If anything, her experiences serve only to heighten her awareness of death's ruthlessness, its complete lack of favoritism.

"So, I need you to know how much you mean to me." Shane takes her by the shoulders, his eyes boring into hers. "Watching you these past weeks, seeing you step up to what is being asked … I know you're afraid, but you're doing it anyway. It's made me realize how much I care for you."

She searches his gaze. "It has?"

"Yes." Even in the thin light, she can see the flush shadowing his rugged features. His eyes dart away and then back. "I don't suppose you might feel the same way?"

Heat floods her cheeks. Shane is the first man she's allowed herself to feel any kind of attraction to since TJ. And though she knows

Shane isn't her soul-match in the same way TJ was, she doubts any-one could be.

With Shane, she sometimes believes her cold heart might be flickering to life, though she's had no idea whether he felt the same. If it is meant to happen, she's told herself, it will.

And now, in a most unexpected way, it has. She surprises herself by smiling. "I might."

Shane grins back and cups her face in his hands. "I can't tell you how happy I am to hear you say that." His lips press warmly to hers. She leans into his kiss.

CHAPTER 6

Sarah has one more goodbye to make before she leaves. She waits until the day of her departure to do it.

She times her visit for just before noon, knowing he'll be back by then from his morning inspection of the vines. As expected, she finds him in his shop tucked behind the stables, a spacious storage shed renovated into a workroom.

He's propped open the door to let in the crystalline September sunshine. Scents of mellow oak and tangy, spent wine drift to her, along with the sound of his quiet, off-key humming. At his workbench, he crouches over a plank pulled from an old wine barrel. Barrels can house wine for only three or four years before the liquid saturates the wood, preventing the oaky flavor from making its way into new wine. But Tomaso, who believes in second chances if nothing else, finds a way to breathe new life into the lovely old barrels by using their wood to create furniture, knick knacks, wine racks—anything he can imagine, really.

As her footfall sounds on the smooth cement floor, the humming stops. Tomaso looks up. "So." His square, seamed face softens into a smile. "You haven't forgotten the old man after all."

She smiles back. "Saved the best for last."

He spreads his arms and she goes to him, wrapping her arms around his girth, relaxing against his solid strength. She owes Tomaso so much. Her soul survived after the accident thanks to him.

She gives Tomaso a squeeze and steps back, her glance traveling to his latest project. "What are you working on?"

"Memorial plaque for Jenna. What do you think?"

Laid across the workbench is a rectangle of curved oak. Its concave surface holds a deep red stain into which Tomaso has begun to carve Jenna's name and the dates bookending her life. "Harrison is choosing some poetry for beneath. Thought I'd add some etching along the edges."

"It's perfect." She looks into his brown eyes. "How are you doing, Tomaso? And Vina?" She's hardly seen the couple in the last two weeks.

"We are … managing." A shadow clouds his face. "Your papa, though." He shakes his head. "He needs to give himself time to mourn, not continue on as if nothing has changed."

Yes. She is worried about Dad, too. But this is his way: full speed ahead, no matter what.

Tomaso pulls a three-legged stool from beneath his workbench and invites her to sit. "And you, *mijita*? I hope you are managing some rest, for you have a very long journey ahead."

"I'm okay." She hasn't been sleeping well, actually, images of TJ and Shane and Jenna tumbling together, playing across the unending movie screen of her mind.

"You miss her. More than you thought you would, no?"

Throat tightening, she's warmed by a rush of affection. Thank God for Tomaso. He seems to understand better than anyone that being Jenna's little sister was no simple thing. "I can't stop thinking about our—about everything we missed." She blinks away a sudden film of tears. "Jenna and I didn't end well, you know. And now we've lost the chance to ever make it right."

"*Nunca digas nunca.* 'Never' is rarely a part of God's vocabulary. Sometimes we find healing long after we stop looking for it." Tomaso regards her soberly. "The truth is, Jenna cared for you. More than you realize."

"How do you know?" She grabs onto his words, hoping they are true.

He turns back to his workbench. "The same way I know when the grapes are ripe for harvest. I just do."

She frowns, sensing a sidestep from her question. "Did Jenna talk to you? If you know something, please tell me."

"What is there to tell? I have known and loved you both deeply. That is all."

From a nearby rack, she picks up a cheese plate, a gorgeous burgundy stain forming a smooth oval at its center. "I guess maybe I'm afraid."

"Of what?"

She closes her eyes. Though she knows the weeks of travel ahead will contain their share of risk, that's not what worries her. "I don't know why Jenna asked for me. She must have had a reason. But what if I don't discover it? What if I fail? I've got only one chance to get it right." She opens her eyes. "Shane wants to go with me."

"You don't need Shane," Tomaso says firmly. "You are the woman who used to fly across the earth on her horse and speed through the backcountry on her skis, taking risks no one else would dare."

"And look where that landed us."

Tomaso levels her a look. "It does no good for you to continue blaming yourself in this way, mijita."

"I know you and Vina don't hold it against me. Every day I'm grateful for that." Her gaze travels to the framed photo he keeps above his working space. Vina snapped the candid on Sarah and TJ's high school graduation day. His dark curls are tousled beneath his cap, his thickly lashed, black eyes snapping. She and Jenna stand on either side of him, his arms draped across their shoulders—she in her kelly-green cap and gown, Jenna in a teal sundress.

Had she been falling in love with TJ even then? Maybe. Only weeks before, on a whim, they'd gone to prom together, neither of them having a preferred date. They went as friends, best friends. Only … she couldn't remember ever feeling as happy as she did that night, with him, dancing until midnight, then coming home to the vineyard stables, each taking a blanket for warmth and curling up in the hay to talk and talk for hours. When dawn appeared, they saddled Sassy and Honey and rode out, still wearing their prom finery, until exhaustion finally caught up and chased them home at last.

Perhaps that's when her feelings for him began to shift, though she didn't recognize that until they started attending Central in the fall. It certainly seems she might have been in love with him on graduation day by the way she's smiling up at him.

She grips the cheese plate until her knuckles whiten. "No matter how *you* feel about me, we both know who's responsible for losing TJ. If I hadn't been such an idiot, showing off—" She's wished a million times she could live that day over again, make different choices. Not that she remembers them. It required Jenna's reluctant, painful recollections to fill in the missing blanks of what happened that day. Sarah deliberately skiing into an area clearly marked for avalanche danger, simply so she could claim the thrill. Ignoring TJ's pleas to turn back, taunting him to come after her, to try to stop her. Which he did. So the avalanche, when it came, caught them both—and jeopardized Jenna's life besides. "You may be able to forgive, but I can't. Because I was reckless and stupid, your grandson died."

Silence stretches out. "At risk of repeating myself," Tomaso says at last, "that is all in the past. Long forgiven. The point I was trying to make is that for you, no challenge was ever too great. And not just in a dangerous way, either. Who was the young woman who planned to study abroad for a year, all on her own? You."

She shakes her head. "I was just a girl then, with big ambitions. I'm not that girl anymore."

"That girl still lives inside you. You have only to believe she exists. Jenna was your sister, and you loved her. You love her still. Too often, we see only what we expect to see and become blind to everything else." When he touches his work-hardened palm to her face, she leans her cheek into its warmth. "You want my advice? It is this: be willing to believe the best about your sister. Because that is what love is, *sí*? Believing the best, even when we can't always see that goodness. If you can manage to do that, I think you will return with what you were sent to find."

CHAPTER 7

Hours later, Sarah and Shane speed toward the rising Cascade foothills and Sea-Tac Airport beyond. Windmills, appearing sleekly extraterrestrial against an azure sky, surround the ribbon of highway, their spindly, white blades churning air. Shane whistles in harmony to a Brad Paisley tune turned low on the radio.

Jenna cared for you, Tomaso said. *Too often, we see only what we expect to see and become blind to everything else.* His words coil through Sarah's thoughts, tightening a thick band around her chest.

Her eyes pinch shut at the memory of the last time she saw Jenna alive, four years ago.

Her sister had been home a week into her planned month-long furlough from Bolivia, her first since she'd left home two years earlier. But Jenna spent most of her time away from the vineyard, with old friends, while Sarah had winery business to occupy her. If she was perfectly honest, she hadn't minded Jenna's absence, still nursing the hurt she felt over Jenna's abrupt departure—and her silence ever since.

On this night, with a gorgeous salmon sunset painting the summer sky, Jenna's social circle decided to hang out at the winery for a change. With harvest only weeks away, the vineyard was a magical place, a foretaste of heaven. Lush vines surrounded the patio, where fairy lights twinkled overhead on the crossbeams. As the sun sank behind the mountains, Jenna and five of her friends talked and laughed around the fire pit while they shared a bottle of Dad's best cab sauv reserve and a platter of savories from Vina's kitchen.

In her office overlooking the patio, Sarah had cracked the window to relieve the stuffy space. Working only by the muted light of her computer screen, she finished logging the last of a batch of invoices as laughter erupted outside. She glanced up in time to see her sister's face light up as Jared, an old high school chum, put his arm around her waist and tugged her close. Sarah muted the soft rock station on her computer to eavesdrop on the conversation outside.

"The good news is I've only actually crashed twice." Jenna was talking about her motorbike, her buoyant voice carrying on a breeze. "The last time was the day before I left. I've still got the bruises."

She held out a slim brown arm, flexing it at the elbow. "See? Motorbikes are really the only way to get around in the country, but I swear, it's like being on some kind of twisted circus ride, dodging spiny cactus, loose rocks, feral pigs and more cow poop than you'll find in the whole of the Palouse." She gestured again with her bruised arm. "And this is nothing compared to what I sometimes look like. Sometimes, I arrive for a home visit looking like an assault victim, bruises all up my legs and face." She shook her head, levity slipping away. "The worst part is, they don't even ask about my injuries, assuming I have a boyfriend who beats me. But here's the silver lining: I get instant rapport with the women, most of whom are victims of domestic violence themselves."

"And yet you actually like this place," Jared said.

"I love it," Jenna replied softly. "Sometimes, I think it's what saved me."

"I thought only Jesus saves," Jared quipped.

Jenna didn't join the ripple of laughter that followed. "But that's what I mean. Jesus found me there. Or I found Him. Or both."

As silence drew out, Sarah's curiosity grew. Jenna knew Jesus too? She'd never heard her talk like this before.

Someone else finally murmured a response, too low for Sarah to hear. Longing tugged on her. If only she could be one of those listening to Jenna's stories. A member of her inner circle.

Not allowing time to second-guess herself, Sarah closed her laptop and rose from her desk. Jenna and her crowd had polished off their plates of nibblies. If she brought them a platter of fresh ones, maybe Jenna would invite her to join in.

As she crossed the patio with a tray full of hors d'oeuvres a few minutes later, Sarah took in the faces gathered around the fire pit. Pretty, dark-haired Samantha, Jenna's roommate during her last two years at Eastern. And lanky Jared, Selah High's star pitcher who had led their baseball team to State Championships her sophomore year. The others' names she didn't recall. Sarah's gaze skimmed past them to rest on Jenna. Her sister turned toward her, taking in the tray of refreshments and Sarah's hopeful smile. Jenna's lips curved upward, and for a split second, Sarah could have sworn she saw a longing in Jenna's eyes that mirrored her own.

Then Sarah's right toe caught on an uneven patio tile. She stumbled forward, her weak left leg buckling beneath her. With a nerve-tingling crash, she and the tray sprawled across the tiles.

In an instant, Samantha was at her side, helping her up. Sarah began a stammered apology. "I—I'm so sorry, my knee—" She stuttered to a stop when she glanced up to see embarrassment on the averted faces. Jenna was the only one looking directly at Sarah, her features twisted in an expression that soured Sarah's insides. Abruptly, Jenna stood and walked to the edge of the patio.

As Sarah stooped to collect the mess, the door of Dad's office swung open and he stepped outside. "What happened?" he demanded, his powerful form silhouetted by lamplight.

"Dad!" Jenna wheeled around. "I … uh, Sarah tripped."

In her crouched position, Sarah kept her eyes lowered so as not to see her father's response. They'd grown closer since Jenna had left. He knew how hard she'd worked to walk almost normally again after the accident while assuming a full load of vineyard responsibilities. My Girl Friday, he called her now. With the new nickname came an affection previously reserved for Jenna. She didn't want to see the moment that changed.

After a pause, Dad spoke again. "Well, don't just stand there, Jenna. Help her clean it up."

Seconds later, her sister knelt beside her, picking up the larger shards while Samantha scuttled inside to fetch a broom and dustpan from the kitchen. Heat flooded Sarah's face. Had Dad really spoken so sharply to Jenna, to his darling girl? If she wasn't beside her now, doing his bidding, Sarah might not have believed it. "I'm sorry," she whispered. Jenna gave only the barest of nods.

The rubbish was swept away. The party disbanded shortly after. Sarah went to her room without saying goodnight to Jenna or her friends. In the morning, Sarah learned Jenna had gone home with Samantha.

For the rest of her furlough, Jenna found one reason or another to stay away from Silverwood, eventually returning to Bolivia without laying eyes on Sarah again.

Four years ago, but Sarah remembers clearly what she saw on Jenna's face in the moments before their father appeared. The color that flamed in her cheeks. The way she turned away. She knew that look, firsthand.

Shame.

Her sister was ashamed of her. For her. Her clumsiness like a scar, her weakness a permanent reminder of the loss she'd caused so many.

Blood is blood. For the first time, Sarah understood the dark side of family fealty. Jenna took on Sarah's shame, the guilt of her action that day in backcountry. But for her, evidently, it was too much. Sarah wouldn't have believed Jenna could desert her, except that she had years of silence as evidence. Jenna put as much distance between them as possible.

Shane's hand finds hers, and she opens her eyes. "You okay?"

She manages a smile. "Fine." The Chevy Blazer climbs deeper into the Cascade foothills, the landscape changing from brown to green. She hesitates, then swallows. "Can I ask you something?"

"Shoot."

"What kind of person was Jenna to you?"

He flinches. "What do you mean?"

"What attracted you to her? What made you ask her out?"

A pause. "She asked me out, actually."

"She did?"

"Invited me to go cross-country skiing." A small smile raises the corners of his mouth. "I didn't cross-country ski. She offered to teach me."

"And?"

"She was an awesome teacher. Patient and smart, with a wicked sense of—" He breaks off.

"What?"

"Does it really matter? It was a long time ago."

"I'm just trying to get a better picture of who my sister was. I feel as if my impressions are so one-dimensional." She pauses. "Do you still ski?"

He shrugs. "Not so much."

"Why not?"

"Just … lost my taste for it, I guess."

"Before or after you and Jenna broke up?"

"I don't remember." Shane lets go of her hand. "Could we talk about something else?"

"Okay. Like what?"

"Like how much I'm going to miss you. You have no idea how much. I wish you didn't have to do this." He fishes in the pocket of his denim jacket. "I have a surprise." He pulls her cell phone from his pocket and drops it into her lap. She blinks. In the scurry of last-minute preparations, she didn't realize it was missing. "I got you an international SIM card. Now we can talk every day."

"Thank you, Shane." She turns the phone over in her hands, her heart lifting. It'll make a difference, allowing her to feel connected to home.

He takes her hand again, holding it to his chest, where she feels the steady thump of his heartbeat. "You do what you need to do in Bolivia, then hurry home." His intense gaze makes her flush as he presses a kiss into her palm.

$\mathcal{C}$HAPTER 8

The Avianca Airlines captain announces their approach to the El Alto airport as they circle the sprawling layers of La Paz. From her window seat, Sarah blinks eyes that feel scraped by sandpaper and gazes down at an impossibly long runway. It seems to stretch on forever. Already, Shane seems another planet away.

Shane. Shutting the barely begun novel in her lap, Sarah allows her thoughts to wander toward home … and him.

She met Shane at harvesttime during Jenna's senior year at Eastern, when Jenna brought him home to meet the family. A few weeks later, they'd evidently broken up. Then the accident in January. By February, Jenna had left the country. Sarah hadn't given Shane Ferrell a second thought until Dad's winemaker retired two years ago and Shane applied for the position.

Shane worked at Silverwood for a year before Sarah began going out with him casually, an occasional drink together or a movie in town after a long day, often with Ana and her boyfriend. Gradually, they began seeing each other more frequently.

Fun. Smart. Ambitious, but not in an all-consuming way. Though he has plans for his career and for the vineyard, he makes time to savor life. Their rural community has little to offer by way of nightlife, but he knows where to find what fun there is.

She doesn't spend all her waking hours dreaming about him, but when they are together, she enjoys his easy company. And when she kisses him, she's reminded that the woman in her didn't completely die on that mountain with TJ.

Plus, Dad adores him. Within months of his arrival at the vineyard, Dad was treating him like a member of the family. He revels in Shane's intuitive winemaking skills, the way his innovations have rocketed Silverwood onto the Washington wine map. She admits Dad's devotion sometimes unsettles her, leaves her unsure about where exactly she fits in. But as the plane banks left over the city, it occurs to Sarah that if things get serious between her and Shane it would make her father very happy.

She drinks in the rugged landscape below, almost disbelieving that she is finally seeing what she's only known from online research—and Jenna's stories, of course. When Jenna chose to spend the first half of her college junior year here, Sarah never had any notion of seeing it for herself, even though she spent hours poring over articles about the people and the terrain. The distance that had sprung up between them drove Sarah to learn everything she could about this place, as if gaining a better picture Jenna's experience would somehow explain her sister's aloofness.

Her seatmate, a quiet Japanese businessman whose skin seeps garlic, leans in for a better view. The pilot appears to be passing intentionally close to the snow-covered, triple-peaked Illimani towering over the canyon city. She wonders if he's attempting to give them a close-up of the four climbers making their careful way to the summit. They look so tiny, mere dots against the great expanse of white.

Despite their evident proficiency, they strike Sarah as dangerously exposed. Defenseless. She turns away with a shiver.

Inside the airport, feeling grimy and slightly light-headed after her twenty-one hour journey, she allows the sea of people to sweep her along the concourse through passport control. Languages swirl around her, from which she can pick out an occasional stream of Spanish.

In baggage claim, amid the throng of eager people awaiting new arrivals, a woman holds a hand-lettered sign emblazoned with Sarah's name. Beck told her one of Jenna's colleagues would meet her and host her overnight before Sarah continued on to Santa Cruz. This woman has fair, freckled skin, a square face and chin-length, auburn curls. Sarah hesitates, but the woman's brown eyes light up.

"Sarah?" she mouths. At Sarah's nod, the woman closes the distance to envelop her in a tight hug. "Sarah." She speaks against her ear. "*Bienvenidas a Bolivia.*" She holds her at arm's length. "Welcome."

"You must be Abby."

"I am and very happy to meet you." She speaks with a crisp British accent. "I only wish it were under different circumstances."

"Thank you."

"I can't tell you how Jenna's death has affected us. We're devastated, all of us. Everyone who knew Jenna absolutely adored her."

"We appreciate that."

Abby takes her arm and leads her toward the baggage carousels. "I'm sure you must be exhausted. We'll get you out of here just as quick as we can. How many suitcases do you have?"

"Just the one. There it is." She grabs the bag as it spits from the chute.

"Right then." Abby takes it from her. "Let's go someplace where we can hear ourselves think."

"I understand you're a midwife," Sarah says as they pull away from the airport in Abby's midnight-blue Toyota Camry.

"Among other things." She merges skillfully with traffic flowing toward the city. "My husband and I run a mobile clinic, so I wear many hats." She smiles. "But delivering babies is by far my favorite."

"Sounds like hard work."

"It is, most days. Long hours, tough situations. But incredibly rewarding, too. I'm sure Jenna told you all about that."

"Actually, no, she hasn't. Didn't. We, um, didn't talk much in recent years."

Abby's glance slides sideways. "I'm sorry to hear that."

Sarah stares straight ahead. "Me too, actually."

They talk about her flight and things back at home until Abby draws to the curb in front of a long block of square office buildings. Part of the reason Sarah flew into La Paz instead of directly into Santa Cruz is to visit the offices of La Fuente, the non-profit through which Jenna worked, and to meet its president, Rand Caldwell.

Abby leads her inside a nondescript building, where they climb rough cement stairs to the fifth floor. Halfway up, Sarah stops, embarrassed to have to lean against the stairwell wall to stay upright. She hauls in air as if waking from one of her nightmares.

"It's the altitude." Abby touches her shoulder. "Takes some getting used to. I can give you something if it doesn't improve soon. They say unless you're born here, you never completely adjust."

Sarah nods, concentrating on drawing each new breath until finally a measure of equilibrium returns. Still lightheaded, she follows Abby up the remaining flights and then down a short hall, where they pass through a wooden door marked with a simple sign. *La Fuente.* The Wellspring.

Inside, on the terracotta-painted wall facing the door, are several lines in Spanish, written in a calligraphic hand: *Va a ser como un jardín bien regado, como un manantial cuyas aguas no se agotan.* You will be like a well-watered garden, like a spring whose waters never fail.

Beneath this, a waterfall splashes into a turquoise basin of water. The lilting notes of pan pipes and violins float above the burble of moving water.

Nearby, discreet track lighting illuminates a framed painting in the modern Bolivian style. Bold, bright colors form highly stylized human figures, a man and a woman standing near a waist-high stone structure. Beside the woman rests a large purple jug. Her petticoats swish beneath a red skirt and on her head rests a blue bowler hat. The man wears sandals and a yellow stocking cap with earflaps.

Despite their traditional Bolivian garb, something seems familiar about these characters, this pose. Then she realizes: It's Jesus and the Samaritan woman at the well.

"Like it?" Abby asks.

"It's wonderful." Admiration expands inside her chest as she takes in this artist's wildly imaginative re-creation of the well-known Biblical scene. She scans the perimeter for a signature. "Who did this?"

"A local artist. Rand had it commissioned shortly after La Fuente opened." She pauses. "Jenna told me you're a gifted artist yourself."

She said I was gifted? The news rustles uncomfortably beneath her sternum. "Another lifetime ago, maybe."

Abby cocks her head. "Not anymore?"

She shrugs, and suddenly another thought hits. The quote from the book of Isaiah. The depiction of Jesus. "Is La Fuente a faith-based organization?"

"The hands and feet of Jesus." Abby's mouth tips up at both corners. "You didn't know?"

"No." She is embarrassed to admit how little she knows about Jenna's work.

"She'd been with us for about a year. Before that she worked with a secular NGO."

"I see." An unexpected rise of hope makes her momentarily forget her mind-numbing fatigue and discomfiting inability to draw a full breath. Had Jenna come to know the same Jesus she knew? Her mind spins back to that hot summer evening four years before, when Jenna sat with her friends on the vineyard patio. *He found me there,* Jenna said. *Or I found Him. Or both.* In the blur of shame that followed, Sarah had all but forgotten it. Maybe Jenna did know Jesus. Not just the accept-Him-into-your-heart milquetoast Christ of their Sunday school upbringing but the real One. The One who, after the accident, gave Sarah Someone to live for besides her broken self.

Before she can fully process this, a middle-aged man with sleek, low-profile glasses emerges from a room off the foyer. He approaches, hand outstretched. "You must be Sarah. Rand Caldwell." His accent, like Abby's, labels him a Brit. He takes her hand, cupping it between both of his. "We are so deeply, deeply sorry for your loss."

"Thank you."

"How is your father?"

"Struggling."

"I am sure. The loss of a child. Incomprehensible, really. You both have our very deepest sympathies. And you, my dear, how are you? How was your journey?"

"Long."

"Yes. Only three time zones away, but it seems halfway around the world, doesn't it?" Another man appears from a different room. "Sarah, may I introduce Marcos Aliguerra, our attorney." As they shake hands, Rand continues. "We know you must be exhausted, so we won't keep you long." He gestures for her to precede him into his office. Abby and the attorney follow.

The space is small, no more than twenty feet square, two of its terracotta walls adorned by framed landscapes, another by a map of Bolivia dotted with dozens of color-capped straight pins. The small window overlooking the street is closed, blocking the traffic noise.

The object at the center of Rand's desk draws Sarah's attention. The size and shape of a vase, it's silver with a Celtic cross etched into its face. "Your sister's ashes," Rand says quietly. Her stomach lurches as he lifts the urn and gently offers it to her. When she has accepted it, Rand places his hands on top of hers for several seconds in a kind of benediction.

HAPTER 9

JENNA
Age 16
Selah, Washington

"It's obscene."
"I completely agree," Mom said calmly.

From across the dining room table, Sarah stared at me, wide-eyed. Dad glanced away, clearly unsettled though he tried to cover by taking another sip of wine.

I looked down at the steaming enchilada in *molé* sauce on my plate before pushing it away, untouched. What I'd learned in my current events class still swirled through my brain. We were studying various cultural practices around the world.

Though I don't think Mr. Abramson meant the conversation to veer in this direction, once Selma Hawkins brought up female circumcision, there was no stopping it. Clitoridectomy. Such a cold, clinical term for the methodical, deliberate removal of a young girl's most intimate parts. Irrevocable. And devastating. Happening not to some small pockets of people in developing countries but every year, every day. On today's planet, it had happened in twenty-eight countries to 125 million girls. 125 million!

The knowledge made me sick. In class, I'd had a hard time keeping my lunch down.

What made it even more ghastly was that people outside these communities knew about the practice but did nothing to stop it. Or at least too little to change it. It was still going on.

I picked up my fork. "It's cruel and barbaric. The girls hardly know what's happening to them. Most are only six years old. They strap them to tables, then leave them there without water for a whole day so they won't pee into the incision. They cut them then they torture them. No one should be allowed to get away with that."

"I agree," Mom repeated. "So what are you going to do about it?"

"What can I do?"

"Well, I doubt Mr. Abramson exposed you to all that just so you could get angry about it."

I rolled my eyes. "Of course he wants us to *do* something. A five-page paper, due next Friday, about anything we've discussed in class these last few weeks."

"And?"

"And that's it."

"So I repeat: What are you going to do about it?"

"I can't do anything. I'm only one person."

"Don't let not being able to solve the problem keep you from being part of the solution." Mom smiled. "One person can't do everything, but everyone can do one thing. What's your one thing?"

I shrugged. "What one thing could I do that would make any sort of difference?"

"Why don't you write these girls' stories? The ones you say are being mutilated."

"Their stories?"

"That's what you're good at, isn't it? Telling stories. Give these girls a voice. Advocate for them."

"But who would read what I write? Only Mr. Abramson."

"Start where you are, Jenna." She smiled again. "I think Mr. Abramson might be just the beginning."

That night after dinner, with Mom's words buzzing through my brain, I went online to research female genital mutilation. There was a ton of information about it—a shocking amount. Books, magazine articles, documentaries. Later, from the library, I checked out the Pulitzer-Prize winning *Half the Sky* and read it over a single weekend. Those girls' stories changed me. I watched movies like *Girl Rising* and *Not My Life*, which made me further realize that what was happening to these girls wasn't some deep, dark secret. Why wasn't more being done to stop it? Maybe, I thought, because not enough of everyone was doing their one thing. I determined not to let that be me.

My research taught me that one of the most practical, basic ways to empower girls was to provide their families easy access to clean water. If children—almost always girls—could get water from a convenient, safe location nearby, they had more time to go to school. To be educated. Educated girls tended to marry later, give birth later, have healthier pregnancies and children, and contribute more substantially to their family's income. Which made them more valued members of their communities.

When girls were raised up, whole communities were, too.

For my senior project, I organized a 10K run to raise money for clean water in Bolivia, building wells and installing purification systems in a Quechua village. I chose Bolivia for its reputation as "a beggar on a throne of gold," so called because of its ongoing, pervasive poverty despite its vast wealth of natural resources. I had no idea then that my appreciation for the metaphor would begin Bolivia's siren call on my life.

But that came later. Before any of that, I wrote my essay—earning an A from Mr. Abramson—then re-formatted it into an article and sold it to *The Seattle Times*. They published it in their Sunday paper with my byline: Special to *The Seattle Times* by Jenna Lanning.

CHAPTER 10

SARAH
La Paz, Bolivia
Present day

Sinking into the nearest chair, Sarah cradles the urn in her lap. Then Rand hands her a single white envelope. "We closed Jenna's post office box in Cortadera and instructed the postmaster to forward to us any mail that might have been en route. There has been only this."

Sarah takes it, noting the typewritten direction but no return address. It bears a Washington state postmark. After tucking it inside her tote, she turns to Rand. "Do you mind if I ask you something about the night Jenna died? There's something I haven't been able to understand."

"Yes, of course," Rand says. "Anything you need to know we will try to answer."

"That night—" She glances from Rand to Abby, whose unwavering brown gaze encourages her to continue. "Can you tell me exactly what time the accident happened?"

"About twenty-three-thirty, local time."

Twenty-three-thirty. That was half-past eleven, or eight-thirty p.m., Pacific Time. What had Sarah been doing at that precise moment? Nothing very significant. Reading or readying herself for bed. She was awake, for certain, yet she hadn't sensed anything amiss. Shouldn't she have felt something when her sister's spirit left the earth? Why had those odd sensations, those strong impressions of Jenna, not come until hours later when Cork awakened her?

"And when did you learn about the accident?" Sarah traces the urn's smooth contours. It feels impossibly heavy, a lead weight in her lap.

"About two hours later. Another bus passed along the same road about an hour after it happened. Some of the survivors had climbed out of the ravine and flagged it down. A few of the passengers of this second bus stayed to help the victims, while the driver continued to the next town and alerted authorities. Eventually, they got word to us."

"And then you called our house. But why did you hang up before we could answer?"

"We didn't—" Rand begins but stops when Aliguerra puts out a hand.

"That was me," he admits. "I dialed and then thought better of it. I realized it would be … kinder for you to hear such terrible news from someone you knew. Jenna listed Beck Lawson as an emergency contact. I am sorry if that was the wrong decision."

"No, it wasn't the wrong decision. I was just wondering. I was awake at the time, you see. Our dog had gotten me up, he was acting very strangely, and—" From the corner of her eye, she sees Abby stiffen beside Aliguerra on the brown leather loveseat. Sarah glances over and finds Abby's gaze locked on hers. "That's the first time I thought something might be wrong. I felt the call must have been about Jenna, even though—" The three of them are staring at her, and she wonders if the lack of oxygen is affecting her brain. Is she not making sense? "Sorry, I'm only trying to understand the timeline. So then, Señor Aliguerra, you waited until morning to call Beck?"

"I didn't wait, no. I phoned him immediately after calling your house."

"As soon as you found out?"

"Sí, of course."

She sits back in her chair. Had Beck really known about Jenna since before dawn that morning? And yet he'd waited nearly twelve hours before coming to the house to tell Dad. Why the delay? She shakes her head. Beck must have had his reasons, though she can't puzzle one out. Surely waiting only made the news harder to tell. "So what happens now?"

"Tomorrow Chase Maddox, our pilot, will fly you to Santa Cruz," Rand answers. "From there, he and another La Fuente employee, Rachael Gray, will take you by vehicle to Magdalena, where your sister and her husband were living."

Sarah blinks. "I'm sorry—her *husband*?"

"Yes, of course. Jonas." Rand's brow furrows. "You didn't know your sister had married?"

"I—we had no idea." She glances again at Abby, whose eyes have widened. The attorney shifts, recrossing his legs. Sarah swallows. "How long? I mean, how long had they been married?"

Rand looks to Abby.

"A year? No, not quite that. About nine months, I'd say."

"Jonas is another of our employees," Rand explains. "He was traveling with Jenna when she was—when the accident occurred. He's been in hospital in Santa Cruz these last two weeks, recovering from his injuries. Abby has been in touch with his doctors. They expect to release him tomorrow. Chase will take you to meet him."

"I see." But she doesn't see. Jenna, married? Without a word to anyone back home? Why keep her marriage a secret? *Was she coming home to tell us? But why did she wait so long to share the news? And why come alone?* Jenna asked Dad to buy her one plane ticket, not two. Unless her husband was traveling separately—but that made little sense either.

"Which brings us to the issue of her inheritance." Rand shifts his attention to the attorney. "Marcos?"

Aliguerra uncrosses his legs and leans forward. "Before she married, your sister informed us of the terms of your mother's will."

Monica Ridgely Lanning, their mother, came from a family of means. When she and Dad married, her money stayed in her name. When she died, the terms of her will stipulated that her daughters would each receive equal portions of her inheritance when they married or turned thirty, whichever came first. As Jenna had been only twenty-eight, her marriage meant she would inherit.

"Jenna wanted the funds to remain in the U.S. She also wanted to ensure that no one other than the legal entities involved should know she had inherited. She put me in touch with your attorney. He helped work out the details."

So Beck knew Jenna had married. He never let on, not even a hint.

Aliguerra continues. "La Fuente requires each employee to leave instructions in the event of their deaths. Your presence here today is because Jenna specifically requested it. In addition to such instructions, we also require our employees to make a will. Leaving a will saves time and eliminates red tape. It was all the more necessary in this case, as your sister chose not to leave her estate to her husband."

Sarah nods. So Jenna has left her half of Mom's money to La Fuente instead of her husband. Are they worried she'll contest it?

"In addition to what she inherited from your mother, she also had a life insurance policy. It's not insubstantial, and this she left to her husband." Aliguerra says. "But all the rest, she left to you."

She blinks. "To me."

"*Señorita* Lanning." He smiles faintly. "Your sister has left you a very wealthy young woman."

She shakes her head, stunned. "Why?"

"Jenna did not say. We only know her wishes, which are what I have stated."

Sarah's brain feels packed with cotton, her thinking thick and fuzzy. "This makes no sense. I don't need her money, but surely her husband—Jonas, right?—surely he does. Or he will. You said he's been injured. Can he return to work?"

"We don't know the answer to that yet. From what the doctors say, it will largely be up to him."

"What about La Fuente? She didn't leave any of the money to you? Surely you could put it to good use."

A corner of Rand's mouth tips. "We never turn away donations from those who feel led to make them, but for whatever reason, this was not your sister's wish."

A thought, small and unpleasant, uncurls at the back of Sarah's mind. She shakes if off, unwilling to let it play out in front of these strangers. Instead, she asks, "Does Jonas know about these terms?"

"Presumably."

She certainly hopes so. If not—well, she hates to think how he will react when he learns the heiress he married left her inheritance to someone he hasn't even met.

CHAPTER 11

As Abby weaves her Toyota through the steep streets of La Paz, Sarah balances the urn of Jenna's remains in her lap and tries to ignore the headache starting in dime-sized patches at her temples.

Her sister was married.

Her family is clueless.

She is rich.

None of it makes any sense.

Then the thought that began in Rand's office stretches itself out, demanding her attention. This scheme of Jenna's, leaving Sarah all her assets, is so typical of her tendency to not consider consequences. Had she not thought this could very well alienate her from Jenna's as-yet-unmet husband? Because surely he has more right to—and need of—Jenna's money than Sarah. Unless he is wealthy himself. But even if that were true, why give it to Sarah and not to La Fuente?

She kneads her forehead with a finger and thumb.

"Headache?" Abby asks.

She nods.

"It's an awful lot to take in all at once."

"I can't believe Jenna was married. Why didn't she say so?" She twists in her seat to face Abby. "Is Jonas well off?"

Abby's eyebrows shoot up. "Well off?"

"You know, wealthy."

She chuckles. "Not one bit, except in spirit."

"What about his family?"

"I don't know much about them, only that he was raised by a single mother, so I doubt it."

Maybe Sarah can simply *give* him the money. "Were they happy? Jenna and Jonas, I mean."

"Very." Abby's eyes leave the road to spare her a glance. "Jonas is a good guy, Sarah. They were completely besotted with each other from the very start. It breaks our hearts knowing what Jenna's loss means to him."

"How long had they known each other?"

"Not very long. A little over a year."

"It happened pretty fast then."

"Attachments tend to form very quickly around here. They met when they were both doing their culture and medical training here in La Paz, prior to their field assignments." She pauses. "While we're talking about Jonas, there is one more thing you need to know." She maneuvers through a busy intersection before continuing. "He sustained a head injury in the accident. While we certainly hope it's a temporary thing, it's left him unable to remember."

Sarah startles. "He has amnesia?"

"Correct."

With a swirling sense of *déjà vu*, Sarah is back in a narrow hospital room, seeing her own gruff doctor's thinning hair, hearing his voice that sounds like too many years of cigarettes. Absorbing his warning that she might never remember the events that changed her life so drastically. At the time, they'd hoped she would remember eventually, but six years later, her mind remains as blank as if the accident had never happened. A black hole swallowed her memories, leaving only the damage to her body and the absence of TJ to prove it.

"Jonas was conscious immediately after the accident," Abby says. "He tried to help Jenna. After he knew he'd lost her, he helped some of the other victims. We know all this from other survivors. Jonas recalls nothing. It seems he's lost his memory for as far back as two or three weeks before the accident. Not terribly uncommon, of course. Chances are good, however, that he will remember, in time."

"Or he may not." When Abby says nothing, she adds, "I know it from personal experience."

"You—you suffer amnesia?"

"After an accident, six years ago. A skiing accident. I was fortunate. I lived." She swallows. "The boy I was with did not."

"I'm so sorry to hear that." Abby pauses. "You know about survivor's guilt, then."

She winces. "Yes." *And then some.* "Some people have tried to tell me it's a mercy I don't remember, but I've never been able to believe that."

"Why not?"

"Because it makes it more difficult to accept what really happened. I dream about it now, but it's more my brain piecing together what I've been told than actual memories, my subconscious trying to make sense of it."

Abby nods. "I agree with Jonas's doctors that it would help him to remember at least a portion of the accident. He's wrapped pretty deeply in denial at the moment. Which is also perhaps a mercy." A sigh escapes. "The full reality will hit him soon enough."

Abby pulls her car to the curb in front of a wrought-iron fence surrounding a long, stucco house with a tiled roof. A stone fountain in the shape of a fluted flower trickles prettily in the courtyard. Sarah carries the urn while Abby gathers Sarah's suitcase from the trunk and leads her through the gate.

A Jack Russell terrier greets them at the door. "Meet Jake." Abby bends to pet the exuberant dog. "I am sorry my husband is not here to meet you as well. He is in Eastern Europe meeting with supporters who want to begin a ministry like La Fuente in Romania. It was planned long in advance, and Luca had no way of getting out of it."

Abby kicks off her low-heeled sandals, leaving them in a basket by the door. Sarah follows suit. The smooth floor tiles chill her toes as she follows her hostess past a comfortable living room, its deep-red walls covered in richly colored tapestries.

"You'd probably like some time to yourself." Abby speaks over her shoulder as she opens the door to a spacious, sun-dappled room at the end of a long hallway. Despite the bars at the window, it is a lovely, inviting space with lush, potted plants tucked into corners. A Quaker-style dresser holds a jug of water, the matching bedside table a lamp and a Mason jar of fresh daisies. A butter-yellow duvet covers the double bed. The whole effect makes Sarah want to crawl beneath the covers and sleep for hours. "Can I get you a bite to eat, Sarah?"

"Thank you, but I'm fine." She places the urn on the dresser, glad to relieve herself of the burden.

"How's your headache?"

She grimaces. "Not much better. I'm sure I just need to lie down for a bit."

"It's altitude sickness, I imagine. Let me get you something for that, then you can rest until dinner."

Abby returns a few minutes later with a mug, hands the steaming beverage to Sarah. "See if this helps." The dog, which has followed Abby into the room, sniffs at a navy knapsack leaning against the wall. "Jake, come away from that." To Sarah, she adds, "Chase brought it with him when he flew over today. They're your ... it's what Jenna had with her when she died. We thought it might be easier for you to deal with it than Jonas."

"Yes, of course." She eyes the bundle, her headache intensifying as a new heaviness settles across her shoulders. She has almost managed to forget that collecting Jenna's belongings is part of why she's here.

Shooed from Jenna's knapsack, Jake makes a beeline for the bed and jumps on it. "Oh, for heaven's sake, Jake, not again. How naughty you are today." Abby snaps her fingers. "Get down."

He wags his tail, an absurdly pleased grin lighting his whiskered face.

With an exasperated sigh, Abby lifts him from the bed. "I am so sorry, Sarah. I hope you like dogs. I'm afraid we have a very ill-mannered one."

"I love dogs. I've been missing mine, in fact. His name is Cork."

"Ah yes. I know about Cork. Jenna missed him still, I remember. And she was nuts about Jake. I have a sneaking suspicion that when she stayed with us, Jake slept with her on the bed." Abby shakes a finger at the dog. "And you've never forgotten it, have you, boy? Silly old mutt."

Hiding a smile, Sarah sips the beverage Abby has given her. It's mild, like green tea only sweeter. "Thank you for this. It's good." Already she feels the coil of tension unwinding.

"*Maté de coca* almost always does the trick. Now, enjoy your rest and we will see you when we see you." Abby ushers Jake ahead of her and gently shuts the door.

CHAPTER 12

Scooching herself to the center of the bed, Sarah tucks her feet beneath her and circles her hands around the warmth of the ceramic mug. On the dresser, the urn reflects the sunlight shafting through the window. She stares, unable to believe that compact vessel holds the remains of her sister. Jenna was larger than life. How could something so small contain all of her? With effort, she averts her gaze and concentrates on her tea. She's just finished the last sip when her phone rings.

Shane.

"You made it."

"I'm here." She smiles. "Your timing is perfect."

"Everything going okay?"

"Fine." She exhales. "Just exhausting."

"I miss you."

"Miss you too." The connection is surprisingly clear. She wishes she could wrap herself in the warmth of his voice, like a blanket.

"What are you doing?"

"Just resting."

"No, I mean who have you talked to so far?"

Her brows draw together. Something in his direct question unsettles her, makes her want to draw back. "Well, Abby met me at the airport, then we went to La Fuente headquarters and met the guy Jenna worked for." Her thumb picks at a tiny chip in the mug. "Rand Caldwell."

"What was that like?"

"He gave me a bit of a surprise, actually."

"What kind of surprise?"

"Jenna was married."

"*What?*"

"I know." She imagines his face as blank with astonishment as hers must have been when she heard the news. "She got married nine months ago."

"I don't know what to say. That's … shocking. Why do you suppose she'd keep something like that a secret?"

"I have no idea." She hears a soft pop against the window. Outside, a big, black fly bounces off the pane. "Her husband was with her in the accident, hurt pretty badly, sounds like. He's still in the hospital. I'm going to meet him tomorrow."

"That'll be interesting."

"I know. But Shane, there's something else." The fly reappears at the bottom of the pane. Her eyes follow its progress as it traces a diagonal path, disappearing into foliage at the far corner. "I've told you about the terms of my mother's will, right?"

"Sure, a little. Something about how when you either turn thirty or get mar—oh. Oh wow. Jenna was *married*. She came into her inheritance."

"Exactly." It disturbs her again to realize Beck has known this for months and never let on. She remembers how she sensed he was holding something back when he told her about Jenna's death. Now she knows what.

"So what happens to her money now?" His tone sharpens. "I guess the husband gets it all?"

"No, that's the other surprise." She closes her eyes, still not wanting to accept it. "He gets her life insurance. She gave the rest to me."

"What?"

"I know. I want to give it back. Or away, somehow."

"Why would you do that?"

"Because it doesn't belong to me. She shouldn't have done it."

"Why not? You're her sister."

"Which didn't seem to matter much when she was alive, did it?" The words spurt out before she can stop them. They hang there, forming a barrier she can almost see. A hedge around her heart. She sighs. "Sorry. Didn't mean to take it out on you. I know I need to just get over it. What's past is behind, right? It's just that she ignored me for the last six years. How does any amount of money change that?"

"It doesn't." Shane is quiet a moment. "But I guess in the end, it doesn't matter why she gave you her money, only that she did. Right?"

"I suppose." She lifts her gaze to the window again. The fly is gone, and beyond the barred window, a fading sun washes the blue sky with pink. "I can't help but wonder if Jonas knows."

"Jonas?"

"Her husband."

"Oh. Right. Well, does it matter? Unless—do you think he'll fight it?"

"Wouldn't you?"

This makes him pause. "But the will is legal, right?"

"Of course it's legal." Suddenly she's tired of talking about it. Her head feels so stuffed with new information that she fears it might explode. "I should probably call Dad. How is he?"

"Keeping busy. We decided the chardonnays should come in tomorrow. They're going to be good. Really good. Maybe our best harvest ever." He hesitates. "I think it helps him knowing you're there."

Her heart lifts a little. "Then I'm glad I came."

After they hang up, she flops back on a plump pillow, staring at sunlight and shadow dancing across the ceiling as she replays their conversation. Something about it niggles at her. Shane zeroed in on the money, sure, but she could almost expect that. He's a businessman, after all. No, it was something else. Something in his reaction to the news of Jenna's marriage. It seemed off, somehow. She sensed him withdrawing, putting distance between himself and her news. And was it her imagination or did he not seem quite as surprised as he should have been?

A new thought strikes her: Could he have known? Maybe. Perhaps Jenna told Dad. And if she told him, he could have told Shane.

But that doesn't make sense, either. Why would Dad tell Shane and not her?

She rubs her forehead. Though the headache is fading, her thinking remains murky. Jet lag, no doubt. That and the altitude sickness Abby talked about.

A snuffle sounds from the hallway. She rises and opens her door. Jake makes a beeline for the bed and jumps. She peers down the hall for sign of Abby. Seeing none, she closes the door.

Nudging Jake over, she lifts one corner of the duvet and stretches between the cool sheets. When the little dog curls against her, she strokes his soft form, missing her animals back home: Sassy Britches and Cork. It hits her suddenly that when Jenna moved to Bolivia, she left not only her family but her dog, which she'd raised from puppyhood. This place must have called to her very strongly for her to do that.

Sarah places her phone beside her on the bed. She'll call Dad after she rests her eyes a few minutes. She knows she won't sleep. Too many unanswered questions swirling inside her head for that.

CHAPTER 13

Sarah opens her eyes to a darkened room. She sits up, pushing tousled hair from her face. What time is it? She blinks, adjusting to the gloom. Jake is gone. Abby must have discovered and removed him. Sarah hopes she hasn't gotten the little dog into too much trouble.

Voices penetrate the quiet—Abby's and a man's. She glances at the luminous clock on her bedside table. Eight o'clock. She's been out for nearly three hours. Fragrant tendrils of something savory waft beneath her door. The hollow rumble of her stomach makes her hope she hasn't missed dinner.

She flicks on a cream-shaded lamp and stands at the dresser mirror to repair her hair, finally pulling the whole mass into a ponytail before adding a light coat of gloss to her dry lips. She heads for the kitchen and pauses at the threshold. A pot of stew, thick and brown, simmers on the stove, and three fat, beeswax candles plus a small light over an old ceramic sink bathe the room in an amber glow. But Sarah finds no occupant.

A shuffle from the corner makes her step farther in. She discovers a petite, copper-skinned girl on the floor bent over a strip of butcher paper, black hair hiding her face.

"*Hola.*" Sarah speaks softly so as not to startle her, unsure whether the child has heard her enter. As the girl looks up, Sarah catches her breath.

Beneath a pair of beautifully black-fringed eyes, a gaping cleft yawns beneath a twisted nose. The child sucks in a breath as she quickly hides her deformity behind one hand. Onyx eyes dart toward the back door as she springs to her feet.

"*Está bien.*" Sarah holds out a hand. The girl stills, though her eyes remain alert, wary. Still in Spanish, Sarah offers her own name and asks the child for hers.

The girl shakes her head. Does she not understand? Maybe she speaks Quechua or Aymara. Or perhaps she cannot speak at all. Sarah is about to try English when the girl crouches again over the roll of paper. In one corner, she writes swiftly in tidy script: *Sofía.*

"Sofía," Sarah murmurs. "What a lovely name. *Qué bonita.*" Then she looks at the drawings that cover the paper.

With colored pencils, Sofía has sketched an elaborate scene, one Sarah recognizes, having seen it fleetingly from the car window earlier: La Paz's famed witches market. At the center of her piece, Sofía has placed a heavyset woman dozing beside her wares, her black eyes slitted at half-mast, at her feet a basket of hideously desiccated objects. A green-swathed table beside the woman holds an array of bowls with dried herbs, insects and frog parts. Just behind her, tucked into a dozen cubbyholes, an army of soapstone statues glares at passersby. Each figurine claims a distinct look of surprise or malice or mischief, which Sofía has conveyed in a single stroke—an arched eyebrow or rounded mouth.

But the ultimate expression of Sofía's whimsy is the sly, round face peeking from behind the somnolent woman's unsuspecting shoulder, the small brown hand reaching to pluck a piece of fresh fruit from a basket. Though this face is only visible nose to forehead, the thief looks exactly like Sofia.

"You drew this?" Sarah asks softly. Sofia drops her head in a modest nod. "*Excepcional.* Sofia, this is so very, very good."

She starts to say more, but the back door opens and Jake darts inside to dance a circle around Sarah's feet. Abby steps in behind him, followed by a tall-ish man, maybe six feet, with dark blond, wavy hair. He wears a wrinkled black t-shirt that reads: *Wag more, bark less.* Dark circles ring his hazel eyes. He needs a shave, possibly a haircut, and looks as if he hasn't slept in days.

"You're awake," Abby says to Sarah, sounding pleased. Then, "Jake, leave that poor woman alone."

"He's okay." Sarah nudges him with a bare toe. "Hope I didn't get him into trouble, letting him on the bed."

"Guess I can't make too much of a fuss if you don't." Abby touches the top of Sofia's head on her way past. The child spares her a glance before fastening her gaze on the man. He gives her a wink before turning his attention to Sarah as Abby introduces them.

"Sarah Lanning, Chase Maddox."

Chase takes her hand, pressing it between both of his in a warm, firm grip. "We're all so sorry about Jenna." He speaks in a plain American accent, a welcome change to her homesick ears. "Your sister was an amazing person. I—we all miss her so much." Though he releases her hand, his eyes hold hers with an openness she finds instantly appealing.

"Chase does a little bit of everything around here," Abby puts in. "Agricultural engineering, medical care, piloting our plane. He'll be flying you to Santa Cruz tomorrow."

"Hope you're up for an early morning." A faint smile tugs one corner of his well-shaped mouth. "Once we reach Santa Cruz, we still have a long drive ahead of us, so we need to start at oh-zero-thirty if we're going to reach Magdalena before dinner."

"I'll be up whenever you need me to be," she answers and watches as his eyes warm in approval.

Then he turns his attention from her. In one fluid motion, he scrapes a chair away from the table and sits, beckoning Sofia to his lap with a crook of his finger. She scampers over, trailing her artwork behind her.

"What have we here?" he asks in Spanish, taking the sheet of paper from her and smoothing it across the table.

She points and utters an unintelligible grunt.

"Yes, I can see it's a witch woman. But who's this?" He indicates the sly urchin reaching for the fruit.

Sofia's black eyes dance toward his.

"Thought so. Up to your usual tricks." He tickles under her ribs, prompting squeals and wriggles but no attempt to get away.

Abby watches with an indulgent smile before turning to Sarah. "Did you have a nice rest?"

"Very."

"Good. How's your headache?"

"Gone."

"I'm so glad." She pulls silverware from a drawer. "I was beginning to question whether to wake you. Glad I didn't have to make that decision. Hope you're hungry."

Sarah is opening her mouth to answer when her stomach emits a growl loud and long enough to be heard above Chase's one-sided banter. Her face warms as Sofia darts her a startled glance and Chase tucks his chin to his chest, unsuccessfully hiding a smile.

Abby chuckles. "Right-o. Guess that answers my question. Let's eat!"

～〜～

They dine by candlelight around the kitchen table, eating thick pork stew with root vegetables and fluffy cornbread, conversing in Spanish for Sofia's sake. The girl, her chair shoved against Chase's, carefully mashes every morsel of food with her spoon before delivering it to her mangled mouth. Sarah finds herself smiling at Sofia's wide-eyed interest in their conversation, which Abby keeps carefully centered around life on an Eastern Washington vineyard.

Following Abby's prompting, Sarah tells of her father's gamble in converting his family's apple orchard into a vineyard a decade before other Washington fruit-growers followed suit. She describes Vina's award-winning recipes and explains how Tomaso still conducts his inspections of the grapes the old-fashioned way—on the back of Old Romeo. How, thanks to them, she and Jenna grew up in a bilingual home. She also talks about Shane, whose innovative varietal blends have made him a living legend among Washington winemakers.

When Sofia's face lights up over Sarah's description of Cork's victorious encounter with a rattler, Sarah can't resist running a hand down the girl's smooth fall of hair. Her heart lifts when Sofia catches her hand and presses it to her cheek. When Sarah raises her eyes, she finds Chase watching her over the top of Sofia's head, a half-smile tugging at his mouth.

They are nearing the end of their meal when Sofia begins darting glances at the wall clock over the door. As soon as her plate is cleared, she taps Abby's bare forearm and lifts her delicate black eyebrows.

"Is it that time already?" Abby looks at her watch. "Okay, yes, you may be excused. We'll have our pudding in a little while. I'll call you when we're ready, sí?"

After delivering her empty plate to the sink, the child scampers off to the next room. A moment later, the TV warbles to life. "She does love television." Abby rolls her eyes and switches to English. "I give her only half-an-hour a day. You'd think I was giving her gold." Then she sobers. "She admired your sister so much, Sarah. She can't verbalize her grief, but she's taken Jenna's death very hard." She gestures to Sofia's drawing, now coiled into a scroll on the counter. "She wouldn't do any of her usual artwork for a week after receiving the news. Only terrible scribbles, her way of expressing her rage, I think. This drawing today is only the second she's done since receiving the news. I am very relieved." She adds quietly, "No one who knew Jenna could remain unaffected by her passing."

"Not even the dog." Chase reaches for a third piece of cornbread and drops a dollop of butter onto it.

"Jake?" Sarah glances at the little dog curled up on his pad in the corner.

"Oh yes. In fact, he gave me my first inkling something was wrong. That something might have happened to Jenna." Abby's eyes narrow. "I had the impression today in Rand's office that you may have had a similar experience."

A tiny prickle climbs Sarah's spine. "Why do you say that?"

"The night Jenna died, Jake woke me up from a very sound sleep. He doesn't normally get me up at night, so of course I thought he needed to go out. Instead, he went straight to the room where you're staying, where Jenna also slept when she was with us. He jumped on the bed and wouldn't get down no matter what I tried. Finally, I gave up and left him there. I went back to bed. But it got me wondering."

"It made you wonder … about Jenna?" Sarah swallows over a suddenly dry mouth.

A burst of canned, televised laughter comes from the other room. Abby waits for it to settle before answering. "Bolivians believe newly departed spirits return to places they knew as home during their life, and that dogs recognize their presence."

Sarah laughs a little, rubbing her hands against the chill that has erupted along her arms. "That's a little creepy."

Chase studies Sarah's face. "Is Abby right? Did something similar happen to you?"

"Something very similar, actually." She frowns, poking her fork at a piece of discarded fat. "Are you suggesting Jenna's spirit came to visit us both?"

He shrugs. "Why not?"

"But the bus crashed hours before the episode at my house with Cork. I thought she died instantly."

Abby nods. "Given her injuries, the coroner thinks it happened very quickly. Mercifully."

"So what happened in between? Did her spirit just linger?"

"I guess no one really has the answer to that. Where was Lazarus' spirit after it left his body and before Jesus brought him back to life? Had he been to heaven already?" Abby smiles as she reaches for the bread and helps herself to another small sliver. "I've always imagined he wasn't very happy to get wrenched from there to here again. Or could he have dwelled in an in-between place for an unknown period of time? We can't know, can we?"

"Tell her about the Solanos," Chase urges.

"Oh yes. The Solanos are originally from Peru. They used to work with us but left La Paz about two years ago and returned to Lima. Not long before they left, they were all eating dinner together when their youngest daughter, Cristina, saw a woman dressed all in white walking outside in their garden. When she investigated, no one was there. This happened several more times throughout the evening, other family members catching the flash of white as well. They all saw it, but like before, when anyone went to look, nothing."

Chase takes up the story. "The next morning they got the news their grandmother had passed away the night before, a few hours before the time Cristina first saw the woman in white."

"Her ghost?" Sarah asks.

"Her spirit, more like," Abby says. "Grandma Solano, whenever she came to visit her family in La Paz, always spent a lot of time in the garden. It's where she felt the most at home."

Sarah's scalp tingles. Had her sister's spirit, like Grandma Solano's, really lingered in the places she loved the night she died? The possibility fills Sarah with wonder, and oddly, with hope. Because if it's true, then Jenna still cherished home and family. Including, perhaps, her sister.

CHAPTER 14

JENNA
Age 17
Selah, Washington

Sarah and I followed TJ off the school bus that dropped us at the end of our lane. TJ had almost skipped school that day to help in the fields, but in the end, Tomaso had told him to go, promising Dad he himself would work extra hours to make up for it. With Mom's funeral only a month ago, things had gotten behind in the vineyard. Now Dad was barely getting any sleep, worried that on top of everything, we might lose the harvest.

A pickup pulling a horse trailer rumbled down the lane toward us from the house. We stepped onto the soft shoulder to let it pass in a hot swirl of dirt and exhaust. I let it go by without comment, my mind on my first day back at school since Mom died. It hadn't been as bad as I anticipated. Though I'd not wanted to return to school, Tomaso had encouraged Sarah and me to go. He said it would help get our minds off Mom being gone. And he'd been right. I almost dreaded leaving school to return home, where reminders of our loss lurked everywhere.

"Why was that trailer here?" Fifteen-year-old Sarah broke into my thoughts, her gaze following the dust plume rising in the truck's wake.

I shrugged.

Sarah frowned after the trailer another moment, then looked toward the house. Her lips turned white and she broke into a run, her pack bobbing against her back.

I shared a glance with TJ before taking off after her, not understanding the panic rising in my throat as I struggled to catch up. Sarah was fast. It was all I could do to keep a steady distance, especially with a backpack of books weighting every step. TJ's footfall pounded behind. He overtook me as we rounded the last bend in the lane. A second trailer waited in the courtyard, a horse handler leading Sassy Britches up a ramp into it. Dad stood beside the trailer, his face set like stone.

"No!" Sarah screamed. TJ hesitated as I drew abreast of her, panting. Without even shrugging out of her backpack, my sister flung herself at our father. "Dad! You can't do this! Not Sassy!"

Though he caught her from falling, his expression remained implacable. "Stop, Sarah," he commanded. "We have to."

"But why?" Not so much a question as a wail.

"Your mother is not coming back."

"So you're getting rid of the horses? All of them?"

"Even Honey?" I leaned over my knees, my breath still coming in sharp gasps. Honey was Sarah's favorite.

Sarah rounded on me, her face pink. "I'd rather have Sassy!" Then she turned back to Dad. "Mom wouldn't like this, Dad. Please?"

"I'm sorry, Sarah, my mind is made up." He nodded to the handler, who closed the trailer doors, securing Sassy and three other horses inside.

Tears streaming, Sarah ran into the house, slamming the door behind her.

At the edge of the courtyard, TJ shifted from foot to foot, lip caught between his teeth as he glanced from me to the house and back. When I, too, looked toward the front door, he seemed to take that as his cue. He dropped his backpack and ran into the house after Sarah.

I crept closer to Dad as the trailer crawled away, watching his face fall into inexpressively sad lines.

Later that night, after listening to Sarah cry herself to sleep, I found Dad in his study staring into the crackling fire in the hearth. It was April, springtime, much too warm to need the heat. Odd that he'd taken the trouble to lay and light it. I stared, thinking I'd never seen Dad look old before. In fact, I'd always taken pride in how young and handsome both my parents looked. He seemed to have aged twenty years since he'd laid Mom's ashes in the ground. Dead. Thrown by her horse. By Sassy Britches.

"Dad?"

He held out a hand, his face softening. I went to him, curled myself onto the floor beside his chair, the heat from the fire at my back. I laid my cheek on his knee, and he gently stroked my hair. Silence reigned for several long minutes. I swallowed. "Dad? Maybe you shouldn't have done that."

"Done what, Jen?"

"Gotten rid of Sassy."

He sighed. "Jenna, while your sister may not be a realist, I am. There's no point in keeping Sassy. Who's going to ride her? You and I don't ride, and she's too much horse for Sarah. It's better to let go of the past. To move on as soon as we can."

I raised my face and searched his eyes, feeling a bead of sweat run down my spine. "Do it for me. Please?"

Pain squeezing his strong features, he didn't answer for a long minute. Then, "It means that much to you?"

I thought of Sarah's agonized weeping from behind her closed door. My sister didn't have to tell me that the loss of Sassy on top of the loss of Mom was almost more than she could bear. "It means that much."

He sighed. "I'll see what I can do."

A tiny bubble rose in me. Relief? A sliver of happiness? I laid my cheek back on his knee.

Two days later, the handler returned Sassy to her stall, along with Honey and the other two horses. Though the stable wasn't filled to capacity as it had been before, it was enough for Sarah. It fell to TJ to exercise Sassy. At fifteen, he was nearly as capable on a horse as Mom had been. And most days when he took Sassy out, Sarah took Honey and rode along with him.

CHAPTER 15

SARAH
La Paz, Bolivia
Present day

Back in Sarah's room, lamplight illuminates the bed's fluffy duvet in an amber pool, leaving the corners in shadow. Abby's soothing tones as she tucks in Sofia seep through the shared wall. Sarah finds she's not at all sleepy and regrets her long nap.

Hearing Sofia's girlish giggle, she smiles, then sighs as she recalls her jolt when the child lifted her ravaged face. It's the first cleft palate Sarah has ever seen beyond magazine ads for humanitarian non-profits. The brutal reality of the condition unnerves her, stirring an old, familiar ache. The ache she first felt the year she turned six.

She and Mom were walking home from the bus stop after a half-day of kindergarten when Sarah spied roadkill rotting at the side of the pavement. She froze in horror at the poor creature, flattened and battered almost beyond recognition. Almost. It was a rabbit. A bunny that must have been soft and brown and impossibly adorable in life. She burst into tears, sobbing as her mother led her away.

Later, the storm of weeping past, Sarah sipped a glass of frosty lemonade on the front porch swing, cuddled against her mother's side. Then she haltingly told Mom what had troubled her. It wasn't so much the senseless death of an innocent creature, for as a girl growing up in ranch country, she was well-familiar with death. No, what distressed her deeply was the ugliness of the smashed animal, its beauty lost beyond all redemption.

"That ache is your spirit's longing for beauty, Sarah," Mom told her. "We won't find perfect beauty here on earth, but our longing for it reminds us that heaven awaits. While all possess that longing, it's more acute in some, perhaps." She gave Sarah a squeeze. "Even more so when you have the spirit of an artist, I think. That's why I paint. As an expression of beauty. But I'll tell you something else, Sarah Beth. Don't ever try to shut down that ache, no matter how much it hurts, because it's a good thing."

"But how, Mommy? How is it a good thing when it makes me feel so bad?"

"Because it's like the ache God feels when He sees His creation destroyed or His people hurting. When the things that hurt God's heart hurt ours too, that keeps us close to Him. And that's always a good thing. You understand?"

She'd nodded, though of course she hadn't understood. Not at age six. Nor at age sixteen. Even now at twenty-six, she feels she is only beginning to catch a glimmer of what her mother may have meant.

From Sofia's room comes the murmuring cadence of Abby reading a book in Spanish. Sarah listens a moment but is unable to pick out distinct words, only the lilt of Abby's voice. Another niggling thought rises to the surface. Abby clearly loves the child, so why allow her deformity to go uncorrected? Abby is a nurse, after all. Surely she has the means to fix what is broken here.

An unexpected hunger for home grips Sarah, a longing for what is safe and familiar and whole. Before she can change her mind, she speed-dials Dad's number.

He answers on the third ring. "Sarah."

She closes her eyes at the timbre of his familiar voice, nearly giving in to the urge to weep. Though at times she's wished she had the same wealth of memories of Dad that she does of Mom, hearing his voice now reminds her she still has the chance to make new ones.

"How's it going down there?" He sounds good, better than she'd hoped, and her heart beats a little more lightly.

"Fine. It's been a long day, lots of stuff to take in. Feeling pretty wrung out at the moment."

"Bet you are. They treating you okay?"

"Everyone's very kind, but how are you?"

"Keeping busy."

"That doesn't answer my question."

"Don't you be worrying 'bout me, that's not your job. I was hoping you'd call. Shane said he spoke to you."

"I meant to call earlier but I fell asleep." She can hear voices ringing out in Spanish across the line. The field workers, she realizes with a fresh twang of homesickness, probably beginning the night harvest of the chardonnays. "What did Shane tell you?"

"He mentioned Jenna named you beneficiary in her will." He clears his throat. "And got herself married down there. That really true?"

"Yes, Dad." So he hadn't known. "Her husband was traveling with her, apparently, and got pretty badly hurt in the accident. I'm meeting him tomorrow in Santa Cruz."

"What's his name, you know?"

"Jonas. Jonas Jackson."

Dad blows out a breath. "He's American then."

"I think so. Guess I'll find out tomorrow." Her bag lies sprawled on the bed beside her. She pulls it toward her and retrieves the envelope Rand gave her, noting again the Washington postmark. "They also gave me the last of Jenna's mail. Who does Jenna know in Chelan?" She hears the present tense of her question but is unable to stop it. So hard to grasp that everything about Jenna now resides in the past.

"Chelan? No one I can think of. "

"She must know someone because there's a letter with a Chelan postmark but no return address."

"Well, why don't you open it and find out?"

"I thought I'd let her husband do that."

"I'd say you have as much business doing it as he does."

"Maybe." But knowing she won't. She doesn't have as much confidence as Dad in her right to do so. Returning the letter to her bag, she says instead, "I wish you could be here. To hear all the nice things people are saying about Jenna. Everyone's so devastated."

A knock sounds at her door.

"Oh, I think that's Abby. Can I call you right back?"

"How 'bout you give me call tomorrow when you get to Santa Cruz? After you've met this Jonas person, you can fill me in. Okay?"

"Sure, sounds good. Tomorrow, then."

As she sets the phone on the dresser, the soft tapping comes again. She hastens to open the door. Only it isn't Abby standing in the doorway.

"Chase, hi." She resists the urge to smooth back her hair, trying not to notice the attractive tilt of his smile. She clears her throat. "Was there something you needed?"

"Just came to wish you a good night's sleep. And to say I hope your first day here hasn't been too difficult."

"Not too bad, all things considered."

"All things considered, I'm glad." His eyes crinkle in sympathy. "I know the adjustment to the altitude can be a little rough. It won't be like this in Santa Cruz."

"Good to know." From next door, Abby's voice has fallen silent. "Um, was there anything else?"

"Just—well, I also wanted to thank you."

"To thank me? For what?" She notes his eyes are more green than hazel, a dark cyan, the color of the Columbia River in midwinter. She has a fleeting thought to paint them.

"For being so accepting of Sofia." He glances at the girl's closed door. "As you might imagine, not everyone reacts the way you did."

"Maybe it helps that I have some experience with less-than-perfect children. I teach art to kids with special needs." She smiles. "Sometimes I think they teach me more than I teach them."

"Funny how that works." He returns her smile and starts to say something more when Sofia's door opens and Abby emerges. She draws up short finding Chase in the hallway.

"Thought you'd left already." Amusement quirks her eyebrows as she glances from Chase to Sarah and back again.

"Leaving in a sec." He reaches for Sofia's door. "Realized I forgot to say goodnight to Sofe."

"I just got her settled, Chase. Don't go getting her all worked up again."

"Would I do that?" He winks at Sarah and disappears. A moment later, Sofia's throaty laugh filters into the hall.

Abby rolls her eyes. "That man is impossible." But she smiles as she says it.

CHAPTER 16

"Sarah?" Abby calls softly, rapping on the door.

Sarah rouses, glancing at the alarm clock, set to go off in another hour. Propping herself on an elbow, she invites Abby to come in.

Abby cracks open the door, allowing a thin band of light to stream in from the hallway. "Sorry to get you up so early, but Chase has been listening to the weather report. An unexpected front from the west is headed our way. He's concerned about getting out."

"Do we need to wait?" She swallows a yawn, forcing sleep from her brain.

"Well, that's what he wants to talk to you about. Can you get dressed and come out?"

"Sure. Be there in a minute." Sarah hastens into jeans and a striped yellow tee before sliding her feet into sandals.

In the kitchen, Chase is on the phone, speaking rapidly in Spanish. He offers her a distracted smile as she accepts the mug of fragrant coffee Abby presses into her hands. She blows on the steam and waits for him to finish his call.

Finally, he turns, rubbing the back of his neck. "Mornin'. Sorry to wake you, but we've got a potential hitch in our plans. Big storm heading our way. Started brewing yesterday, now looks as if La Paz is smack in its path. Once we clear the Andes, we should be okay, but we'll have to race to make it."

"What's our other option? Delay?"

"Yes. But there's another storm piled up behind this one. If we wait, it could be days before we're able to get out."

"And if we leave now?"

"If we leave immediately, we will probably beat the worst of it."

"What do you want to do?"

He doesn't hesitate. "I say we go for it."

She sets her mug on the counter. "Then let's go."

～ ○ ～

Leaving Sofia to slumber in peace, they return not to El Alto but to a smaller municipal airport, where a lithe Kodiak waits on the tarmac. Abby parks in a dusty lot outside a gated enclosure as the first, fat raindrops fall from the predawn sky. Chase hurries inside the low building to file his flight plan while Sarah and Abby grab the luggage from the Toyota's trunk. They meet Chase at the plane, where he stashes their bags in the back before running through his pre-flight checklist.

As Sarah mounts the plane's steps, Abby hands her a paper bag. "Snacks for the road. Also some more of that tea in case you need it." Then she hugs Sarah tight, the easy affection causing a lump to rise in Sarah's throat. "*Vaya con Dios.* Stay safe."

Blinking hard, she joins Chase in the cockpit. Harnessed in beside him, she listens as he instructs her in a few basic safety procedures, then shows her how to use the headgear to communicate in flight. He also demonstrates how to strap into a parachute, giving

～ 116 ～

her the first real twinge of unease. She must telegraph her doubt because he grins and squeezes her shoulder. "Just a safety precaution. We'll be fine."

She expels a nervous breath, then chides herself. Before her accident, she wouldn't have thought twice about the risk. She'd have seen only the adventure. The thrill.

Time to recapture some of that spirit.

As the sky begins to lighten, billows of black clouds crest the peaks of the snow-tipped Andes. They lift off the tarmac. Chase tips his wings in a goodbye to Abby, who is waving to them from the ground. Then they head east.

For several minutes, they travel in silence as the little plane climbs. Below, the sprawling city escapes the bounds of the vast canyon formed by the three-peaked Illimani. Despite the urgency of their departure, Chase's motions remain smooth and unrushed. His calm seems to envelop the small cockpit. Even when turbulence jars the aircraft and they slip altitude, Chase is unfazed. Drawing from his confidence, Sarah concentrates on keeping her hands unclenched in her lap.

As the aircraft breaks through the clouds, the day's first light comes over the horizon. Chase levels off the plane, his shoulders relaxing as he glances over at her. "Doing okay?" His voice, soothing and low, sounds through her headset.

"Fine."

"Small planes make some people nervous, even in the best conditions."

"No, I'm good." Better than good, actually. Her gaze sweeps the clear, sapphire sky. Despite the knowledge of what awaits when they land, a ripple of exhilaration expands inside her chest.

"You been in a small plane before?"

"Not since I was a child. Sometimes we'd catch a hop from Wenatchee to Spokane or Seattle on our way to Europe."

"What were you doing in Europe?"

"My parents were learning how to operate a vineyard. They liked to soak up firsthand knowledge from Old World vintners. Sometimes they took Jenna and me with them."

"I'd love to get there myself, someday."

"You've not been?"

"Never. Hoping I might find myself over there pretty soon, though, if Rand's plans pan out." He glances at her. "In any case, sounds like your dad's venture paid off."

"It did." The interest in his gaze warms her, making it easy to want to share the story with him. "Most of our neighbors thought he was crazy. I mean, everyone knows Washington can grow apples, but grapes? A lot of people thought we were far too north to be successful."

She relates one of Dad's favorite tales: how millennia ago, the great Spokane Flood changed in only a matter of hours everything that had taken thousands of years to create, altering the land's form, its very soil, forever. And how this seemingly shattering devastation turned out to be a blessing for the future farmers of Washington, laying vast deposits of well-drained, alluvial soil.

Chase tilts his head thoughtfully. "In other words, leaving a lot of highly fertile land."

She nods. "Perfect for growing wheat, apples, pears—and grapes. But when Dad was looking to make the change, no one knew that yet. It took him six tries before he found a bank that would lend him the start-up money. Now, of course, we've got tons of competition— and more new wineries opening every year. Washington has become the second-biggest wine-producing state in the country. Only California does more."

"I understand wine-making is quite an art."

She can't hold back a small smile. "Shane would say the best wines are the result of art and science combined."

"That's the guy you mentioned last night. Your winemaker, right? Guess he's pretty good at what he does."

"That's what they say."

"You don't say it yourself?"

"I'm not an expert."

"A vintner's daughter, and you're not an expert?"

"No." Her fingers pick at a loose thread on the shoulder harness. "I only live there."

"I see." As his eyes lock on hers, she can't help but notice his eyelashes—long and thick, but not a bit girlish. "So you can't say for sure how good this guy is at making wines, but you like him anyway."

"Why would you say that?"

One muscled shoulder lifts in a slight shrug. "Not hard to guess, the way you've talked about him. He likes you too?"

"So he says."

"And what makes you think he's not telling the truth?" He holds her gaze a moment longer before looking out the cockpit window.

The loose thread tugs free, and she wads it into a tiny ball. Though she meant it as a light remark, she may have spoken some truth in jest. Was this what niggled at her when she and Shane spoke last night? A sense that, though he said all the right words, he was holding something back?

Or am I the one holding back?

She shakes off the nagging doubt. It's hardly something she can talk about with a man she's just met. "And you? Anyone special around here or back home?"

"Not at the moment." He seems not to notice the abrupt change in subject. Or more likely, is too polite to comment on it.

"That's too bad."

He grins. "My mother would agree with you."

She lifts an eyebrow. "But you don't?"

He shrugs. "It's not that I don't want it. Just haven't found it. Yet."

"So there's still hope." She sends him a teasing smile.

His laugh comes as a low rumble through the headset into her ears. "There's always hope."

"An optimist, I see."

"I've learned to be." He makes an adjustment to his control panel. "You warm enough? I can turn up the heat a bit."

"I'm fine." She peers down at the changing landscape, at the fields of crops dotted by the occasional dwelling. "So where is home, by the way?"

"Colorado. Though I haven't lived there for nearly a decade."

"How long have you been with La Fuente?"

"About four years."

"And before that?"

"Afghanistan, mostly."

"Army or Air Force?

"Army."

"And that's where you learned to fly?"

"Good guess."

She settles back into her seat, oddly content. With the clouds slipping behind them, they can see for miles. The little plane's size and speed makes her think of the movement and freedom she used to know when she flew across the land on Honey. Something Mom used to say pops into her head. *The air of heaven is that which blows between a horse's ears.*

And maybe that which flows beneath a small plane, too. "It's glorious up here."

"I couldn't agree with you more." He glances at her and smiles, his gaze holding hers a moment longer. She hopes the warmth at the back of her neck doesn't mean she's blushing.

CHAPTER 17

After they land and disembark, Chase peels off his navy North Face sweatshirt to reveal a white t-shirt reading *eschew obfuscation* across the front in neon orange. The weather in Santa Cruz is nothing like what they've left. Here it's at least twenty degrees warmer, sunny, and so muggy the air feels like a second skin.

While Chase disappears into the flight office, another La Fuente employee, Rachael Gray, meets Sarah on the tarmac. Tanned, tall and slim, Rachael wears her long, chestnut waves pulled into a messy ponytail. She carries a basket, a bright-eyed, golden puppy with a stiff white cast on its front leg nestled inside. After setting down the basket, she gives Sarah a warm hug. "Jenna was like a sister to me." Rachael has an Aussie accent and smells of lavender. "I miss her more every day." When she pulls away, tears pool in her brown eyes. "I hope we'll be friends, too."

Sarah smiles, crouching to pet the puppy. "What happened to this little guy?"

"This is Miski," she says, as if that explains it all.

"Miski?" She squints up at Rachael as the puppy's small pink tongue caresses her fingers.

"Jenna's dog."

"I didn't know she had a dog." Sarah straightens, wiping her hand across the seat of her jeans. "Jenna and I didn't talk a lot."

"Oh." A small furrow puckers her brow. "Well. Miski was traveling with Jonas and Jenna the night of the accident. He got hurt, too, but doc said he's going to be fine." She bends to tug on one of Miski's golden ears. "Right, mate?"

A shadow slants across Miski's basket. Rachael turns to greet Chase, who clutches several sheets of paper fluttering in the breeze. He scoops Rachael into a bear hug. When he releases her, she smiles up at him. "How was your trip, Chase Maddox?"

"Thrilling."

"Sure, if you relish flying in a tin can. *I* don't." She picks up Miski's basket, and Sarah and Chase follow her to a faded brown Ford pickup with extended cab. Rachael stows the puppy in the backseat. When Sarah offers to sit with him, Rachael tosses the keys to Chase and takes the passenger seat.

"So," Chase merges skillfully into the traffic flowing away from the airport. "How's Jonas?"

"Not great." Rachael angles herself so Sarah can hear her above the roar of wind through the open windows. "Physically, he's ready to be discharged, but his heart is breaking. I think it's really starting to hit him that his wife's not coming back."

Not coming back. The words strike Sarah like a slap, the truth always lingering in her periphery and darting at her sideways when she's not expecting it.

"He remember anything yet?" Chase asks.

"No. Not since I talked to him last night, anyway."

Sarah gazes out the window, suddenly off-kilter, almost jittery, knowing she is about to meet her sister's secret husband. She is also terribly curious. What kind of man married headstrong Jenna?

To distract herself, she adjusts Miski in his basket and strokes fur the color of butterscotch. *Miski*—Chase told her it means "sweet" in Quechua, a touch of whimsy so like Jenna. "What's going to happen to the puppy?"

"Kind of depends on what Jonas wants to do," Rachael says, "whether he decides to keep him. If he even chooses to stay here. Miski really was Jenna's dog. She took him everywhere with her. Even had a special basket installed on her motorbike."

"If Jonas doesn't want to hang on to him, he's always welcome with me," Chase says.

"Kinda figured as much." Rachael gives his arm a squeeze.

They leave the freeway and weave through city streets, Rachael maintaining a steady stream of conversation, asking Sarah about her trip and her stay with Abby. "She gave up everything to marry Luca and move here," she says after Sarah mentions how welcome Abby has made her feel. "Her family actually has some connection to British nobility."

Sarah's eyebrows rise. Chase glances in the rearview at her, amused.

Rachael chuckles. "I know, right? She never drops a clue. Her dad and mum are lord and lady something-or-other, wanted Abby to marry an earl, but she fell in love with Luca while traveling in Italy during her gap year. 'Course, this was like a thousand years ago, but she's absolutely my hero. I want to be just like her when I grow up. In fact—" She glances down at her phone. "Oh! Jonas just texted. Wants to know where we are."

Chase flicks on his turn signal and prepares to change lanes. "Almost there."

They wait in the crowded hospital lobby until a white-coated man pushes through the double-doors separating them from the hospital's interior. His badge reads Dr. Manuel Martinez. He has light, smooth skin, brown hair and John Lennon-esque glasses perched on a thin nose. After greeting them in Spanish, he leads them to a closet-sized consulting room furnished with a rickety card table and three stiff, plastic chairs. Everyone chooses to remain standing.

"Jonas wanted me to explain a few things," Dr. Martinez begins once he has closed the door behind them. He shoves his hands deep into his lab coat pockets while his eyes scan the room as if anticipating the next emergency. "I spoke again with Abby Carmichael this morning. She said you have been informed of his amnesia. Unfortunately, in the last day or two, another situation has come up. Jonas has begun to experience what we call petit mal seizures, sometimes called absence seizures because the person 'goes absent,' mentally speaking, for a period of time. The ones we've seen in Jonas have been of short duration. These are not violent episodes. Instead, motion ceases and cognitive thinking is interrupted, like someone pressing the pause button."

Sarah glances at the others, whose stunned expressions reflect what she feels. She doesn't even know this man, Jonas, but she aches for him. He loses his wife, then his memory, and now this.

Chase finds his voice first. "How long will he experience these absence seizures?"

"Impossible to say without further tests. When he returns to the States, he will undergo an EEG to determine whether he sustained permanent brain damage or if this is an anomaly connected to his head injury. If it is permanent damage, he'll have to take precautions when driving or operating heavy machinery, and he'll be on anti-seizure medication for the rest of his life."

Sarah's heart twists, understanding perhaps better than anyone else in the room the double burden Jonas might now have to live with: both the not-knowing *and* the knowing that nothing will ever be the same again.

Chase clears his throat. "What about his memory loss? Will these seizures make his amnesia permanent?"

"I would not yet give up hope." The doctor gives a small, tight smile. "In many, perhaps even most cases, memory is recovered in time. But there are no guarantees. The brain is an incredibly complex organ. We are not even close to being able to unlock all its secrets. There is a very real possibility Jonas may never remember." Dr. Martinez glances at his watch. "One more thing." He looks at each of them in turn. "Do any of you know why his wife was leaving Bolivia?"

"She was coming home for a visit," Sarah says.

"Yes, but do you know why?"

"No," she admits. "Not really. Is it important?"

"The thing is," Dr. Martinez says, "Jonas recalls his wife being very upset about something, perhaps some unexpected news, but he doesn't know what. This troubles him deeply." He sighs, as if this additional unsolved mystery troubles him too. "Regardless of how much or little Jonas remembers, he will need to receive counseling. Grief therapy."

"I assume you've told him all this," Rachael says.

"Of course. But he cannot be responsible for his own care right now. That's why I'm telling you." He turns his head and looks at Sarah. "You are his wife's sister, yes?"

She nods. Chase moves closer. A warm hand rests against her lower back, offering unspoken support. "How well do you know your brother-in-law?"

"I've never met him." She lifts both hands. "My family wasn't informed of the marriage." The pressure of Chase's palm increases slightly.

The doctor's expression shows surprise. "You will get to know him well, then, I think. For his own good, sí?" He doesn't wait for her answer. "I will go get him now. He is very eager to leave here." He moves toward the door, but then turns back. "Oh, I almost forgot. He has repeatedly mentioned a dog. Miski?"

"Jenna's puppy," Rachael says. "He was with them in the accident and was injured but is doing okay now."

"And where is Miski?"

"Waiting for us in the car."

"Well, this may be a good sign that he's asking about her dog. Perhaps it indicates the tiniest glimmer of memory."

As they move to follow the doctor from the room, Chase's hand gently slides from Sarah's back. In the main waiting room, they form a cluster and exchange uncomfortable glances. Perhaps the others, like Sarah, are beginning to realize that Jonas's recovery could prove more complicated than they imagined.

"Do you have any idea what may have upset Jenna?" Rachael asks. Chase shrugs, Sarah shakes her head. If she knew, it might give her a clue to … so many things. "I wish Abby were here," Rachael murmurs. "She'd know what to do."

"We'll call her tonight." When Chase squeezes Sarah's shoulders in a one-armed hug, she shoots him a grateful look, glad to not be facing this alone.

"Should we go and get him?" Rachael asks. "Or do you think they'll just send him out?"

Sarah swivels around, looking for the doctor so they can ask. There's no sign of him, but at that moment, a towering, black man with hair shaved close and his left arm in a sling pushes through the swinging door that separates the waiting room from the patient ward. He pulls up short as his eyes lock on hers. Her pulse jumps and accelerates as Rachael gasps and lunges across the room toward him.

Jonas?

When Rachael circles her arm around his lean waist, Sarah shoots a questioning glance at Chase. His kind smile provides the answer.

CHAPTER 18

JENNA
Age 18
Selah, Washington

"So?" I twirled in front of the mirror. "What do you think?"

"Nice," Sarah said.

I stopped spinning to frown at my sister, sitting cross-legged on Nana's quilt. "Nice?" I ran a hand down the satiny length of the lavender sheath. "That's all you got?"

Sarah offered an absent smile, absorbed with fiddling with Mom's old camera.

I stared for a moment at the crooked part jagging along the top of Sarah's bent head. Despite her distraction, I felt grateful for her company while I dressed. It was my senior prom, after all. Mom wasn't here to see it, Dad out in the fields. He was clueless anyway, and I needed someone to take pictures when Mike got here.

I turned back to my reflection. Sarah didn't have to tell me I looked awesome in this dress. Mike was gonna love it.

Mike. Just focus on Mike. In an hour, we'd be together with the whole night in front of us.

I glanced at the carved mahogany box on my bookshelf, thinking of the bundle of notes—love notes, from *him*—hidden inside, away from Sarah's inquisitive eyes. She thought she was so subtle, but I knew she'd never given up trying to get inside that box. For some reason, she obsessed over anything special Dad gave me. Instinctively, I touched the silver charm bracelet dangling from my wrist. Maybe she fixated on my stuff because she so easily lost hers. Her own quinceañera charm bracelet had vanished only months after Dad gave it to her. At any rate, I knew she could never open that box, not without the key. And I was the only one who knew the secret of its whereabouts.

My pulse quickened as I thought about Mike's last note. He wrote things I never dreamed a guy would even think to write to a girl. He knew me like no one else, seeing all the way down to my *soul*. He wrote about our future together as if it were already settled. His life experience had grown him up fast—one of the things I loved best about him.

I began to style my hair, having already decided on an upsweep with tendrils on the sides. The first time I met Mike, I'd had my hair in a ponytail, and he always said he liked it up.

We'd met when I'd gone with some friends to an away basketball game, the first game I'd gone to in the six months since Mom had died. I'd been surprised to find myself noticing the hot guy with the gorgeous brown eyes working behind the concessions counter. Of course, it was hard *not* to notice a six-foot-three guy who had to duck to get his head beneath the service window. Plus, he was so thoughtful, making sure I knew I could get a popcorn refill if I brought my empty tub back before the game was over.

At halftime, I told Monica I was going for my free refill. She gave me a look. "They don't give free popcorn refills."

"Sure, they do," I insisted. "The guy behind the counter told me."

"He did, huh?" Monica narrowed her eyes. "He just said that to get you to come back."

Monica was right. Not until our second date, though, did Mike confess his fib.

That was last February. We'd been dating nearly four months now, though, strangely, tonight would be the first time he'd meet anyone in my family. If Mom were alive, she would have had him over for dinner a dozen times already, eager to know everything about him. But Dad was too busy getting on with his life to notice that someone was making me smile again.

When I was finally ready, I stepped into the courtyard to wait. I held Mike's boutonniere, a lavender rosebud that matched my dress. A perfect evening, the sun bathing the vineyard in warm, peach light, a breeze wafting the fragrance of honeysuckle blossoms. And then there was Mike. I didn't even notice the rusted dents in his sky-blue pickup anymore. I saw only him. He slid from behind the wheel, unbelievably tall and shockingly handsome in a dove-gray tux that complemented his coppery skin. In his boots, with his jet-black hair parted down the middle and pulled into a ponytail, Mike Niceleaf looked every inch the full-blooded Yakima Indian he was. His smile brought a rush of desire so thick and fast I nearly forgot to breathe.

Sarah must have heard the truck because she emerged from the house with Mom's camera. For the next ten minutes, she shot frame after frame. My sister knew her way around a camera, just like Mom. Mike couldn't take his eyes off me. His stare created a tingle low in my belly, one that set up a dizzying anticipation for what might happen *after* the dance.

When we were finishing up, Dad came out of his office. I made introductions. Dad nodded and shook Mike's hand and told him to keep me safe and to have a good time. But Dad's tight smile told me something wasn't right. I saw him in the side-view mirror, standing in the courtyard, arms crossed, watching as we drove down the lane toward town. An uneasy foreboding crept into my spirit like fog creeping over the foothills.

I tried to push Dad from my thoughts, but the vision of his frown kept flitting across my memory, hobbling my happiness. Though I wasn't thinking about him when Mike brought me home at 3 a.m.—until I let myself into the house, still weak-kneed from Mike's last kiss. Dad was waiting in the living room. He rose from the cold hearth. "Have a good time?"

"It was great, Dad." Ignoring the nervous thudding of my heart, I tried on a smile, hoping to shift the mood. "But you didn't need to wait up for me."

"No trouble. That boy treat you well? With respect?"

"Mike?" I didn't like Dad calling him a *boy*. "Of course. He always does. He's a gentleman." I emphasized the last syllable.

"You like him then."

I love him. My skin still burning from where Mike had touched me, I almost said so, but the lowering of Dad's brow told me to steer wide. "I do, actually."

"I see." He pointed to the couch. "Have a seat."

"Now? Dad, I'm really tired, and—"

"This won't take long. Should have said it before now." I obeyed. True to his word, he got straight to the point. "Jen, do you see a future with this boy?"

"I—I don't know. Dad, we're in high school."

"And next year, you'll be in college. If you're not thinking about the future now, you will be then. I suppose you think yourself in love with this Mike." I started to answer, but he didn't pause. "Listen, this may be hard for you to hear, but I'm trying to spare you pain down the road. Whatever you think you have with this guy will never last. I guarantee you that. His kind can never go the distance with one of our kind."

"One of our—?" I choked, the happiness I'd tasted only minutes before evaporating like vapor in the wind. "Is this because he's Native?"

"No, no it's not. I don't care what color his skin is. I care about what he's made of, who his people are, and how that's going to affect you down the road."

"I don't believe you."

"You don't believe it will affect your future?"

"No." I narrowed my eyes. "That it's not about skin color."

His face darkened. "Don't speak to me like that. Not while you're living under my roof."

I drew back, pressing myself into the couch cushions.

"Look." Apparently sensing my fear, he softened. "I know it's hard, and I'm sorry that it hurts you. I also know it's more ... politically correct now than it was, but mixing different cultures gets tricky."

"Why should it be tricky?" In his softening, I saw the chance to plead my case. "Because we don't have the same standard of living? Or vision for the future? Mike's not like that, Dad. He's different than a lot of ... others on the rez. He's not going to be stuck there forever, if that's what you're afraid of. He's smart and ambitious. Like you. He has plans. He's going to WSU to study engineering—computers—and he already has his first year paid for with scholarships." I stumbled to a halt as Dad set his jaw and glanced away.

The grandfather clock in the foyer must have ticked away a full minute before he looked at me again. "It's one thing to work, or even to socialize, with people like Mike. Beyond that? Well, as I said, I'm trying to spare you greater pain down the road. You understand that, don't you?"

"But shouldn't I be the one who gets to make that decision? If I get hurt, shouldn't that be on me?"

"Not while you're my daughter."

My mind flew to the mahogany box upstairs, to the other secret it contained. With a queasy thud, I felt again the dread of my recent discovery, a dread I'd been able to ignore because of Mike. But all at once, I realized that my fear hadn't disappeared, it had only been thrust away. Though Mike had provided a welcome distraction, he would never be enough to make it vanish altogether.

"What am I supposed to tell Mike?" Hating how small my voice sounded. Defeated already.

"The truth. That you see no future together. That it would be better to end things now, before you get any more involved." He pulled me to him, hard against his chest. I hadn't realized the extent of his tension until I felt his muscles relax. "I'm sorry this is hard, but I know it's what's best. That's what fathers do. It's what *Lannings* do for each other. Right?"

I nodded, wrapping my arms around his middle. Because I needed him. More than I needed anyone else.

~ ⌒ ~

Back in my room, I didn't sleep, too lacerated by loss to lose myself in slumber. Hours later, close to noon, Sarah tapped on my door. When I didn't invite her in, she spoke anyway. "The photos turned out amazing. I ran into town and got the best ones developed. Want to see them?"

"No."

"Why?" Sarah tried the door, found it locked. "What's wrong? Jenna, let me in."

"No." My refusal became the first brick in the wall separating me from my sister.

After I heard her move on down the hall and the quiet closing of her bedroom door, I emerged to use the bathroom. Sarah had left the camera and packet of photos on the hall table. In a moment of weakened resolve, I looked. Sarah was right. The photos were amazing.

I took the best one and left the rest. Closeted again in my room, I stared at the image of Mike and me, tried to imagine his face when I told him I couldn't see him again. And for the first time, I doubted whether I had what it took to be a journalist. The best journalists sought to uncover truth above all else, yet I was afraid to seek out the truth of my own self.

I retrieved my carved wooden box, inserted the key, opened the lid. Pulled out the object that had thrown me into confusion. What if I was wrong about what it meant? That would change everything. I fingered the photo of Mike and me. If only I *knew*. The uncertainty made me weak. But there were ways to find out. I knew what I needed to do. Simple, really. I had only to summon the courage to follow through—and accept the truth no matter what.

CHAPTER 19

SARAH
Santa Cruz, Bolivia
Present day

Seeing her sister's husband sparks a long-buried memory.
Sarah and TJ had started their freshman year at Central Washington. Away from their families for the first time in their lives, they hung out together. A lot. Then they started dating. And then they fell for each other. Hard.

When she returned home for Christmas break that year, she hoped the passage of time might have somehow eased the emotional coolness in her sister that began, as near as Sarah could place it, around the time of Jenna's high school prom. She missed the sleepovers they used to have in each other's room, the late nights in front of the fire with a shared bowl of kettle corn and a chick flick. Throughout the past couple of years, Jenna had kept her door shut and spent more time away from the vineyard than she did with her family. Once, when Sarah heard weeping behind Jenna's door, she stepped inside to find her sister shoving a crumpled sheet of paper behind her pillow. "Don't you ever knock?" Jenna barked. She kept her door locked after that.

With the rift widening, Sarah gambled on confiding in Jenna as a way of bridge building. So she told her she and TJ were in love.

An odd smile twisted Jenna's mouth. "TJ," she repeated. "Tomaso and Vina's full-blooded *Mexican* grandson." When Sarah stared at her, baffled by her reaction, Jenna chuckled without humor. "Didn't you ever wonder why Mike and I split up?"

"No." She'd always assumed they'd simply gone the way of most high school couples.

That's when Jenna told her what happened the night of her prom. The truth dismayed Sarah, though it didn't altogether shock her. Dad had always been clannish. It was the dark side of his loyalty to his family, his tribe, his people. What Mom used to call "the Lanning pride."

So she told Jenna she didn't care what Dad thought. She loved TJ and would not stop seeing him just because her father was a bigot. And she dismissed Jenna's warning as irrelevant.

But now, as she trails Jonas and the others to the double-cabbed pickup truck, she wonders if Jenna had been trying to warn her of something else as well. Maybe her sister hoped that by making sure Sarah saw their father's feet of clay, she wouldn't be tempted to put him on a pedestal as Jenna had done. When her father fell off, as men on pedestals eventually must, had Jenna's heart not survived the fall?

Though Sarah doesn't have the answer, it strikes her that she now knows why Jenna kept her marriage a secret. She must have feared telling Dad she'd married a black man. Could that have been the reason she was coming home? To tell Dad the truth while shielding her husband from his reaction?

It also hits her in a new way that maybe there was more to Jenna's distancing herself than the shame Sarah had brought to the family name. Yes, the accident and Sarah's role in it seemed to be the last straw. That delineation was too plain to miss. But what else might have been going on in Jenna's life that Sarah did not know? What secrets had she been keeping?

All this tumbles through Sarah's mind as Miski squirms in ecstatic reunion with Jonas. Rachael finally manages to get the dog into his basket and into the backseat. Jonas climbs in beside him, and Sarah takes her position on the other side. Once they're underway, Miski now curled on Jonas's lap, Sarah glances over to find Jonas staring at her. He looks so uncertain and confused—just like a little boy. She can't help it. She gives him a smile.

His shy grin in return swells her heart. "I'm so glad to finally meet you," he says. "I don't think I'd have guessed you two were sisters."

"We didn't resemble each other much." Jenna looked like Mom. Sarah looks like Dad. For as long as she can remember, she's wished it were the other way around, that she'd been the one blessed with gorgeous auburn waves, porcelain skin, and generous curves. Although Jenna's facial features may not have been classically beautiful, to Sarah's eye they were infinitely more interesting. Her own light brown hair seems too plain, her fine features too regular and predictable.

"Still," Jonas goes on, "not hard to tell you're both Lannings."

She darts him a quizzical look, sensing something hiding behind his words but not comfortable enough to ask. "She told you about me?"

"Quite a bit, actually."

Unable to control her curiosity, she asks what Jenna said.

"That you've been through the fire and deserve everything good coming your way."

Her mind flits to Jenna's inheritance. Was this why she left her the money? Because she pitied her? She shakes the thought aside and looks down at her hands, clasped in her lap. "I haven't had the chance to say this to you, but I'm awfully sorry for your loss, Jonas. I lost a sister, but you—you lost your wife."

"Thank you." The words are husky, barely there. "I know you can relate, some, to what it's like."

She lifts her gaze to his again, questioning.

"She told me about TJ," he admits softly, his espresso-brown eyes searching hers. "She missed him, too."

A tiny lance stabs beneath her breastbone as it always does at the mention of TJ's name. She blinks, a little stunned by how quickly this stranger has breached her defenses.

A minute passes before Jonas speaks again, his voice barely discernible above the flow of wind through the cab of the truck. "Does it ever get any easier? Being left behind?"

His quiet anguish, the agony on his face squeezes her chest like a vise. She takes in the faint purpling around his jaw, the nearly healed abrasion across his right cheekbone. Thinks of the pain he's already suffered. "It does. Eventually."

"I'm scared," he says, low.

"I know." She swallows. "Me, too."

"Why?"

She looks down at her hands again, picks at the frayed edge of a chipped fingernail. "I'm scared that the way we were with each other toward the end will be my last memories of her. That I'll forget what it was like growing up with her, how much I used to love being her sister."

Jonas says nothing. She looks at him, concerned she may have said too much. But he is nodding, a muscle jumping in his jaw. "And I'm scared I might forget her altogether. We weren't together very long. A little over a year. What if I forget what she was like? Who she was? My *wife*."

"What do you remember now?"

His broad chest rises as he inhales deeply before releasing his breath. "The way her hair looked like cinnamon and smelled like vanilla. That one crooked tooth, which only made her smile more interesting. How her laugh could explode out of her, making everyone in the room turn to look. And how when she found something really funny, her legs couldn't hold her up and she'd collapse on the floor."

"I remember those things, too."

"I'm afraid I'll forget the way her breath sounded when she slept beside me at night. The feel of her skin, like satin, against mine. I'm afraid I'll wake up one day and find all my memories of her erased, like the accident. Or worse, that I'll still remember everything but will go through a whole day without thinking of her once."

"I don't think you need to worry about that. No one who knew Jenna could forget her completely." She reaches for Jonas's hand and holds it. "Even from the other side of eternity, she simply won't allow it."

He returns her gaze for a long moment before turning his face toward the window.

⁓ ᴐ ⌒

As Santa Cruz drops farther behind, Chase remarks on their progress, predicting they'll arrive at Jonas and Jenna's home well before nightfall. As the truck bumps over increasingly rutted pavement, Sarah wonders how far the accident site is from the city. An hour? Three? Will they be able to see it from the road?

Similar thoughts must have been passing through Jonas's mind because after about thirty minutes, he leans forward to speak to Chase. "Where did it happen?"

Chase doesn't pretend to misunderstand Jonas's question. "About two hundred kilometers from the city."

"We'll be driving by it today, won't we?"

"Afraid so," Chase says. "There's really no other way."

Jonas nods. "When we get there, I want to stop."

"What? Why?"

"I want to see it."

Rachael turns around, brown eyes wide and worried. "Jonas, I really don't think—"

"My wife died there. I want to see it. Maybe then I'll remember."

The interior of the cab goes silent, Jonas's words falling around them like rocks tossed into a pool. Finally, Chase speaks. "You're sure, man? It's all still pretty recent. It could be rough."

"Have you been there, Maddox?"

Chase hesitates. "No."

"You, Rae?"

She shakes her head. "I've been by it, but I didn't stop."

"Do you either of you know what it looks like?"

"I've only heard reports," Chase says. "The bus is gone, and it's been mostly cleaned up, but—who knows what we'll find."

"I don't care." Jonas sets his jaw. "I need to see it."

Chase and Rachael exchange glances. "Okay." Chase's shoulders rise and fall in a sigh. "If you feel it's something you need to do. We'll stop."

After their first conversation, Sarah and Jonas don't talk much, though she finds herself watching him when he's not looking. His features are strong, clean-cut, handsome. Even with his arm in a sling, he exudes the powerful presence of a natural athlete.

Another hour drags by. Jonas keeps his face turned toward the window. Guessing what's running through his mind, she pictures the urn gently cradled among soft blankets in the back. She thinks, too, of the letter to Jenna in her tote and wonders when she should give it to Jonas. Or whether it would be kinder to quietly slip it into his bag for him to discover in his own time.

The hot wind roars ceaselessly through the open windows. Their passage over the mostly unpaved road jars Sarah's bones until she fears they will rattle apart. She longs for Abby's guest room, the clean, crisp sheets, the quiet. Jonas somehow manages to drift to sleep, his head against the window padded by a folded sweatshirt.

She closes her eyes and sees Dad the day after Mom's memorial service, hiring packers to remove her belongings from their bedroom—clothes, shoes, books, everything except her paintings, jewelry, and a box of personal mementos, which he sent to gather dust in the attic. Even at fifteen, she sensed him trying to hurry his grief along, as if it could be put on a production schedule, like his grapes.

The truck slows. Sarah opens her eyes as Rachael reaches back to squeeze Jonas's knee. "Almost there."

He straightens, frowning. "Already?"

The truck jerks as it leaves the road and settles onto the scant shoulder. Jonas's gaze finds Sarah's, a tremor shaking his frame.

"You okay?" Her stomach clenches so hard she fears she might throw up.

He closes his eyes and nods.

She hauls in a deep breath. Leaving Miski in the well-ventilated cab, she follows the others from the truck.

Four crosses mark the site where the microbus left the road, a stretch unprotected by a guardrail. The crosses are festooned with plastic flowers, already fading beneath the relentless Bolivian sun. A rut like a scabbed-over wound cuts through the dense brush, marking the removal of the bus.

In the naked heat, birds twitter in shrubs that rise as high as Jonas's head, while yellow daisies sway in a slight breeze. Rachael pauses to pick a small bouquet. The sun's punishing rays make Sarah wish for a hat. Perspiration coats her skin, yet beneath her arms feels cold, clammy.

A rough path has been etched beside the scarred swath caused by the bus, a path that must have been created by rescuers' countless trips up and down the hillside.

Jonas starts the descent, followed by Rachael carrying her clutch of flowers. Chase pauses to look back at Sarah, his eyes questioning: *You okay?* Even after she nods, he hesitates as if he means to wait for her, but she motions him forward. She needs to do this alone.

Picking her way down the hillside, she can't help but imagine the midnight scene. The eerie silence following the crash, the moans of the injured, the whimpering of Miski. The moon, she remembers, had been full. Its light would have guided Jonas and other survivors as they groped among the wounded. Had Jenna gazed upon that full moon in her last dying moments? Had its light brought her any kind of comfort? Did she think of what she was leaving behind, or was she already focused on what lay ahead? Was she even aware?

Sarah looks over at Jonas. Sweat gleams on his smooth forehead, gathering to form a rivulet that runs down his cheek. It splashes darkly from his set jaw onto the shoulder of his gray t-shirt.

Without any memory of that night, Jonas cannot lead them to the location where Jenna died. Rachael turns a slow circle, scanning the area before heading for a thin tree, casting a scant shadow onto the stubbled ground. She places her daisies at the base of the tree. Chase and Jonas join her there, the three of them forming a small semi-circle. Sarah wanders away before they can ask her to join them, though she feels Chase's eyes following her.

Here in the ravine, the heat is even more concentrated than at the top, bearing down on Sarah's head, pressing her into the hard-packed earth. The grass gives off a roasted aroma, not unlike Vina's rosemary bread.

Inhaling, Sarah captures that reminder of her far-away home, aware of a quickening at her core. Releasing her breath in a whoosh, she so viscerally feels a presence beside her that she turns to see if one of the others has come upon her without her realizing.

There is no one. And yet …

The hairs on her arms stand up, a breeze licks her forehead.

Jesus. His nearness brings a settling to her spirit, an easing of tension, as if a coiled spring has sprung. And then, out of nowhere, a tiny lift of joy, so unexpected that her knees soften and she sinks onto the seared ground. Relief washes over her, the kind of relief you feel when you find something precious. Something you haven't even known was lost.

Jesus is here with her. And as surely as she knows her own name, she knows He was with Jenna, too. Here on this hillside. Here when she needed Him.

A drift of wind moves down the slope, rippling the grass. She lifts her face to the breeze, savoring this moment of peace. Placing her hand on the ground, she feels something hard against her palm. Glancing down, a metallic glint catches her eye. She frees the object from its bed of matted weeds, her breath catching in recognition.

Jenna's bracelet.

CHAPTER 20

The bracelet's silver links glimmer in the sunlight. Sarah lost her own quinceañera charm bracelet, a gold one, while out riding Honey, but Jenna had worn hers every day since Dad gave it to her. Sarah turns the delicate chain in her fingers. Dad had added a charm on every birthday after her fifteenth. At least until Jenna left home. But she must have continued on her own, for Sarah counts sixteen charms now, among them a book, a wine bottle, a typewriter, a bunch of grapes, something that looks like a teardrop, a heart, a cross, and an oddly shaped key. The clasp remains undamaged, but one of the links has twisted open. She bends it closed before fastening the bracelet around her left wrist.

A shadow falls across her. She looks up as Jonas squats beside her, holding his injured arm tightly against his body. His gaze settles on her wrist. "Jenna's bracelet," he breathes.

"I found it." Her cheeks warm. "Sorry, I shouldn't have put it on." She moves to undo the clasp but Jonas's big hand stills hers.

"Please," he says. "Keep it."

"You sure?" Squinting against the bright light, she can't read his expression.

"She would have wanted you to have it."

Somehow she knows that, too. "Thank you." Then she reaches behind her neck and undoes her necklace with its simple gold cross. Tomaso gave her this pendant when she was in rehab, but she knows he'd approve of what she has in mind. She lays the cross on the ground in the precise spot where she found Jenna's bracelet.

Jonas seems to understand the gesture. He nods, even manages a faint smile.

They sit in silence a few minutes more before he rises and makes his way back up to the top, where Chase waits with Rachael. When he reaches them, Rachael touches Jonas's arm, looking up into his face as if searching for something, but he shakes his head and Sarah reads his silent message: he still remembers nothing about the accident. Rachael's expression says she doesn't know whether to be relieved or disappointed.

Chase remains where he is, hands shoved into his pockets, patiently waiting. As Rachael and Jonas climb back into the pickup, Sarah begins her ascent. Halfway up, she pauses to look around once more. She stands on the very soil that cradled her sister in her dying moments. This scraggly ravine is hallowed ground. They won't return here, too terrible to dwell long. Yet she is not sorry they've come, after all. Nor does she want to forget it.

You're not the Jenna I knew, are you? She's certain of this now … here. This land, these people changed her sister somehow. *He found me there.* Jenna's long-ago words once more return. *Or I found Him. Or both.*

Sarah lifts her face to the sun, closing her eyes to its intensity. *I don't know what it is you wanted me to see, but I'm willing to look.* To whom is she speaking—Jesus? Jenna? Sarah addresses the wind. *And I'm willing to believe what I see when it appears. Okay?*

Opening her eyes, she finds Chase's concerned gaze on her. She smiles to show him she's all right, and he holds out his hand to help her the rest of the way.

CHAPTER 21

By the time Chase pulls the old pickup truck into a rutted dirt driveway, exhaustion weights Sarah's limbs. All she wants to do is to lay her head on a pillow and sleep for three days. After leaving the accident site, they all fell silent, cocooned in their own thoughts and fatigued by the constant jarring over pocked roads and the enervating heat. Bad as the main roads are, the less-traveled ones are even worse, often little more than hardpan trails. Throughout the last hour, they've often slowed to a crawl to navigate through small herds of llamas and goats, the pungent musk settling thickly in their throats. As they drew closer to Magdalena, where Jonas and Jenna made their home, Sarah caught glimpses of squat houses lining the road, sensing more than seeing the inquisitive gazes of colorfully garbed people.

Rachael hops out to open a gate built into a barbed-wire fence surrounding an adobe house with a red-tiled roof, as squatty as any of those they passed along the way. Made of mud and straw and cement, the whole thing looks as if it would melt in the first good rain. Shriveled fruit trees waste in the dry heat, while a pile of bricks lies in a corner beside a nearly dead vegetable garden. Goats foraging among the roots raise curious eyes as the truck rolls to a stop in front of the house.

When Chase kills the engine, no one moves. Sarah can do nothing but stare. This junk heap was Jenna's home?

Jonas's gentle gaze meets hers, a ghost of a smile playing around his mouth. "It depressed Jenna the first time she saw it, too," he says.

They pile out of the cab, stretching cramped limbs. Miski limps off and relieves himself, creating a miniature yellow river in the dust. An occasional bird calls, and from not too far away comes the rush of moving water.

"Well," Chase starts, "I suppose we go in, see what we can scrounge for dinner? Jonas, I assume you still have the key somewh—" He breaks off as a new sound reaches their ears, a rhythmic scrape above a thread of tuneless humming. A moment later, a woman rounds the bend of what appears to be a communal path, a well-worn trail sloping down the hillside behind the house. She wears a full red skirt and a yellow cotton blouse. Her waist is as stout as a tree trunk, her silver-and-black hair in two thick braids down her back. She pushes an ancient wheelbarrow containing two orange, five-gallon buckets.

Seeing them, she freezes.

Jonas calls out. "Dolores? Dolores!"

With extreme reluctance, she continues her approach, only the steady squeak of the wheel penetrating the silence. Finally, she stops before them, her gaze downcast.

"Dolores, it's good to see you," Jonas begins in Spanish. When she does not immediately respond, he continues awkwardly. "You remember Chase and Rachael? From La Fuente."

"Sí, sí." She nods without meeting their eyes. "Rachael came last week to tell us. About Jenna."

Jonas stiffens, and Sarah's heart breaks for him. He goes on with his introductions. "This is Sarah, Jenna's sister. Sarah, this is Dolores Salamanca, our nearest neighbor."

The ice seems to break a bit as Dolores lifts her gaze to Sarah's, her shrewd black eyes assessing Sarah's face and form. Looking for what? A family resemblance that would link her to the neighbor she lost? Without waiting for Dolores to find whatever she is searching for, Sarah offers her hand. The older woman takes it shyly, dropping it almost as soon as their fingers touch. "I am so sorry for your loss," she says, so quietly Sarah has to strain to hear. "And you, Jonas," she says, turning aside to him. "We have all lost so much, but you, most of all. And I am sorry you are hurt as well."

"Thank you, Dolores." By the softening of his features, it seems her words touch something more than their stiff formality would warrant. Then his tone sharpens as he focuses on the five-gallon jugs in her barrow. "But why are you carrying water up from the river? What's wrong with your well?"

The woman's brow knots. "You don't remember?"

His body freezes. "I, uh—no."

Rachael steps forward. "The accident caused some memory loss, Dolores," she explains. "While the doctors hope his memory will come back, no one knows for sure whether it will."

Dolores nods, clasping her work-roughened hands in front of her.

The silence grows strained. Finally, Jonas says, "Tell me what's wrong. Why are you carrying water from the river like this?"

In a monotone, she explains how just prior to Jonas and Jenna's departure from Magdalena, her daughter and son-in-law's hand pump had been broken, evidently sabotaged. Then, only a week ago, days after learning about Jenna's death, several other members of the Magdalena community awakened to discover their water wells destroyed. Most of the hand pumps were merely dismantled, but one family, who had an old-fashioned drilled well instead of a modern Mark II, found a lame, blind horse tossed into its depths to drown. They'd been unable to pull out the corpse. Now it rots there, poisoning the water.

A sudden lump rises in Sarah's throat, squeezing out a tiny sound. Chase glances at her, touches her shoulder lightly before asking, "Do we know who's responsible?"

"It was done at night," Dolores says. "No one saw."

Jonas starts to say something but closes his mouth again, an odd expression twisting his features.

"I suppose we should check it out." As Chase's shoulders sag, sympathy twangs Sarah's heart. His fatigue must be even worse than hers, having been up hours earlier, then flying and driving countless kilometers of abysmal roads. "We should see if anything can be done to restore these people's water supply ASAP."

"It can wait until morning, surely," Rachael says in English.

"I'm sure it can, but I'd rather see what we're in for now. We don't have a lot of time here. If we can do something to help, we'll need to plan for it." Falling back into Spanish, he asks Dolores if they may stop by her place to take a look. She gives permission before taking up the handles of her wheelbarrow and plodding down the road toward her home.

After she has gone, Jonas turns to Chase. "Jenna thought this might happen."

"What? When? Why didn't she say something to Rand?"

Jonas rubs his forehead, pinching his eyes closed. "It was—on the microbus. That night. I remember she said something about it. She was worried."

"Jonas." Rachael clutches his arm. "Is it coming back?"

"I—I don't know. Maybe. I have this impression—no, an actual memory. She wanted me to get back to Magdalena as soon as I could. She thought if I was here, maybe I could stop it. As Dolores said,

Sixto and Matilde's pump had been damaged, and Jenna was afraid it might happen to others. Matilde is Dolores's daughter. She and Jenna were very close, but Matilde's husband was not happy about some of the changes happening here." He sighs. "I suspect Dolores thinks her son-in-law had something to do with it but won't say so. Not to us, anyway. She'd only tell someone she trusted."

Someone like Jenna, Sarah thinks.

Chase blows out a breath. "Okay. We should probably get to the bottom of this tonight if we can. Sarah, will you be all right if we leave you here with Jonas?"

"Of course."

He nods. "Good. We'll be back as soon as possible."

CHAPTER 22

After the dust plume settles behind the receding truck, Sarah looks to Jonas for a signal as to what to do next. He makes no move to approach the house. Instead, he trails Miski as he noses among the neglected garden. A pair of mud-splattered motorbikes, one with a basket rigged across the handlebars, rests alongside the fence. A goat bleats when Sarah passes the scraggly trees to mount the surprisingly sturdy steps to the tiny dwelling. She scans the length of the porch, mosquitoes buzzing in fly-by's around her head. A green nylon hammock swings in a slight breeze. The ripple of moving water reaches her ears, and fields of crops she can't begin to identify stretch to the horizon. Jenna's home, she thinks, her heart squeezing.

A footfall sounds on the wooden stairs. With Miski cradled in his good arm, Jonas hesitates on the top step, his face creased in uncertainty. She doubts he is prepared for the company of a sister-in-law he barely knows as he re-enters the home he and Jenna so recently shared.

"Would you like me to go in first?" Sarah asks quietly.

His tight expression relaxes in relief, and he nods. "I don't think I can." He fishes out a beaded key ring from his pocket and hands it to her. The heavy, old-fashioned key is warm. The lock scratches when she turns the key. The door opens stiffly, as if resisting her unfamiliar touch.

Inside, the heat feels thinner. The room's two windows are shuttered from the inside. She opens them. As light streams in, she glances around and remembers Rachael said she hadn't touched anything inside the house when she was here last week. Which means everything is exactly as Jenna left it. The thought shoots a warm current along Sarah's limbs.

The house is a single large room, its windows cut into the adobe. Elegant tapestries cover the white, plastered walls. Two antique armoires separate the living space from the bedroom, where a quilted bedspread and plump pillows create a warm and welcoming space. In the opposite corner, a stained sink and an ancient stove form the kitchen, while a red-checked tablecloth on the table brightens the dining area.

Along the far wall, rows of wide planks supported by cinder blocks create a makeshift bookshelf, spilling over with books. Sarah moves farther into the room to scan the spines. Some authors are familiar, others not: Maya Angelou, Henri Nouwen, Luci Shaw, Holly Burkhalter, Nicholas Kristoff, William Butler Yeats, C.S. Lewis, Dietrich Bonhoeffer.

There are also tomes of a different tenor. *The Survival Medicine Handbook, Alternative Water Sources and Wastewater Management, Transnational Peasants of the Andes, The Encyclopedia of Country Living.*

She shifts a book leaning at a cock-eyed angle, then jerks her hand back with a gasp. Behind the book stands a jar containing a fist-sized, hairy spider suspended in amber fluid.

"You found Thor." Jonas speaks from the open door. Backlit by the setting sun, his large frame fills the doorway, his long shadow slanting across the hard-packed floor. "Jenna's tarantula."

"Is that what it is?" She leans in for a closer look.

Jonas chuckles as he sets Miski on the floor. "She never lost her fascination for those guys."

"I see that." Sarah's mind spins back to their childhood. Long before TJ was her best friend, he was Jenna's. Though two years younger than Jenna, they were closely matched in interests and temperament. Tomboy Jenna became his go-to girl for outdoor play, cemented by what Dad called her creepy-crawly stage. Most summers until they hit junior high, they collected an assortment of garter snakes, salamanders, lizards, and frogs. They kept them alive in home-fashioned terrariums until the fall, when, with great ceremony, they'd release them back into the wild.

Sarah examines the preserved tarantula from all angles, less squeamish now that the shock has worn off. How like Jenna to capture something potentially dangerous and render it harmless so she could indulge her obsession.

Sarah closes her eyes. Here, where tangible evidence speaks of her personality and passions, Jenna's presence is very strong.

She wanders into the kitchen. The small pantry contains plastic bins filled with stuff that can survive without refrigeration: sugar, flour, cocoa, olive oil, powdered milk, tea, spices. On the center of the kitchen table, a small earthenware jar holds a withered flower, long dead. On the stove rests a sunny yellow teapot. She picks it up and feels the slosh of water, as if it were ready and waiting to welcome visitors.

I'll hand this to you, Jen. You knew how to make even this armpit of a place feel like home.

Jonas crosses to the larger of the two armoires. Aside from the bed, it is the most substantial piece of furniture in the room.

Cobwebs crackle as he sweeps them aside before opening the doors. He brushes his fingers over neatly hung clothes, a vibrant array of cotton shirts and flowing skirts.

Hoping to give him whatever emotional space he needs, Sarah turns away. A small wood plaque gracing the opposite wall catches her eye. Recognizing Tomaso's handiwork, she looks to Jonas, a remark balanced on her tongue, but the words die in her mouth. Her brother-in-law stares down at the vast bed with its gorgeous quilt and layers of inviting pillows. She freezes at the look on his face, his expression too private for her glance.

Abruptly, he wheels around and heads for the door. "We'll need water for dinner tonight," he rasps, snatching an empty plastic bucket from beside the sink. The little house shudders as the door slams behind him.

⌒ ᦡ ⌒

Sarah rushes after him, making it to the porch before common sense slows her steps. A copse of trees swallows Jonas from view, Miski hobbling at his heels. Staring at the spot where they disappeared, Sarah realizes being alone is probably exactly what Jonas needs right now.

Back inside, she stands in the kitchen, momentarily at a loss for what to do. Then the uncomfortable hollow of her stomach reminds her they have yet to eat.

Glad to have something to occupy her hands, she finds enough in Jenna's pantry to pull together a simple spaghetti dinner. She can't help but smile as she searches her sister's cupboards, all of them obsessively organized. Clearly, Jenna lost none of her control-freak tendencies after leaving home.

While cooking the pasta will have to wait for Jonas to return with water, she opens two cans of pureed tomatoes, which she dumps into a pan and sets to simmer on the propane stove. Then she steps outside to scrounge in the garden for vegetables, immoderately pleased to find some carrots, scallions, and a pepper plant that have managed to survive days without water.

She rinses the veggies in the small amount of water reserved beside the sink. After dicing and tossing them into the simmering marinara, she adds spices and dried herbs. With every motion of her wrist, Jenna's silver charm bracelet lends musical accompaniment.

Looking for more to add to their meal, she roots in the back of the pantry to see what other non-perishables Jenna kept on hand. At the back of the top shelf, Sarah's fingers brush cool glass. She withdraws the object and stares in disbelief. An apple-shaped canning jar filled with applesauce—Vina's homemade applesauce with cinnamon, created from scratch every fall using fruit from their orchard. Sarah special-orders a case of these jars every year from a company on the East Coast. The handcrafted Silverwood Cellars label reveals that this batch is from last year. A note attached to the lid by a length of raffia reads: *Buen apetito! T. also sends his love. ~ V.*

She stares at this mute evidence of Jenna's contact with home, a connection Sarah never even suspected. Why have neither Tomaso nor Vina hinted they kept in touch with her sister? And not just in touch—sending her care packages, no less. She can't imagine what small fortune they must have spent to insure something as fragile as this arrived in Jenna's hands unbroken.

Obviously, Jenna wasn't the only one keeping secrets.

Sarah rubs circles at her temples, fearing the start of another headache. She needs food. They all do. She glances at her watch, feels a pang of alarm. Nearly an hour has passed since Jonas disappeared down the path. She wants to give him his space, but shouldn't he be back by now?

What if he suffered one of those absence seizures Dr. Martinez talked about and fell into the river? She's about decided to go in search of him when above the steady gurgle of the river comes the rumble of an engine. A moment later, the truck pulls in front of the house. She runs out and blurts her concern to Chase.

"How long has he been gone?" He gets out of the truck. On the other side, Rachael does the same.

"Almost an hour." Realizing she's gripping his arm, she lets her hand fall to her side.

Chase exchanges glances with Rachael. "I'll go find him," she says. "Poor mate." She takes off at a jog toward the river.

Chase shakes his head as Rachael disappears into the trees, a grim set to his mouth. Sarah recalls the attempt to learn more about the damaged wells. "Bad news?" She follows him to the house.

"Not good," he admits. He briefly removes his blue Canucks cap to push fingers through his sandy hair. "Tell you more later. Right now, I'd better do some debugging."

"Debugging?"

"Spraying to get rid of scorpions and beetles so you and Rae can sleep inside tonight." From the far corner of the porch, he lifts a large metal tank with a hose attached to it and heads for the door. "The critters like to lurk in corners."

"Scorpions and beetles?"

"Vinchuca beetles, mainly."

She's read about vinchuca beetles, living in the walls of primitive dwellings, threatening rural populations with their threat of incurable, deadly Chagas disease. Then she thinks of the hour-plus she's already spent inside the house in sandals, poking her fingers into dark pantry recesses, and shudders, an involuntary reaction that elicits a chuckle from Chase, the first she's heard since they've arrived in Magdalena. "I take it you don't share Jenna's fascination of creepy-crawlies?"

"Not even close." She crosses to the bookshelves. "Have you seen this?" With two fingers, she holds up the jar containing the giant arachnid suspended in liquid.

He takes it and lifts the jar to the light, turning it to view the specimen from every angle. "That's a beaut. Don't usually see them so big, even down here." He hands it back to her. "Couple of months ago, a spray netted Jenna fifteen dead scorpions, twelve beetles, and two tarantulas. A personal record."

Sarah wrinkles her nose and offers to wait on the porch while he sprays, hoping to catch a glimpse of Jonas and Rachael returning from the river. Five minutes later, Chase joins her again. "Dinner smells great, by the way." He sets the tank back in the corner. "Thanks for getting something started."

"Just some marinara. It was all I could find." She glances toward the river again. Still no sign of the others. "It's going to be dark soon. Should we be worried?"

"Nah. I'm more concerned about losing our light. Rae said the solar panel was out when she was here last week, so I'd better get the generator running before we can't see what we're doing."

She goes inside to light what candles she can find. Chase returns in minutes, lips pressed together. "I know Jonas usually keeps a couple of gallons of petrol in reserve for the generator, but they're not there now. Someone must have lifted them." He shakes his head ruefully. "Will this day never end?" He sighs and pulls the truck keys once more from his pocket. "Don't suppose you'd like to come with?"

"Yes, please," she says, maybe a bit too quickly, which earns her Chase's wry smile. She doesn't like the idea of being left alone, not in the fading light, not with the ghosts of whatever scorpions, beetles and spiders Chase has slain.

She scribbles a quick note for Jonas and Rachael, then follows Chase to the truck.

CHAPTER 23

As they drive to the nearest petrol pump several minutes up the road, Chase tells her what he and Rachael have learned about the community's wells. "They were definitely sabotaged. I was hoping Dolores might have been exaggerating, but if anything, it's worse than she said. It'll take weeks to get the parts needed to repair the hand pumps, not to mention what it's going to cost these people. Money they don't have."

"And what about the other well? The one with the—the horse?"

Chase shakes his head. "Unless we can figure out a way to haul the poor beast out, that one's lost for good."

The thought turns her stomach. "Why would someone do that?"

Chase lets a minute pass before responding. "I have the deepest respect for these people. Their culture, their history. Bolivians are overcomers, some of the strongest, most creative people I've ever met. But strengths can become weaknesses. People become ingrained in ways of thinking that aren't always healthy. When La Fuente comes into a community, we have to move very slowly. The first thing is to build trust, which we do by forging relationships with them. I suspect in this case, we moved too quickly, tried to change things before the community was ready to accept those changes."

"What kind of changes? Weren't the wells a good thing?"

"Attitudes, mainly, many of which run along gender lines. Accepted roles of men and women. The way men and women think about each other and themselves."

While Sarah knows that women in Bolivia, as in so many parts of the developing world, are often relegated to the lowest rung of the societal ladder, she still isn't sure what he's getting at. "But why go after the wells?"

"The women and children—girl children mostly—are responsible for hauling the family's water supply."

She nods, picturing Dolores and her wheelbarrow of water jugs.

"So, when we put in water wells, they are the ones most immediately and obviously helped. Some men find this threatening, because all of a sudden, their women, who before had to spend most of their days carrying water to provide for their family's most basic needs, now have a lot more free time. Time they can use to make their lives a little bit better. Or even a lot better. Time to educate themselves. To learn to read and write. Children, especially the girls who were once pressed into helping their mothers, can now go to school. If they stay in school long enough, they can consider college. And find jobs. Move away. It's the ripple effect of one small change, such as getting water from wells."

"Surely not all men resist."

"Of course not. Many, even most, embrace these changes wholeheartedly. But sometimes you find a community with pockets of stubborn attitudes. They are hard to shift." He glances at her. "I'd hate for you to get the wrong idea, Sarah. These guys don't mean to be exploitative. But we're meddling with generations of a certain kind of thinking. In many ways, it's thinking that's existed in almost every society since the beginning of time. Adam and Eve were perhaps the only two people on this planet who ever knew what it meant to exist in perfect gender equality the way God designed it. It's only in the last several decades that a more egalitarian kind of thinking has taken hold, even a little bit. And even now, it's far from perfect."

"So, do you have an idea who sabotaged the wells?"

"Not for certain. Though we believe Sixto knows. That's Dolores's son-in-law. He won't give up his *amigos*, though."

A beat passes as she considers this. She had no idea Jenna's life included this kind of strife. "What happens now?"

"Don't know yet. We tried calling Rand from town—sometimes, there's reception in Cortadera—but we didn't have any luck. We can't do anything more without the go-ahead from him. For now, we'll have to leave things as they are."

Sarah returns to something else he said. "If La Fuente moved too fast to try to change things in this community, are you saying it's La Fuente's fault this happened?"

He tilts his head, a contemplative look in his eye. "I'm saying it's complicated."

Complicated. Yes. Her mind jumps to her jumbled feelings about the little girl they left in La Paz. "And what about Sofia?"

"What about her?" His eyebrows lift, obviously surprised by the non sequitur.

She pictures Sofia's small, ravaged face. "I don't know a lot about cleft palates, but I know they're easily corrected by surgery."

"True."

"So why hasn't anything been done for her? I mean, Abby's a nurse."

"Abby and Luca would have done something long ago, only Sofia's father won't allow it."

"She's not an orphan?"

"No. Both her parents live in La Paz. But her mother is too ill to get out of bed most days; her father too drunk. So Sofia spends many of her nights with Abby and Luca."

"Oh." A moment slips by as she thinks about this. "And the father won't let her have the surgery because he can't afford it?"

"Luca is a surgeon. He's offered to perform the operation for free. But Carlos refuses because he believes Sofia's deformity is God's punishment for a sin he or his wife committed."

This silences her for several seconds. She's angered that this kind of thinking still exists in the world and begins to understand what La Fuente is up against. "Sofia's mother believes this too?"

"She does, though she'd be willing to let Sofia undergo corrective surgery. She doesn't believe their child should be made to suffer for her sin. But she can't stand up to Carlos. When she tries, he beats her. She's already lost half her teeth to his fists."

It matches her memory of Jenna's stories of widespread domestic violence, the way it's winked at and ignored. "Does he beat Sofia too?"

"Sometimes. That's why Abby lets her stay with them whenever she wants. Every once in a while, Sofia will return home to her parents, although why she goes, I have no idea. Maybe she goes to spend time with her mother. Sofia usually comes back with bruises she won't explain. Abby and Luca do what they can. Feed her, clothe her, love her. Abby homeschools her, too." An affectionate grin tugs at his mouth. "She's extremely bright, an excellent reader. And, as you saw, a gifted artist."

When they reach the small outpost of civilization, Chase pulls into a primitive gas station. Sarah waits in the truck while he purchases the petrol and drops the filled jug into the back of the truck. Night has fallen quickly, almost skipping dusk. On the drive back, their headlights provide the only illumination, cutting a narrow swath through the darkness. Chase is silent, and she can't stop thinking about Sofia. Though she barely knows the child, she's seen her art-work. Seen her spirit. How much abuse would it take to permanently bruise that bright and tender soul?

CHAPTER 24

Jonas and Rachael are back at the house by the time Sarah and Chase return. Too exhausted to power up the generator, they eat dinner by candlelight. No one says much. Afterward, Jonas and Chase take a lantern and pitch a tent behind the house, where they will spend the night.

As Sarah helps Rachael change the sheets of the queen-sized bed they'll be sharing, she can't help but think about the last time Jenna slept here. With Jonas. How can he stand to be in this place, where every single object speaks so clearly of Jenna? How does he endure each pointed reminder of her presence, now gone from earth forever?

As if reading her thoughts, Rachael tells her that Jonas has decided to leave Bolivia. "When he saw the house, he realized he couldn't stay. Rand had thought he might consider relocating, like to La Paz or Santa Cruz, but Jonas wants to go home. He needs time and space to figure out what to do next." Rachael tugs the corner of the sheet into place. "Though I appreciate Rand wanting to give Jonas options, too much has changed for him to stay here. I am amazed he was even willing to consider it."

"Where's home for Jonas?"

"Los Angeles, I think. Not much family to speak of, though. Never knew his dad, and his mom has early-onset Alzheimer's. Lives in an assisted-living home."

"So he can't live with her."

"No. He has a half-sister, though. Janice. They're fairly close. She would have come down after the accident but she has four kids under the age of six and didn't feel she could leave them for so long. Jonas told her not to come, anyway."

"So what's he going to do?"

"Stay with Janice while he figures out what's next."

Sarah bites her lip, thinking of her inheritance. Jonas needs it so much more than she does. "Did you know Jenna left me her money? Except the life insurance, which Jonas gets."

Rachael looks up sharply. "No."

"Why would she do that? Don't most people make their spouse their beneficiary?"

"Yes." She smiles. "But Jenna wasn't most people. She must have had her reasons."

"I wish she'd told me what they were. It's driving me nuts. She and I weren't close these last few years, you know. That's why it doesn't make any sense. I suppose I could simply give the money to Jonas."

"Jonas won't take your money."

"It's not my money, it's Jenna's."

"Not anymore." Rachael slips beneath the covers on her side of the bed and snuffs out the candle.

Within minutes, Sarah can tell that Rachael has fallen asleep. It isn't so easy for her. She lies awake, staring into the darkness, remembering sharing a bed with Jenna on family vacations, taking turns giving each other backrubs and whispering long past bedtime.

"What do you want to be when you grow up?" Jenna's fingers spider-step across Sarah's shoulders.

"An artist." Sarah suppresses a delicious shiver. "Like Mom."

"You gonna do murals, like her?"

"Maybe. Maybe I'll do more paintings, though. And get good enough to sell them in galleries in Seattle or San Francisco."

"Or New York!"

"Yes. And if that doesn't work out, I can be a teacher." Jenna gives her back a tap, indicating her turn is over and it's time to flip. Sarah's palms knead her sister's spine the way she likes. "What about you?"

"I think I'm going to be a journalist," Jenna says. "So I can tell stories."

"You write people's stories, and I'll paint them."

"Perfect."

"I'll go to study in Paris, or Rome, and you can come visit me," Sarah adds.

"After I go to London to get my master's, where you can come visit me."

"Deal."

They both curl onto their sides like spoons, her sister's warmth at her back and pooling comfortably behind her knees. And Sarah drifts to sleep, content because it seems that with Jenna's approval, her dreams will surely come true.

$\sim \backsim \frown$

In the morning, as they share a simple breakfast of scrambled eggs wrapped in corn tortillas, Chase suggests the four of them walk to Cortadera. It's Sunday. Market day. A good chance, he says, to spread the word about Jonas's decision to return to the States as well as to invite Magdalena residents to an informal memorial service.

"What do you say, Sarah?" He confers an easy grin over the top of his coffee mug. "Up for a walk into town?"

She manages a return smile that probably looks more like a grimace. "Sure." She had not slept well, memories and churning questions keeping her awake long after lights-out. Plus, Rachael mumbled in her sleep, reminding Sarah of Jenna, whose sleep-talking had often kept her from slumber. Finally fatigue overruled and she dozed, but her dreams felt shallow and unsatisfying.

A sympathetic crease appears between Chase's eyes, showing she's revealed more of her thoughts than she meant to. But maybe the fresh air will revive her. Besides, she doesn't relish the idea of being alone for long in Jenna's house, where her presence remains palpable.

At the last minute, though, Jonas decides to stay behind. "You sure, man?" Chase asks. "Folks will want to say goodbye."

"I'm not so certain of that," Jonas counters.

"What? How can you—"

"Did you see the way Dolores acted yesterday? She shut me out."

"I wouldn't say that."

"I would."

Chase's mouth thins. "What I saw was a grieving woman upset about what's happening in her community."

"I know these people, Maddox, and Dolores has never acted like that around me. I think she blames me for what happened to Jenna."

"Now, Jonas," Rachael jumps in. "Why would she do that?"

"Maybe she thinks I could have done something to save her. And who knows? Maybe I could. I have no idea because I can't remember any blasted thing!"

The other three exchange looks, Sarah unsure whether to be alarmed or relieved that Jonas is venting.

"You remembered that Jenna was worried about the wells," Rachael offers. "Your memories are there, just taking a while to all come back."

Jonas says nothing.

Chase clears his throat. "About Dolores. Maybe you were seeing her natural reserve," he suggests quietly. "Her way of grieving."

"Whatever." Jonas's expression becomes shuttered as he rubs his forehead with his big right hand. "I'm just not up for socializing right now, okay?"

"All right," Chase agrees reluctantly, rubbing his chin. "You stay and get some rest. We'll catch up with you this afternoon."

CHAPTER 25

The sun is approaching its midday zenith when the three of them start out. They join a parade of people filling the dusty road, steering clear of cow dung and spiny cacti as they move among chickens, pigs and goats destined for barter at the market.

Magdalena has no village center but is a community comprised of fifty or so families sprawled along the Magdalena River. It has only the small general store and gas station Sarah and Chase visited yesterday to supply its everyday needs. Cortadera, the nearest real town, boasts a church, a hotel, an Internet cafe, and a cantina. The weekly Sunday market serves as the gathering place for the wider community.

In Cortadera's town square, vendors' stalls sprawl out like spokes on a wheel from the market cross at its center. Stretching into random alleyways and side streets, in makeshift structures and on blankets spread across the cobbled pavement, hawkers display their wares: vine-ripe tomatoes and giant peppers, herbs and spices, potatoes and yuccas and golden grains.

Chase and Rachael split up to cover ground more quickly, with Rachael focusing on getting word of Jenna's memorial service to as many women as possible. "Sarah, why don't you go with Chase?" she suggests. "These women are hurting. I'd like them to be able to express that, but they may not around a stranger. You mind?"

Sarah assures her she doesn't. Rachael heads for the far end of the labyrinthine market, while Chase starts at the center. Sarah trails slightly behind him as he moves from stall to stall. He typically converses with the vendors in Spanish but also occasionally in a language she doesn't understand. Quechua, she guesses.

With some bolivianos from Chase, Sarah purchases enough fruit and vegetables to last them for rest of their stay at the adobe house. With her own coins, she also buys a tiny, carved wooden dog that reminds her of Jake, which she thinks Sofia might like.

As they move through the market, Sarah is haunted by Jonas's face, the haggard look of someone who hasn't slept in days. She wonders if he's had any more absence seizures. Though she's not witnessed one, at least not that she knows, that doesn't mean they haven't occurred. Would he even say if he'd had one? She needs to ask Chase his opinion when she has a chance.

After an hour under the broiling sun, she's thankful she took Rachael's advice and donned a floppy, wide-brimmed straw hat from Jenna's closet. Even in her lightest sundress and sandals, the heat is draining. The constant push of people, in front and behind, the din of hawkers and the stench of animals for sale don't help.

Chase turns to ask her a question, his eyes crinkling with concern as he takes in her wilted appearance. "Thirsty?" He digs into the pocket of his cargo shorts. "Washington doesn't prepare you for Bolivia, does it?"

"Not much." She nudges the hat up and wipes her wrist across her sweaty forehead.

"Wait here." He crosses the street. The thin fabric of his faded lime-green t-shirt stretches across his well-toned shoulders. She tilts her head, trying to define him. Kind, but not meek. Possessing strength that makes people want to lean against him in a storm. A safe harbor. He steps into a beverage line and she smiles at what's emblazoned across his chest: *If all the people who fell asleep in church were laid end to end, they'd be a lot more comfortable.* He catches her smile and grins back.

Her thoughts drift toward home, to Shane. She's wanted to call but hasn't seen bars since Santa Cruz and has not talked to anyone back home since La Paz. So much for Shane's international SIM card.

What if he'd come with her? Would she want to lean against him in this storm? Does he make her feel safe? She bites her lip, suddenly unsure. Maybe when she leaves this country, with all traces of Jenna left behind, she'll be able to discover what Shane means to her.

Thinking to buy him a souvenir, her gaze skims from a bin of cheap ballpoint pens to a nearby straw basket brimming with unidentifiable objects—skeletal, long-necked animals with legs curled beneath their bodies. When Chase returns a minute later, she points to one. "What're those?"

"Dried llama fetuses. Or is it feti? Every market seems to have them."

"Why?"

"Why do they sell them?"

"Yes. And what are they used for?"

"Bolivians traditionally bury them in the foundation of a new home. They're believed to bring good luck."

"Not for cooking, then."

"Not for cooking, no." He smiles. "Were you worried?"

"Well, would you want that thing swimming in your soup?"

He laughs and holds out a cup containing a deep burgundy beverage. "Try some api."

She catches a thick whiff of spice. "What's in it?"

"Ground purple corn, cinnamon, sugar. No dried llama babies, I promise."

She eyes the concoction dubiously. She'd been expecting something a little more liquid but gamely brings the cup to her lips. The beverage tastes sweet, slightly fermented, reminding her of the spiced mulled wine Vina serves at Christmastime. "It's good."

"You sound surprised."

"Just not what I expected." She sips again. "Who knows, in time I might even accept the possibility of dried llama-fetus soup."

He chuckles. She's raising the cup to her mouth again just as a little boy in a t-shirt and no pants sprints past. Almost before she can register what she's seen, an older girl, the boy's sister perhaps, runs by, shouting after him and holding out his missing trousers. The flapping clothing snaps Sarah's wrist and sends a spray of api across her face. She sputters and bursts out laughing.

"You okay?" Chase, holding back his own laughter, is quick to move in with a Kleenex pulled from his shorts pocket. "Don't worry, it's clean."

"Thank you." Sarah swipes the liquid from her skin. "That's one way to enjoy a cool drink." She lifts her face for inspection. "Did I get it all?"

"Not quite." He smiles as he wipes the last dribble from her chin with a finger.

A bark of rough laughter makes them both turn. Sarah follows Chase's gaze to a group of men gathered outside the door of a corner cantina. There are five of them, two seated at a small plastic table, three standing beside it. Each man wears grimy khaki pants or jeans and a t-shirt of indeterminate color. They drink from brown bottles. One of the men sitting at the table, more barrel-chested than the others, says something that makes his companions shout with laughter again. With a gap-toothed grin, he raises his bottle and smiles right at Sarah.

His mouth set in a grim line, Chase grabs her hand and pulls her in the opposite direction. His swift mood change alarms her.

"Who are they?"

"One of them is Sixto. Don't know the others."

"Sixto?" she repeats. The name rings a bell.

"Dolores's son-in-law."

Now she remembers. "He had something to do with wrecking the wells, right?"

"Maybe not directly, but I'm sure he knows who did. Very likely one or more of his drinking buddies." Chase shoots a glance over his shoulder. His expression relaxes and he releases her hand. "Sixto and I exchanged some rather heated words last night. Ordinarily, I wouldn't be concerned about running into him here, but they've probably been drinking since they arrived. Best stay clear for now."

"Shouldn't be too hard."

"Right." His lips tighten. "Let's finish up so we can get back to the house."

Some twenty minutes later, she's poking through a bin of zucchini squash when she becomes aware of an odd kind of stillness emanating from the stall where Chase has stopped. Although most of the villagers have greeted Chase with a certain stoic concern, this vendor's reticence has a different feel.

The man presiding over tables displaying woven totes and tapestries wears brown trousers belted at the waist with a length of twine. He barely meets Chase's eyes and only shrugs in response to what Chase says. The woman with a baby at her breast sitting behind the man likewise shows no visible interest. But as Sarah approaches the stall, the woman looks up sharply, locking gazes with Sarah for one fleeting second before her coal-black eyes flood and she drops her gaze. Two tears trace across her square cheekbones to fall, one after the other, onto the smooth, brown forehead of her suckling child.

Apparently unaware of the woman's reaction, Chase finishes his one-sided exchange with the man and moves on. Sarah hesitates, transfixed by her glimpse of the woman's emotion, before hastening to catch up with him. Just before they turn the corner into the next alley, Sarah glances back and finds the woman's eyes on her.

Should she say something to Chase? She doesn't know what the woman's look means, but she thinks it's important. She waits impatiently while Chase finishes his exchange with a trinket vendor. This man and his bowler-hat-wearing wife are more loquacious, but finally Chase turns away.

"Chase." She plucks at his shirt. "At that last stall, the one with all the woven goods, did you notice the woman sitting in back, nursing a baby?"

"I'm not sure—" His gaze travels behind her and he breaks off. "Wait, you mean her?"

Sarah wheels around as the woman in question enters the alley, her eyes darting from side to side. Seeing Sarah and Chase, she pulls to a halt for a brief moment before continuing toward them. Her baby now sleeps in the sling across her chest. In her hand she carries a woven aguayo. She rushes at them and presses the serape tote into Sarah's hands before hastening back the way she came.

Sarah's eyes meet Chase's for one second before he hurries after the woman, stopping her at the top of the alley. He speaks to her. She answers. But her gaze never rises to meet his. Some minutes pass before she hastens away. Chase returns to Sarah.

"What did she say?" Sarah runs her fingers across the fine weaving of the bag.

"Her name is Luz. She's new to the community, having left her family to move here when she married. She was a member of Jenna's women's co-op. Once, soon after Jenna and Jonas came to

Magdalena, she missed a co-op meeting because she had become very ill. The next day, Jenna went to her house, miles away, to check on her, something not even her nearest neighbors had done. The fact that Jenna noticed, that she cared—Luz had never experienced that kind of concern before. When Jenna saw how sick Luz was, she spent the entire day with her, making her tea, cleaning her house, baking bread, washing her clothes."

Chase lifts the aguayo from her hands. "She knows you're Jenna's sister and wanted you to have this, her way of showing gratitude. She told me what it means. Purple yarn, the color of beauty. With a puma woven on this side, and a gazelle on this one, symbols of strength and grace."

He hands it back and she hugs it to herself, warmed by the woman's gesture. "May I tell her thanks?"

"Not with her husband there. He seems pretty resentful of the La Fuente presence here. Took some courage for her to chase us down."

"That doesn't sound good."

"Many of these women don't have it very good. Jenna was doing what she could to change that." He pauses. "I feel for Luz. For all these women. Jenna's was a voice of hope for so many of them."

And what will happen to them now? Sarah wonders but does not ask aloud, afraid she already knows the answer.

CHAPTER 26

JENNA
Age 21
Selah, Washington

Unable to sleep, I finally gave up and turned on my bedside lamp. More than jet-lag and travel fatigue, it was the email I'd gotten a few hours earlier that kept me from rest.

Come, it had said. *You are welcome anytime.*

Two days before, I'd returned from my semester-long work-study course in Bolivia. I'd chosen Bolivia because of my fascination that had begun during my high school years. Now, having spent three months of my junior year there, I'd witnessed firsthand what they meant when they called the country a beggar on a golden throne. And I fell in love. With the culture, the land ... the people.

I began to plot my return even before leaving La Paz, using the airport's free WiFi to research humanitarian organizations that might accept me. On impulse, I'd reached out to the most promising of the three, a well-respected international NGO. In a one-page introductory letter, I explained my long-held interest, my Spanish fluency, and other skills I thought relevant. A shot in the dark, I thought. Hoping, at best, to hear from them in a few months. So I was shocked when a personal email from the organization's president landed in my inbox. A response that included that single magic word: *Come.*

And now my mental wheels wouldn't stop spinning. How would I raise my support? Or could I convince Dad to fund me so that I wouldn't have to waste time fundraising, devoting instead all my energies to work on the ground? Would they be willing to hold a spot until after I graduated so I could finish school on schedule?

Before we'd left the States for Bolivia, Professor Wilkinson had said our experience there would teach us empathy, a helpful quality for a journalist. But to me that implied a kind of hands-off, observational approach. I longed to get my hands dirty.

I'd never been squeamish about bugs and dirt and having to rough it. The primitive conditions in Bolivia had been hard on some of my fellow students. One had even waved the white flag and hightailed it home after three weeks. Not me. I'd never felt myself more in my element. Never felt more alive. I had found my people.

Rising from my bed, I went to the window. Across the courtyard, a light shined from Mom's studio. Sarah.

I think I was the only one who knew my sister sometimes sneaked in there—one of the few reminders of Mom that Dad hadn't touched. I felt the familiar tug of guilt as I thought of Sarah, heavier now because of the vow I'd made in Bolivia—one I hadn't been able to keep so far.

My glance slid to my mahogany box as I pictured what it contained—and what it didn't. Before leaving for Bolivia, I'd removed Mike's letters, read each and every one of them, then burned them. All except one, which I couldn't persuade myself to part with. Mike would never know that every time I thought of him, I ached. Of all the mistakes I'd made in life—and at twenty-one years old, I'd already managed quite a few—letting him go was the greatest. I feared I would lament it for the rest of my life. I'd known what I was sacrificing yet still believed it necessary. But that didn't mean it came with no regrets.

And then there was Sarah. I can't say exactly how it started, how her presence became such a complicated force within me, how things got so twisted up in my heart. It began shortly after the discovery I made about a year after Mom died. Since then, I knew my behavior toward Sarah was unjust, but I couldn't seem to stop myself. Jesus, help me, I couldn't.

I'd pleaded with Him about it, the Jesus I'd encountered in Bolivia, One like I'd never known during my Sunday school upbringing. This One did more than extol moral behavior, He told stories. And such stories! Convicting, truth-filled, life-giving. That Man was One I could get behind. From the safety of thousands of miles away, I felt sure He would help me overcome this block that kept me from loving Sarah the way she deserved.

But here, Sarah was once again an ever-present reminder. I couldn't stand it. Even while I hated myself for being so small.

On my first night home after my return, her eyes had never left my face as I'd shared my Bolivian adventures at the table. I'd told of sleeping in hammocks to keep out disease-carrying beetles, and the confusing swirl of the Quechua and Aymara languages, plus the energizing music, vibrant colors, piquant food. Her face lit up as I described the Basilica Menor de San Lorenzo, Santa Cruz's iconic Baroque cathedral, where I liked to go to snack on *salteñas* and people watch. I could practically see Sarah's fingers reaching for her brushes to paint the pictures my words created.

Across the courtyard, a slender form filled the studio window. I ducked back, out of sight. When I looked again, the light had blinked out. Had she seen me? Hastily, I turned off my lamp and slid back into bed. Moments later, I heard Sarah's soft tread on the stairs. When she tapped on my door, Cork, stretched out at the foot of my bed, lifted his head and whined.

"Jenna?" Sarah whispered. "You awake?"

I held my breath, didn't answer.

"I wish you would let me in. Tell me what I've done. Or what's bothering you. Either way, we can work it through. We're sisters. I can help you. But you have to let me."

It was the opening I'd been looking for. I tossed back the covers, about to swing my feet to the floor when she sighed and moved on down the hall.

I flopped back on my bed, carrying on the imagined conversation. *It's not you, it's me,* I would say, and then I would lay out before her all the ugly details.

But I didn't. Instead, the words I longed to say remained trapped in my heart. And I failed to imagine what it would take to finally set them free.

CHAPTER 27

SARAH
Cortadera, Bolivia
Present day

When they come to an Internet café, Chase pauses. "Mind if we stop here a minute?" he asks. "Since I've not been able to reach Rand by phone, I'd like to send him an email while we're in town."

"You go ahead, I'll wait here." Sarah finds a bench nearby, in partial shade, and pulls out her phone to check the display, without much hope.

"Hey." It's Rachael, slipping onto the bench beside her, clutching a brown paper bag dotted with spreading grease stains.

"Hey." Sarah holds up her phone. "Anywhere around here I can get bars on this thing?"

"Not until we get back to the city. Sorry." Rachael holds out a salteña from her bag. "Want one?"

Sarah takes the flaky pastry, pocketing her phone and scooting to make more room on the bench. "So, how'd it go?"

"Well, I'm glad I'm not asked to do anything like this very often. The women are taking it hard."

"I know." As she relates their encounter with Luz, she pulls the aguayo from her tote for Rachael to inspect.

"Gorgeous." Rachael runs her fingers along the patterns woven into the cloth.

"How long did she live here?" Sarah folds the aguayo on her lap. "Jenna, I mean."

"About six months. She and Jonas came soon after they were married."

"They grew attached to her quickly."

"It takes time to earn people's trust, but the women loved Jenna's spirit. When she told them Jesus adored them, they believed it because they saw Him in the way she smiled at them. She didn't expect more from the women than they could give. People are naturally attracted to that kind of grace. Being around her felt like a kind of blessing, a warmth or light you could feel."

"I wish I got to see more of that side of her." She feels again that melancholy tug of might-have-been. "Recently, I mean."

"Sometimes, it's hard to see such things in those we're closest to. Of course, the real beauty of Jenna's light was the way it shined through her broken places. Women can relate to that. To suffering."

"Suffering?" The word catches her off guard. It's not one she often connects to her sister. "How did Jenna suffer?"

"She never told me details, really. Except your mom died when you were teenagers, didn't she?"

"Yes, and that was awful. But I never thought it affected Jenna in quite the same way it did me. Jenna was always closer to our dad."

"Well, there was something. A darkness you could just catch glimpse of. Like a shadow flitting across the sun. I don't mean that in a bad way. As I say, it was part of her strength, the reason women were drawn to her. They knew she understood what it meant to be broken."

A picture flashes through Sarah's mind, an image from her childhood, of the horse trainer taking Sassy away to spend months being broken. Saddle-broken, her mother explained. Because unless a horse was broken to the saddle, it could never fulfill its purpose: to carry humans.

Perhaps taking her silence as a sign of unease, Rachael changes the subject. "So, where's Chase?"

Sarah points to the café. "Sending Rand an email."

They both look toward the plate-glass window that fronts the building. Sarah sees the outline of Chase in his ball cap, hunched over a computer.

"Maybe I should get in there, too. There are a few things I need to let Rand know about." Rachael finishes the last of her salteña and stands. "How're you doing? Holding up in this heat?"

"A little tired." She squints up at Rachael. "I'm a bit concerned about leaving Jonas alone too long. You don't think he's had any more absence seizures, do you?"

"He hasn't mentioned any."

"Would he?"

"Maybe not to us, but I'm pretty sure he would tell Chase."

"You think I could head back now? I'd like to check on him, and if I go now, you won't have to rush."

"Not a bad idea. You know the way?"

"Straight down the main road out of town, then left at the corner where that road marker is."

"You got it. We'll try not to be too long. See you at the house."

A half-mile out of town, however, Sarah begins to think she should have waited for the others. The earlier crowds have vanished. The slap of her sandals on the hardpan road is all that presides over the silence, underscoring her aloneness. The sun beams directly over-head, seemingly hot enough to melt metal. The bag holding their fresh produce thumps heavily against her hip. Her left leg aches too, unaccustomed to so much walking, plus the meaty salteña has left her parched, making her wish she'd thought to purchase bottled wa-ter before leaving town.

She feels almost grateful when a pebble lodges inside her sandal, giving an excuse to sit for a moment. She searches the roadside, fi-nally settling on a large rock. Unseen insects churr monotonously as she slips her sandal off and shakes the pebble free.

But now another noise intrudes on the quiet. Voices, too loud. Glancing over her shoulder, she sees a couple of men rounding the bend from the direction of town. Her heart skips a beat. She recog-nizes them as two of Sixto's companions from the cantina. Hastily replacing her sandal, she stands. Catching sight of her, they break into wide smiles. *Best to stay clear of Sixto and his amigos.* Chase's words trip across her mind as she starts walking again.

The men quicken their pace and soon draw alongside her. The shorter of the pair rattles off something in Quechua. When she doesn't respond, he does it again. Without making eye contact, she shakes her head and slows her pace, hoping they'll walk on ahead.

Instead, they press closer, shortening their steps to match hers. She catches their scent—sour sweat and beer breath. A panicky awareness of her vulnerability prickles her skin as she searches the area for another passerby.

Hope rises inside her chest as she spots a woman in a volumi-nous blue skirt and bowler hat coming up a nearby path toward the main road. Her graying black hair is twisted into two braids, and her bulging aguayo bends her shoulders with its weight. *"¡Hola!"* Sarah calls out, waving to get her attention. *"¡Como está!"*

The woman lifts her eyes in surprise, her mouth rounding in a small O. Her glance takes in the men, who fell back a pace when

Sarah called out her greeting. Dropping her gaze again to the dirt path in front of her, the woman turns from Sarah and shuffles back the way she came.

Stunned, Sarah darts a look at the men, whose leers have returned as they realize the woman has no intention of interfering. Adrenaline flutters beneath her breastbone as she considers what chance she has of outrunning the inebriated pair.

"Sarah!"

Chase and Rachael round the bend at a jog. Sarah's knees wobble with relief as they rapidly close the distance. As soon as they reach her, Rachael puts an arm around her waist. Chase steps up to the men and releases a stream of heated words in Quechua. The men argue, the other two waving arms and gesticulating. Chase steps nearer the taller of the two, his expression taut. Finally, Sixto's friends back away and stalk toward town. Only then does Sarah realize the extent of her fear.

Once they've disappeared around the bend, Chase spins to Sarah. "Don't do that again!" His brows nearly meet, his jaw tight.

Rachael's hand on Sarah's waist tightens reflexively. "Chase, stop." Rachael softens her voice. "It's not her fault. I told her it was okay. If you want to get mad at someone, get mad at me. Better yet, get mad at *them*." She jerks a thumb in the direction of town.

Chase plants his hands on his hips and glances away.

Rachael squeezes Sarah lightly. "I wouldn't have let you go if I'd known you'd seen Sixto and his mates in town. I'm so sorry. As soon as Chase realized you'd gone ahead, we ran after you." She steps back, looking into Sarah's eyes. "You okay?"

"Fine." She attempts to laugh it off. "I doubt they intended any real harm."

"They didn't intend any good either." Chase glances back at her, frowning. "Most men around here are gentlemen when they're sober, but when they've been drinking, all bets are off. And I'm afraid

Sixto's compadres would think little of hurting a pretty *gringa* like you."

"Sorry." Her heart hammers. She doesn't know which unsettles her more—Sixto's men or Chase's protectiveness. "It won't happen again."

"Good." He steps forward and grips her shoulders with both hands, sparking a warmth she's not prepared for. His gaze boring into hers, he seems to wrestle with whether to say more. Finally, he shakes his head and abruptly releases her.

As he sets off toward Magdalena, he calls over his shoulder. "You ladies coming?"

CHAPTER 28

When they arrive back at the house, they find Jonas asleep inside the tent in the backyard. "It doesn't look like he's even moved." Rachael's forehead puckers with concern. "Is this much sleep normal?"

"It's grief," Sarah says.

"And his body still healing," Chase puts in. "I'd say it's normal. But if it keeps up, we'll call Abby."

Rachael nods, her anxious look fading as they file into the house. "Where should we start?"

Sarah glances around at the life to dismantle.

"You up for this?" The gentleness of Chase's voice nearly undoes her. She swallows hard and nods.

He takes a step toward her as if sensing the hug she needs, but she shakes her head. She's afraid she will crumble. And she didn't come all this way to fall apart.

He hesitates before turning away, appearing to accept her need to stand on her own. After a moment, he says, "I remember how hard it was for my mom." His calm, quiet voice fills the void that has suddenly opened up in front of her. He doesn't look directly at her but moves around the room, touching an item here and there, as if taking stock.

"Her sister died too young. Breast cancer. She left behind a toddler, and a husband so overwhelmed by having the sudden and sole responsibility for a young child he could hardly get up in the morning. It fell to my mom to go in and sort Aunt Kristine's stuff so Uncle Dave could move on again. She said going into their bedroom and giving away her sister's belongings was one of the hardest things she's ever had to do. In some ways, harder than holding Aunt Kristine's hand when she died. At least they'd seen that coming. But sorting through the stuff—that took her by surprise. She said it was like having to say goodbye all over again."

The lump that had risen in Sarah's throat begins to subside until she feels she can breathe again. Their gazes hold for a moment. She hopes he sees in her eyes how grateful she is that he has named her struggle. For his understanding.

The softening in his expression tells her he does.

With Rachael's help, Sarah takes inventory, decides what needs to be packed for shipment back to the States and what can be left behind. Chase and Rachael's companionship makes it easier, and soon she settles into a rhythm that allows her emotions to detach from the task.

After three hours of sorting and crating, Chase straightens from taping up a box of kitchen utensils and pulls the truck keys from his pocket. "It's getting dark, and I need to get back to Cortadera before the Internet café closes. Anyone want to come with?" Though his glance falls on Sarah, it's Rachael who speaks up.

"What for?"

"Need to finish that email to Rand. The one I wasn't able to send because *some*one thought it would be smart to head for home unaccompanied." He catches Sarah's eye, making sure she sees his wink. Warmth floods her body—whether because of the wink or the reminder of the worry she caused, she's unsure.

Rachael unfolds her slender frame from the floor. "I'll go with you. I want to ask Abby about Jonas. Email's probably my best bet for reaching her."

"Sarah?" His eyebrows rise in invitation.

She's tempted, she could use the break, but she glances toward the backyard. "Guess I'll stay here. So someone's around for Jonas."

While Rachael ducks behind the house for a last-minute out-house run, Sarah walks with Chase to the truck. Fresh air flows up from the river. She reaches back with one hand to release her po-nytail, letting the breeze fan through her hair. Miski trots ahead of them, frisking after a blown leaf as if determined not to let his injury slow him down. "Dog's feeling better, I see." Chase climbs inside the cab, then leans an elbow out the window to peer at Sarah from beneath his ball cap. "Feel like taking him for a walk?"

"Sure."

"We're also low on water. Someone needs to bring up more be-fore we can make dinner."

Again, she entertains the fleeting thought to paint his eyes. She brushes it aside to focus on his words. "I can do that."

"Great. Use the two buckets by the back door. Then you can run the water through the filter behind the house."

Rachael returns and climbs into the passenger seat. Chase waits until she's buckled in before turning the engine and shifting into reverse. His gaze lingers on Sarah's face. "Just don't go farther than the river, understand?"

"Yes, sir." She gives him a mock salute and watches them back down the drive before calling to Miski and going in search of buckets and the wheelbarrow.

Another bright afternoon, the breeze ruffling the trees' leaves above her head as she sets off with the dog. Five minutes later, the path opens up onto a pebbly riverbank. Nestled beneath an overhanging tree branch, an enormous boulder hunches like a crouched troll at the river's edge. Sunlight sifts through the trees, sparkling across the clear-flowing water, while birds sing an unceasing chorus. She fills her lungs with the clean air, beginning to understand why Jenna found this place appealing.

She thinks of the jar holding the tarantula up at the house. Despite her privileged upbringing, Jenna always maintained her attachment to the earth. So it isn't such a surprise she'd been able to make a home for herself here, where roughing it is the way of life. In some ways, it seems the life she was born for.

Sarah sheds her sandals and wades into the water up to her calves, enjoying the river's cool caress across her skin as she fills the two buckets. Then she hoists herself onto the sun-dappled boulder to oversee the dog's exploration. While Miski frolics at the river's edge, Sarah lifts her face to the sky, closing her eyes, welcoming the shade-sifted warmth and the chance to let her mind wander. Time here seems to stretch out like an elastic band. She can't believe mere days have passed since she touched down in La Paz. She can count in hours the time she's spent with the La Fuente people, yet already she feels she's known them half her life.

She recalls Abby's comment about bonds forming fast down here. She can well believe it. Everything seems more intense, somehow. Flavors more piquant, colors more vibrant, relationships more authentic. As if without the safety net of unlimited resources, everything matters more. Including people. Especially people.

She remembers, too, what her own mother used to say: the noblest characters, like the best wines, are produced under stress. Perhaps the same is true about relationships. Stress either brings out the best in people, bonding them together and strengthening them, or it tears them apart.

A thought wraps itself around her like a warm blanket: she's glad she came. Glad Jenna summoned her. Whatever Jenna's reasons had been, Sarah would not forget her time here. Nor the people.

Smiling to herself, she calls to Miski, and they make their way back up the hill to the house.

⁓⁓

An hour later, Chase returns alone. "Where's Rachael?" Sarah sits cross-legged in a patch of sunlight, pulling books off the shelf and piling them into boxes.

"She stayed to help with—" He breaks off as Jonas's bulk fills the doorway. "Hey, man." Chase crosses to him. "Catch some good sleep?"

"Too much, probably." Jonas runs a hand across his cropped hair. "Feel drugged."

His espresso-black eyes have that glassy look of someone who's had too much to drink. The mild buoyancy she felt after her walk to the river leaches away as a cold coil of anxiety twists inside her. Jonas does not look good. He moves as if plowing through water, every motion an effort. She closes her eyes. *Jesus, help. Help us help him.*

When she opens her eyes, she finds Chase watching her, the intensity of his gaze igniting a warm glow in her belly. She again hears Abby's words: *Attachments form quickly down here.* And her mind floods with understanding. This is how it happens. The harsh realities creating a crucible for high emotion.

But she is only a visitor. This is not her reality. She finds herself drawn to Chase in a way that's caught her off-guard, but her world—and a different man—waits for her return. She cannot afford to play with this fire.

She breaks the connection, bending to shift a heavy stack of books into a half-filled box. The moment stretches out. She dares not look at Chase. He speaks to Jonas. "How's the shoulder?"

"Sore." Jonas shuffles to the bed, hugging his arm with his good hand. Then he lies back and closes his eyes. Sarah averts her gaze.

Soon Jonas snores softly from the bed, his mouth hanging loosely. She finishes with the books and moves to pack up clothes from the armoire. Chase lays a fire in the fireplace for later that evening, then starts dinner. Jonas rouses when Chase sets food on the table. He looks marginally more alert, though he serves himself only a tiny portion of beans and rice. It isn't until after Chase blesses the food that Sarah realizes Chase never finished answering her question about Rachael.

"Where's Rachael?" Sarah forks a small bite of rice into her mouth.

"Oh." He looks around, as if he's only now noticed her absence. "While we were in town, a woman went into labor. We drove her home. Rae offered to stay until the midwife got there."

"Were you able to get a hold of Rand?"

"Yes, finally." Chase spears a chunk of sautéed pepper with his fork. "We told him about the damaged wells. He's going to talk it over with the board, but right now he wants us to hold off doing anything about it."

"Why? Don't the people need the wells now?"

"Yes, but Rand's not ready to move on it yet."

She scoops some beans onto a tortilla. "And when they do repair them, how much will it cost?"

"Most of the wells need only a few new parts, though some of the older ones need to be replaced entirely. They cost nine thousand to install new."

"Bolivianos?"

"Dollars."

"And how many were destroyed?"

"Four."

Thirty-six thousand dollars. A hefty amount, but not astronomical. "Without new wells, what will they do for water?"

"What they've always done." He holds her eyes with a steady gaze. "Get by."

She looks down at her plate. The words resonate, reverberating through her body like an echo. *Get by.* Isn't that what she's been doing since TJ died?

She risks a glance up and finds him studying her. "What?" She rubs a hand across her mouth, fearing food has gotten stuck there, but when he continues to stare, she realizes his thoughts are far from errant rice grains. He's searching for something. In her? In himself?

He starts to speak, stops himself, lowers his eyes. His lashes hide his thoughts. He picks up his fork and gives a shake of his dark-blond head. "Nothing."

CHAPTER 29

After dinner, Sarah does the dishes while Chase makes a final run to the river for water. Jonas, somewhat revived by food, retreats to the corner where a small desk, chair, and a two-drawer file cabinet function as an office. The metal drawer squeals as he opens it. He pulls out file folders, glancing through each before stacking them inside a cardboard fruit box.

Drying the last dish, she turns to face him, knowing she might not have many more moments alone with him. "Jonas?"

"Yeah?"

"There's something we need to talk about."

"Okay." He barely glances at her, something in the file having caught his attention.

"Why did Jenna leave me her money?"

He looks up then, his face wiped blank by surprise. Whatever he thought she wanted to discuss, it obviously isn't this. "Because you're her sister."

"And you're her husband."

"So?"

"Don't most people name their spouses as beneficiaries in their wills?" Leaving the dish towel to dry on a hook, she pulls a chair from the table and joins him at the desk.

"Probably."

"So why didn't she?"

"Because I didn't want her to."

"Why not? You need it."

The first smile she's seen in a while flits across his face—weak, but there. "Says who?"

"Anyone. Me." She waves her hands around and nods to his arm in a sling. "You've got medical expenses. You'll need something to live on. You won't be working for a while." *You'll need therapy.*

"I'm taken care of. You don't need to worry about me. Jenna and I talked about it." He puts his broad hand on her head, as if she is a little girl needing comfort. "I'm good, Sarah. Really."

His response does little to reassure her. She still feels he hasn't really answered her question, but she asks the next one anyway. "Then what if I give her money to La Fuente? So they can repair the wells and use it to fund whatever else they need around here."

"You could, of course," Jonas agrees. "But then you'd have to ask yourself why Jenna didn't do that in the first place."

"You think I haven't?"

Another tiny smile quirks his mouth. "Okay, then let me ask you something else. Why do you think Rand wants to wait to repair those wells?"

"No money?"

"Maybe. More likely because he sees that something fundamental needs to get fixed first. Say we take the money and rebuild those wells. What's to prevent whoever wrecked them in the first place from coming back and doing it again? Something has to change in this community. Jenna and I thought we'd built enough trust with the people, but apparently we didn't. Not quite. Though a lot of them are ready for change, some are still resisting it. Their collective psyche has to change first. Then and only then do those wells stand a chance of staying built."

"It seems awfully unfair to hold the well-being of an entire community hostage to a few people who are backwards in their thinking."

"Try not to judge them, Sarah," he says, gently. "It's hard. We're talking centuries of superstition and culture to unwind. Not to mention the harm they've suffered, much of it at the hands of people like us. Change happens very, very slowly. But here—" He hands her the manila file he was reading. "This will give you something else to think about."

She reaches for the folder, surprised to find her name written at the top in her sister's confident scrawl.

Inside she finds a scrapbook—all about her. Her breath catches. At a glance, the file seems to hold information covering the six years of Jenna's absence from the vineyard. Including photographs, a couple dozen at least. Who sent them? A handful were taken soon after the accident: Sarah arm-in-arm with her physical therapist, then on her own two feet as she took her first steps without a walker. Another as she shared a toast with Dad in front of the decorated Christmas tree. Candids of Sarah relaxing on the porch with a book or strolling among the vines with Cork or engaging with customers from behind the tasting counter. Then there are copies of articles chronicling the vineyard's latest successes and most recent awards, including a piece about Sarah as the Silverwood Cellars behind-the-scenes maven. There's also that feature about Shane in *The Seattle Times*.

In the possession of anyone but her sister, the whole thing would be creepy. "How did she get these?"

"Most of the articles came from online."

"And the photos?"

He hesitates. "Tomaso."

"She got these from Tomaso?" What the heck? Her sister had been keeping tabs on her? With Tomaso as her accomplice? And he never breathed a word of it. For a moment, she feels angry, but then she sees things as she knows Tomaso does: Jenna cared more than Sarah ever realized.

Sudden tears burn the backs of her eyes. She blinks them away as Jonas hands her another file. "Here's something else you should see."

Jenna had labeled this file Literacy Center. Inside, Sarah finds pages of lined, cream-colored paper that look torn from a stitch-bound journal. Each page holds a thumbnail sketch, a rough outline of an image done in pencil or pen. The people in each are drawn in enough detail that anyone could understand the creator's intent.

The first one shows a woman in a garden setting with what looks like a small cave behind her, her face filled with wonder as she beholds a robed man.

Then there is a woman touching the hem of the garment of a man passing through a crowd.

Another features two women in a small gathering of men around a low table set with food. The woman facing the viewer sits at the feet of a man who is clearly the group's leader, while in the background, the other woman wrings her hands.

The last shows a woman with a jar of water speaking to a man with kind eyes beside an ancient stone well.

Recognition stirs as Sarah flips through the images. Mary Magdalene outside the empty tomb. The woman with the hemorrhage. Mary and Martha. The Samaritan woman at the well. Women of the Bible, who each had a personal encounter with Jesus.

But this is not what causes her pulse to flicker inside her chest as she studies each drawing. She looks up to find Jonas's eyes on her. "Have you seen these?"

"Yes."

"She put me in these drawings. In every one of them, I'm the woman." Even in Jenna's inexpert hand, Sarah's identity is clearly depicted in her heart-shaped face with a smattering of freckles, shoulder-length hair, and the cross pendant around her neck. "What do these mean?"

"Jenna's dream was to build a literacy center for the community here. She wanted all the women in Magdalena to feel at home there. She believed art depicting the way God loves women would remind them that they, too, are empowered to reach for the best for themselves. She envisioned these scenes as murals on the walls of the center. She was always adding to her list. These are just a few of the ones she tucked away."

"And this note?" She points to the back of the file, where Jenna had scrawled Sarah's name.

"She planned to invite you to paint them. Said you would be able to make masterpieces of her mud."

"But I haven't painted anything in years." She has tried to paint since her accident, but something always gets lost between her fingers and the canvas. Colors emerge flat, lifeless. Like trying to translate English into Spanish but having only the consonants.

"Jenna never gave up on people, even when they wanted to give up on themselves." His black eyes mist. "Women around here don't get many messages like that, you know. They're pretty immersed in a culture that teaches them that because they're born female, they're second-class. A means to an end. A way to bring water into the home. A way to produce babies, preferably boy babies, to support the family. They have little or no voice with their husbands or in the community.

"But Jenna wanted women to understand they are accepted. Cherished. And not just as potential wage earners, but as women. Period. That's one reason she loved teaching them to read, so they could see for themselves what God says about women. In story after story—" he points to the thumbnail pictures— "God takes care of women because He loves them. And because He loves them, He plants a dream in each woman's heart and longs for them to fulfill it as part of His plan."

She runs her hand over her sister's inexpert sketch. "Can I ask you something else, Jonas? Did she ever talk about wanting to be a journalist or a writer? It's what she always dreamed of when we were young. But then she came here and that all seemed to vanish."

"She did talk about it, a little. She had regrets."

"Do you have any idea why she quit school?"

"I asked her once. She said when you had your accident, when TJ died, it was too hard to focus. Your dad was distracted, worried about you, and well, lots of things changed, I guess. I think her plan had been to come here for a couple of years and then return to finish her degree. Obviously, that never happened."

"She probably blamed me for that, too," she says quietly.

"Blamed you?" Jonas looks up, startled. "Why would she blame you for a choice she made?"

"Because it was my fault TJ got caught in that avalanche. I was reckless that day, taking stupid chances when I knew better. TJ was her friend too. I know she missed him." She recalls Jenna's expression that evening with her friends on the patio. "She was ashamed for the pain I'd caused so many people. The way it tarnished the family name. TJ's parents used to work for my dad, but after he died, they moved down to Oregon. Couldn't stand the painful reminders every-where. Only Tomaso and Vina were left after that."

Jonas shakes his head. "I knew about your injuries and that TJ died, but beyond that, no. I certainly never got the sense she held you responsible for her quitting school."

Sarah frowns, struggling to make sense of it. She recalls her fleeting realization—was it yesterday?—that there must have been more to Jenna's coolness than just Sarah's actions. She'd been too mired in her own guilt and grief to separate it out, but now it strikes her afresh how much of Jenna's detachment began before the accident. Would she ever untangle the truth?

Remembering she hasn't given him that last letter for Jenna, she retrieves it and hands it to him. "Don't know if this is important since it has no return address, but Rand asked me to pass it along."

He squints at the postmark. "Chelan?"

"Lake town a couple of hours north of us. Don't know who she knows there. Maybe a college friend?"

Jonas tears open one end of the envelope and pulls out the single sheet of paper. It contains only two words:

I'm waiting.

Sarah meets Jonas's eyes. "What does that mean?"

"No idea." His eyebrows draw down as he flips the envelope over. The backside is as blank as his expression.

"Could it be … I don't know, an inside joke?"

"Seems like a lot of trouble for a joke, sending something all the way down here." He stares at the page as if the words might multiply and provide him the answer he's looking for.

The silence draws out. "Jonas?"

"Sorry, it's just—I feel I've seen this before."

"You have?"

"Or maybe something like it. But I can't think where. The answer's locked inside my frozen brain, I guess." He frowns. "But I don't like the looks of this, do you?"

"No. It sounds … I don't know … mean, somehow. Almost like a threat."

Their eyes meet briefly before he glances away, refolding the letter with a shrug and setting it aside. "I suppose it'll eventually come to me." But the shrug and his resigned sigh tell her he doesn't really believe it.

Hoping to change the subject, Sarah returns to the stack of thumbnails. "I didn't know Jenna knew Jesus like this." She flips through the sketches, pausing to study each one. "I mean, we grew up believing in Him the way small children do, but we weren't really taught what it meant to have a personal relationship with Him. Mom knew Him that way, but she mostly kept her faith to herself." She looks up. "How did it happen, do you know?"

"When she first came here in college, she met some students from another school. Their lives, their faith impacted her. That's when she understood Jesus loves stories as much as she did, and it told her He wanted her heart as much as her mind and soul. Which meant something to her."

"Yes," she says softly. "It would. She did love stories." Loved to write them, tell them, read them, listen to them. Which was why quitting college months shy of getting her journalism degree had seemed so shortsighted. Why had Jenna chosen that, when only a few more months of study might have equipped her even more to help these people she loved?

"She liked to say stories had a way of bypassing the intellect and creeping through the backdoor to the soul. She believed that's what gave stories their transforming power. That belief led to her digging into the stories about Jesus, and she noticed how carefully He nurtured a woman's heart. The Bible is full of such stories—" he taps the sketches in Sarah's lap— "but they hadn't ever been explained to her in any really personal way. She started seeing the way Jesus modeled God's love for women in particular. Women standing on the lowest rung of the social ladder, just as they do so often today. She saw how Jesus spoke to women differently than to men. He frequently rebuked men. He never did that to a woman. Have you ever noticed that? Instead, He wooed them, drawing them out, helping them find their voices. Jenna loved that about Him."

She nods, absorbing this new information about her sister. A silence stretches out, broken when Jonas returns the question, asking how Sarah came to know Jesus.

She closes her eyes. "It was when I realized He accepted me exactly as I am. After my accident, I was shattered. Quite literally. I felt so utterly broken and incomplete. Tomaso was the one who showed me I needed to be nothing more than who I was."

"He sounds like quite a guy. Tomaso, I mean. Jenna talked about him a lot."

"He's like a father to me." Only as she speaks the words does she realize their truth. Tomaso *is* like a father to her, in many ways more than her own. Her mind flits back to the countless times she's gone to him for advice or to solve a concern.

And then it hits her: Why does she automatically turn to Tomaso? Because she assumes he has more to offer than her own father? Yes … but why? And is that fair? Or has she simply concluded that because of Dad's bond with Jenna, he has no room left for her?

She sifts through her memories, trying to decide if it's Dad who's given her that impression or if it's sprung from living so many years in Jenna's shadow. She can't decide. But regardless, has Dad seen the way she favors Tomaso? If so, it must hurt him. She's always assumed Dad's been the one keeping her at a distance, but could it be the other way around?

She frowns and opens her eyes. "And you?" Changing the subject. "What's your story?"

"I've known Jesus for as long as I can remember." He turns back to the file cabinet, grabbing files and piling them inside the box at his feet.

She lets another moment slip by before laying a hand on his arm, stilling his activity. "Jonas." She waits until his gaze connects with hers. "When I was at the market today, I caught a glimpse of what Jenna meant to these women. They're not going to forget her."

"Thank you." He searches her eyes. "That's one of my biggest fears, you know. That they would forget. She wasn't here that long."

"They won't forget," she repeats, "and neither will I." She pauses. "I'm so glad I've been able to see this. I didn't know. Jenna never talked about her work here. I—I don't know why, but she wouldn't let me see this side of her."

He looks down, running a finger across a threadbare patch on his cargo shorts. "I know something wasn't right between you two. I don't know why, but sometimes, I thought—" He stops.

"What?"

He shakes his head. "I don't know. Maybe I shouldn't say this, but sometimes there were days when I thought I didn't know my wife at all. There was this side to her … . She'd have these black moods."

"What do you mean, black moods?" Sarah's skin prickles as she hears an echo of Rachael's observation, another acknowledgment of Jenna's dark side. Until recently, Sarah was sure she had been the only one to see it.

"Like—" Jonas pauses. "Like she'd be writing a letter and start crying."

"Who was she writing?"

"I don't know. She always burned the letters before I could see."

Involuntarily, Sarah glances toward the fireplace, where Chase has stacked firewood to light when the temperature drops in a few hours.

"I don't think she mailed a single one," he says.

"She never gave any hint what was troubling her?"

"No. Only, well, sometimes she slept uneasily. Thrashing and mumbling."

"She's always talked in her sleep. Since we were little."

"I could never make out what she was saying. In the morning, she always claimed she didn't remember. Eventually she'd calm down—until the next time. I tried pushing once or twice, but she just shut down. I was afraid she would lock me out for good if I kept at it." He shrugs. "I figured if I was patient, she'd tell me when she was ready, because each time she—"

A clatter sounds on the porch and pounding rattles the door.

CHAPTER 30

Jonas throws back the door. A girl tumbles into the room. "Delia!" he exclaims.

"It's Mama!" she shouts in Spanish. She looks to be about ten years old, wide-eyed and vibrating with anxiety. "She's having the baby!"

Chase reaches the porch in time to hear this, at his heels, Miski, panting and wet from the river. "How long has she been in labor?"

"All day!"

"And where's your grandmother?" Jonas asks.

"With Auntie! Grandmother meant to be back before the baby came, but Mama says the baby's early."

"Did you try Matrona?"

"She's not home!"

Chase and Jonas exchange glances. "The midwife must still be at the other birth, with Rachael," Chase says in English. "Guess that leaves us."

Jonas's eyebrows draw down in worry, his huge hand cupping Delia's head protectively. "Jenna was concerned about Matilde's pregnancy."

"Why?" Chase is already gathering supplies from the kitchen—towels, jugs of water, some food. "What was she worried about?"

"Anemia, from almost the beginning. More recently, preeclampsia."

"And just how early is this baby?"

"A couple of weeks? By Jenna's math, anyway."

"Has she been seen by a doctor anytime during her pregnancy?"

"Abby saw her, but that was months ago."

"Okay, we'd better get over there right away. We'll take the truck."

In another minute, the two men are out the door, ushering Delia ahead of them. The truck's doors slam, the engine roars. Miski cocks his head at the door and whines.

Sarah blinks at the dog, unsettled by the men's abrupt departure. She glances around the darkening house and shudders.

Outside, the truck's door creaks open again before heavy footfalls blast across the porch. She reaches the threshold just as Chase fills the doorway. "You coming? Yes, Miski, you too."

Without waiting for her answer, he scoops up the dog and together they run for the truck.

Five minutes later, Chase pulls into a dirt clearing before an adobe house that looks almost identical to the Jacksons'. Scrawny brown chickens peck among the weeds that rim the dirt, and a mangy goat lifts its head briefly from a mound of compost.

As soon as Sarah opens the passenger door, Delia scampers across her lap to exit the truck and join the children lined up on the sagging porch. Sarah counts five of them besides Delia, ranging in age from tweener to babe-in-arms, all girls, fear blanching their round, dirty faces.

After grabbing as much from the truck bed as he can carry, Chase approaches the house, greeting the girls cheerily. Then another figure steps from the shadows. As light falls on his face, Sarah catches her breath. Sixto.

Seeing Chase, Sixto's eyes widen briefly, then dart to Sarah. She sees in their dark depths a flash of something she doesn't expect. Regret? Shame? The look disappears before she can fix on it. Chase gives the briefest of pauses before giving Sixto a nod and continuing inside.

The girls spy Miski limping behind Chase. Their anxiety vanishes as they descend on the little dog. "Miski!" Excited cries fill the air.

Their exuberance coaxes a smile from Jonas as he and Sixto greet each other with a handshake before they move into the dusty yard, where Sixto lights a cigarette. The low rumble of their voices carries to Sarah as she gathers the remaining supplies from the truck and enters the house.

Inside, it's dark and sour smelling. From the bedroom, Chase calls. "Jonas?"

"No, it's Sarah."

"I could use some fresh water in here. There's no more in the kitchen, so you'll have to bring some from the truck."

She returns outside for one of the water jugs, smiling at the girls as they take turns cuddling the puppy. She hefts a jug, groaning with the effort, wondering if it's occurred to Sixto that because his amigos have damaged his well, his wife has only a limited supply of clean water as she gives birth. Not only that, but the very people they have tried to thwart are now about to usher his child into the world.

Perhaps Sixto does realize it. It could explain the look she saw on his face when they arrived.

Seeing her struggling with the jug, Jonas leaves Sixto to lend a hand. With his good arm, he lugs the water to the porch, saying quietly, "You should know that Matilde has taken Jenna's death very hard. Jenna had meant to be back for the birth. Matilde feels very abandoned. Sixto said he's hardly been able to get her out of bed for days. He's worried about how she's going to manage with the baby." He pauses. "He told her Jenna's death was a sign God was displeased with Matilde for leaving her family to learn to read. She told him that was not God's way, that God is good, His plans for us are always good, even if we can't always see it."

"What did you say to that?"

"What could I say? I told him Matilde was right."

"Did he believe you?"

"I don't know." He runs a hand over his hair. "Why should he? I'm not sure I believe it myself, anymore."

Jonas doesn't wait for a response but deposits the water by the sink and leaves to rejoin Sixto in the yard.

~ ◦ ~

Sarah's gaze sweeps Matilde's kitchen, searching for a vessel to hold the water Chase needs. Jonas's words have set up a hum of anxiety that doesn't stop until her attention snags on a flash of color, out of place among the drab, worn items. A cheery yellow tea kettle— exactly like the one in the Jacksons' adobe home. Without thinking, Sarah places her hand on it. *Jenna.*

"Sarah?" Chase calls.

"Coming." Beneath a rusted metal table she finally locates a large plastic basin and pours water into it. As she carries it into the only bedroom, water sloshes over the rim, darkening a patch on the packed dirt floor. Chase is laying out clean cloths at the foot of the bed. A stale, coppery smell taints the room's cloying air, the temperature at least ten degrees warmer here than outside. Perspiration glosses Chase's forehead.

"Her pains began early this morning." He barely looks up. "Contractions are coming pretty fast now."

Between contractions, the woman has gone still, her eyes closed. She gives no indication she's aware of a new presence in her room. The mound of her belly juts up beneath the thin sheet covering her midriff. Her legs are drawn up, bent at the knee, her ankles thick. "What do you need me to do?" Sarah asks.

"I'm going to check to see how far along she is," he says, switching to Spanish. "Hold her hand, please."

Sarah steps to the head of the bed and wordlessly takes the woman's hand, causing the charm bracelet she's forgotten she's wearing to slide down her arm, chiming gently.

The woman's eyes fly open, darting first to Sarah's face before looking to their clasped hands. Her eyes mist, a sob catching in her throat as she turns her hand to finger the bracelet. Jenna's bracelet. And then she raises her gaze to Sarah's. Looking fully into her eyes, a spark appears. Her chapped lips form a wordless O, before curving into a smile. Tears overflow and slide down her smooth, brown cheeks. In that moment, Sarah catches a glimpse of this woman's beauty: the slim nose and onyx eyes gracing an oval face.

Matilde closes her eyes again, a sound lifting on her breath. "Gracias."

Without warning, her body heaves as a new contraction seizes her. She twists sideways, crumpling the sheet Chase has carefully arranged. "She's close." He's tossed his cap on the floor, and his dark-blond hair lies matted against his head. "I can feel the baby's skull."

A guttural growl begins in Matilde's chest and emerges from between her lips. "Push, Matilde!" Chase urges in Spanish. The laboring woman's body curls upward, her grip on Sarah's hand white-hot as the growl becomes a deep-throated yell, which she sustains until she collapses back against the pillows.

Murmuring words of encouragement, Sarah brushes Matilde's damp hair off her forehead as she pants. Then another contraction grips her, and she coils forward. Chase nods. "Again!"

Sarah loses count of how many times they go through this, her fingers growing numb in Matilde's fierce grasp. Then Chase announces he can see the head. "We're almost there, Matilde. You're doing fine."

Minutes later, a new life tumbles into his waiting hands. "It's a boy, handsome and healthy." He sounds relieved, making Sarah wonder if he'd been more worried about delivering this baby than he let on. He cuts the cord, then smiles as he lays the slick, squalling child on Matilde's chest. "Look at all that hair."

Chase delivers Matilde of the afterbirth, then does a quick clean-up of mother and child. In the other room, the front door crashes open. The men outside must have heard the baby's cry. Smelling of tobacco, Sixto fills the doorway. *"¿Un niño?"* he demands.

"Sí." Matilde's wide smile lights the room. "A boy."

Sixto blinks as if she's hit him. Then, his face crumpling, he crosses the room in two strides and falls to his knees at his wife's bedside. His hands tremble as he takes his son into his arms.

A clamor of rushing feet, then all six girls plus the dog crowd through the doorway. Matilde holds out an inviting hand to her family. *"Vengan,"* she invites. "Come, meet your new baby brother."

The girls gather close to their mother, the younger ones gently touching the baby's tiny feet. Sarah's eyes meet Chase's, his smile spilling warmth over her body. "You did good," he says quietly in English.

"You, too." Their gazes lock, and something expands inside her chest.

Then Jonas fills the doorway. His eyes film with tears as he stands there without a word, swaying slightly, as if an unseen wind keeps him from finding his balance.

An hour later, Sarah escapes the pressing heat of the house and the clamor of the children to lean against the porch rail, Miski cradled against her chest. The puppy is content in her arms, almost as if he, too, is spent from the excitement surrounding the birth. Sarah concentrates on her own steady breathing, taking in Miski's warm, dusty smell. Behind her, she can hear the rustlings and murmurs of the family settling down for the night. She pictures Matilde's face as she last saw it: filled with peace and relief, yes, but something else too, something that seemed to transcend her happiness over her baby's safe delivery. If she had to name it, Sarah would call it hope.

She lifts her eyes to the cloudless sky, where a startlingly infinite number of stars light up the heavens. Then a footfall sounds behind her and Chase draws alongside, handing her a steaming mug. "Thought you could use this." His words fall heavily, as if weighted by the knowledge of Jonas's heartache as he sees the birth of children he will never have with Jenna.

"Thank you." She recognizes the scent. Maté de coca. She shifts the puppy against her shoulder and sets the mug on the rail in front of her. "I wish I could take away his pain, you know?"

"I know." The rail creaks as Chase joins his weight against it, his shoulder brushing hers as he leans forward to stare into the dirt yard.

She feels a bit liquid inside, the effect of being flung from the helium-like euphoria of the birth back into the dredges of reality. She looks toward the truck, where Jonas sits, having escaped after the birth. The outline of his head and shoulders can barely be seen through the open window. "It should have been Jenna here tonight."

"Yes."

She flashes back to what Jonas started to share before little Delia interrupted, the unknown torment Jenna carried. For what, or whom? Though Sarah's not accustomed to thinking of her sister this way, trouble must have existed, at least in Jenna's mind, because Rachael had glimpsed it, too.

Could it have had anything to do with Jenna's sudden decision to return home? Sarah's scalp prickles as she considers the possibility, but then she almost as quickly dismisses it. Because what does any of that matter now? Jenna is gone.

"I don't understand why she was taken from these people." Her eyes seek his. "Do you?"

"No." He blows out the word on a breath, looking so tired. She lifts a hand, wanting to wipe away the fatigue. Catching herself, she picks up her mug instead.

"She wasn't finished with her work. It doesn't make sense." She looks again to the truck. "And now that poor man has to continue on with a Jenna-sized hole he can never hope to fill."

"As do we all."

Shifting her glance, she catches the glint of his green eyes, the sheen of lingering perspiration on his skin. She lifts her mug, takes a sip, the hot tea a painful tingle on her tongue. From inside the house comes the mewl of the infant, followed by his mother's calm shushing. And then, silence.

"Everyone okay in there?" She nods toward the house.

"Everyone's fine." He takes a final swallow of tea before tossing the dregs into the yard. "Mother and child both resting. We can be on our way as soon as we're ready." He leans over to stroke the puppy's head against her shoulder, his head so near she can see the fan of his eyelashes even in the darkness. "I take it you've never seen a birth before."

"Not a human one." A smile tugs at her mouth. "I've seen a horse foal, though."

He chuckles softly. "Not quite the same thing, is it?"

"Not at all."

Miski squirms, and she bends to set him down. As she straightens, her left knee catches, sending her off balance. She grabs for the porch rail but instead finds herself caught in Chase's strong arms. She tenses at first, but as he tightens his hold, she relaxes into him, leaning her head against his chest. She wraps her arms around his middle, willing now to accept the hug she refused earlier. It feels like warm honey in her veins, being held like this. It hits her how little she's been touched these past few weeks. Except for Abby, she can hardly remember the last time someone actually put their arms around her. She's felt she's had to be the strong one, first for Dad, then for these people who knew Jenna so well and are grieving her loss so terribly.

Chase smells of hard work, and beneath that, something spicy and outdoorsy, like the cedar wood of her hope chest back home. His hands warm her skin through her thin dress as her hands slide up his back. Her pulse ratchets a notch and her breath catches.

A cough rasps into the stillness. Sarah stiffens, but Chase does not release his hold until she pushes away, backing to the rail.

"*Lo siento*." It's Sixto, standing in the doorway, holding Miski, who must have nosed his way into the house. "I do not mean to interrupt," he says in Spanish, "but you will not want to forget your dog."

Before Chase says anything, she steps forward, her cheeks warming as she scoops the puppy into her arms and murmurs a thank you. She glances at Chase, his hand brushing her shoulder as she goes down the steps. The men exchange good nights as she joins Jonas in the truck.

CHAPTER 31

"'Jesus said to her, "I am the resurrection and the life. The one who believes in me will live, even though they die; and whoever lives by believing in me will never die. Do you believe this?"'" Chase looks up from his worn, black leather Bible to scan the somber faces around him. The river behind him sings as it flows along the valley floor. Pewter clouds shade the sun, draping the distant Andes like a woolen shawl.

Chase resumes his reading in the Spanish New Testament. "'And Martha answered Him, "Yes, Lord, I do believe."'" Closing his Bible, Chase addresses the people of Magdalena gathered in tight clusters along the river's rocky bank. "And so, my friends, did Jenna also believe. By Jesus Christ's own words, we know that all of us who likewise believe will see her again. God's promise to us, on which we hang our hope. We know this is not the end for Jenna. In fact, for her, it is just the beginning."

The night before, after returning from Matilde's, Sarah and the men collapsed into their beds, Sarah vaguely aware of Rachael's return some time later. They'd all slept until nearly nine in the morning, when the villagers started arriving. By eleven o'clock, the Jacksons' scabby yard was filled with Magdalena residents who had come to say goodbye—to Jenna and to Jonas, who would be leaving their community immediately following the memorial service. They came silently, every single family bearing a gift. A basket of ripe peaches. A plate of sliced tomatoes. A crock of steaming llama stew.

Then, shortly before noon, Chase led the procession to the river. Sarah walked alongside him, cradling Jenna's urn of ashes. She was reminded of how she held Miski the night before, so warm and alive against her body. By contrast, the urn was heavy and cold, exactly what she felt inside.

She and Chase didn't speak as they descended toward the river, but occasionally, she stole glances at him. He'd somehow found time to shave this morning, which helped diminish but could not erase his look of fatigue. The slight stoop to his shoulders told her exhaustion lay just beneath the surface. She remembered her impulse last night to wipe the fatigue from his face. How did he find the strength to carry on, rising to meet everyone's needs but his own? While she's grateful for everything he's doing, it added just a bit to her own heart's ache, knowing the burden he carried.

Standing now by the river, among Jenna's people, Sarah scans their downcast faces. Chase has finished speaking. He catches Sarah's eye and nods. It is time. Without a word, she passes through the crowd. When she reaches Jonas, she twists the urn's lid free and hands it to him.

He takes the vessel in one huge hand and holds it against his body as gently as if it were a baby. Two tears slip free and trace glistening tracks down his burnished cheeks, the only sign of the fierce emotions raging inside. He wades into the river, and when the water reaches his knees, he lifts the urn, its intricate Celtic cross catching the light, and presses the vessel against his full lips. Then he upends it. Ashes cascade free. Jenna's mortal remains hang in the air before drifting onto the river's surface, shimmering, then are drawn into the watery depths.

～ ⌒ ～

Afterward, they return en masse to the Jackson's yard to consume the feast laid out on planks straddling two pairs of sawhorses. Though she has little appetite, Sarah fills her plate with llama stew and a corn tamale before heading for Jonas, who stands on the fringes of the gathering, empty-handed. "Jonas, may I bring you something?"

"No." He keeps his gaze on the people milling nearby. "Thanks."

"A lot of people turned out today."

"With one or two noticeable exceptions."

"Matilde and Sixto, you mean?"

"No." He swallows. "Dolores."

"Is she back in Magdalena?"

"Rae told me she returned early this morning." His mouth tightens. "I told you she blames me. Why else would she stay away?"

"Isn't she likely home taking care of Matilde and the new baby?"

"Matilde herself will be here, you'll see. Bolivian women don't stay in bed any longer than they have to. It's not a preference; it's a reality. I've seen moms walking to market, new babies strapped to their chests, just hours after giving birth. And I've never seen anything keep anyone from a funeral."

"I'm sorry, Jonas." A breeze picks up, flicking her hair around her face, making her wish she'd secured it in a ponytail. She looks for a way to change the subject. "Does your shoulder hurt?"

"It's fine."

"I know this is agony for you."

He looks down at her from his height, his expression inscrutable. "Yes," he agrees. "It is."

"Have you had any more absence seizures?"

"Not since we left the hospital."

"Last night was hard for you, wasn't it?" She knows by the faint tremor in his stubbled chin that she's hit the mark. An ache begins in her throat. "Jonas, I'm so, so sorry."

He nods, swallowing a few times. Finally, he manages the barest of smiles and reaches for her hand, squeezing her fingers lightly. "I know you are. Thank you. It does help. A little." Another moment passes, and he sighs. "Last night, Matilde's baby arrived safely, but they don't always, you know. Last year, two Magdalena moms lost their babies during childbirth, and a mother from Cortadera died the year before that. It's why Jenna said we had to wait to start our family."

From behind them, one of the villagers utters a cry. "Aiii!" Wheeling around, they see it's meant as a greeting for Sixto, who has entered the yard followed by his six daughters and Matilde, holding their new son. But no Dolores.

Sarah's heart thumps as she shoots a glance at Jonas, whose face has gone gray. He gives her a significant look before excusing himself and taking off down the river path. She looks after him helplessly, wondering whether to follow. Then she becomes aware that someone has come up alongside her. Turning, she is surprised to find Matilde, her face made pink by the bursting of tiny capillaries during her labor and birth. Her baby is barely visible inside the crimson aguayo held tightly against her chest.

Matilde accepts Sarah's stammered Spanish greeting and praise for her handsome son. Then she takes Sarah's hand in a calloused grip, her dark gaze seeking. "You are Sarah, sí? Jenna's sister."

Sarah swallows and nods, unable to push a yes past her lips. Somehow, Matilde represents everything Jenna has missed since she's been gone. And what she will continue to miss ever after.

"Your sister meant so much to me." Matilde's husky voice catches. "You perhaps cannot know how much. She was the first person to tell me my life could amount to more than toting water and birthing babies. She taught me to read. Taught me to believe I have something good to offer my family and community. Most of all, she taught me that Jesus has something good to offer me. The freedom to become more than who I am now. The courage to speak. Because of Jenna, I began to envision what my life might be someday."

"I'm glad she was able to give you that, Matilde. It was important to her."

Matilde's eyes, already puffy from childbirth, redden with fresh tears. "When Jenna died, it was more terrible than anything I have ever known. Worse, even, than when our first baby son died eight years ago. That sounds very bad, but I did not know my son as I knew Jenna. He died within minutes of his birth. Jenna was like a sister. I felt abandoned." She clutches Sarah's arm. "You must feel this abandonment too, sí?"

"Sí," Sarah whispers.

"Before our son, *this* son, was born—" Matilde kisses her baby's head. "My husband told me Jenna's death was a sign that God was not pleased with my desire to be more than a wife and mother, my desire to learn to read. I believed him. But, when my birth pains began, all that Jenna told me about Jesus came to me fresh again. How He does not treat us as lesser just because we are women. It was as if my pain, the pain I have because I am a *woman*, caused me to find new strength to remember these truths. And in that moment, I missed your sister so much. More than anything, I wanted her to be with me.

"I prayed to Jesus then. I asked Him to remember me, a woman He loved. I wanted Him, but I also very much wanted Jenna. She'd told me she would be with me at the birth. I felt very lost without her.

"Hours went by. The baby was coming fast. I knew Jesus was with me, but still, I felt so alone. But then—" Matilde's eyes seek hers. "You came."

Sarah swallows. "I came with Chase."

"Chase, yes—but *you*." Matilde's hand lifts Sarah's so the silver links of Jenna's bracelet chime. "When I heard this musical sound, I realized at once you were Jenna's sister, wearing her bracelet. Do you know what she once told me about this jewelry? Each charm was like a piece of what made her heart beat."

A chill races through Sarah. Matilde's features smooth with the same hope Sarah glimpsed on her face the night before. "I'd longed to feel Jenna near me, and God sent me you—with Jenna's heart."

Matilde releases Sarah's hand and presses her cheek against her baby boy's dark, downy head. "Last night, after you went home, I told Sixto, 'You see? God has *not* abandoned me. That is a lie. And with God's help, I will continue to teach the women, as Jenna did. I will teach my daughters to read, and every woman in Magdalena as well.' I also told him someday we will rebuild the wells." She nods and points toward the other side of the yard, where Sixto is talking to Chase. "My husband is right now telling your Chase what he needs to know about who was responsible for destroying our hand pumps. I do not believe it will happen again."

Sarah watches Chase, his head bent close to Sixto's. And though Chase's expression remains carefully neutral, Sarah can tell by the tilt of his broad shoulders, a loosening of his muscles, that Sixto is saying what Chase wants to hear. Her heart lifts, her pulse quickening in gratitude. Suddenly, she knows: she wants this community to succeed. Not only for their own sake, but also for Jenna and Jonas's. That their heavy sacrifice would not be for nothing.

As if sensing her pleasure, Chase glances up at that moment and catches her eye. He smiles, and she can't help the tilt of her own lips in response.

"So." Matilde releases a breath, smiling as well, drawing Sarah back to her. "God blessed us with a healthy son at last, and in my hour of need, He brought me Jenna's sister wearing Jenna's heart. I said to my husband, 'Do not let me hear you say again that God has left us.'" Matilde's baby stirs, and she kisses his cheek. "Indeed, He is very near."

CHAPTER 32

"Here we are." Weariness edges Chase's voice as he stops the truck in front of the La Fuente orphanage in Santa Cruz. "Home sweet home. For tonight, anyway."

"And each of us with our own beds, too." Rachael yawns and stretches her long, brown limbs. Beside Sarah in the backseat, Jonas rouses from his cramped position. All except Chase have dozed for most of the long journey from Magdalena. "None of us will mind that, I think." She smiles at Sarah as she opens the passenger-side door and gets out.

Sarah flexes her shoulders, grateful for the space to move again. They've pulled into a paved courtyard enclosed by eight-foot, wrought-iron fencing. Waning sunlight glints off a sculpted fountain gurgling in front of the set of double-doors leading into a two-story, whitewashed building with a tiled roof. The name of the orphanage is stenciled in blue over the doorway. Los Zapatitos. The Little Shoes.

A plump matron emerges through the front double-doors, her round face splitting into a grin. With a glad cry, she approaches

Rachael first, hugging her tightly before turning to Chase. Then she takes Jonas into her arms, holding him there while she murmurs endearments and pats his back. Smiling sadly, he gently disengages himself and turns to make introductions. "Sarah, this is Lucia. She takes care of everyone here. Lucia, this is Sarah Lanning. Jenna's sister."

With another exclamation, the woman encompasses her into a hug, telling her in Spanish what a dear person her sister was, how deeply she is missed in the community.

Several kids trickle into the courtyard, a small pack of dogs trailing after them. In no time, a band of tail-waving canines and excited children chattering in Spanish surround Chase, Jonas, and Rachael. One of the taller boys scoops up Miski, rescuing him from being trampled. The La Fuente people submit to the attention until Chase suddenly calls out, *"¿Donde está Mowgli?"*

The children fall silent.

"Lucia?" Chase presses. "Where's Mowgli?"

The housekeeper sighs. "He's run off. Again."

"When?"

"Two days ago. He was at breakfast but didn't return for dinner."

Chase swears mildly in English before addressing Lucia again. "Has anyone searched for him?"

"Only the boys. With both you and Rachael gone, there's been no one to spare."

"Okay." He lifts his cap and runs his fingers through his hair before replacing it again. "I'll look for him as soon as we get settled."

It takes a few minutes to sort out which of their bags to carry inside, but soon Sarah enters the orphanage in the wake of Lucia's broad-hipped sway. The older woman leads her through a huge common room set with at least a dozen dining tables, the Panasonic television in one corner surrounded by four worn sofas. The room's single plate-glass window casts slanting sunlight over a battered ping-pong table and foosball game.

As she follows Lucia down a long hallway, Sarah asks about Mowgli. The woman sighs and shakes her head. "Mowgli is Chase's special child. They're all special, but there's always one who captures the heart, no?"

She nods, thinking of Sofia. "Is that really his name? Mowgli?" She knows it only as the name of the feral boy in Rudyard Kipling's story.

Lucia chuckles. "Chase started calling him that for fun and soon had everyone else doing it, too. Now I can hardly recall his real name. When you see him, you'll understand why."

"You're sure Chase will find him then?"

"Oh, he'll find him. Chase has a knack for finding people." She stops at a door at the end of the hall. "Here you go. I hope you'll be comfortable."

"I'm sure I will. Thank you." The room is plain and clean, not much bigger than a walk-in closet. It contains only a dresser and a nightstand set against white walls, with a crucifix centered over the white-draped, twin bed.

"It's not much," Lucia says, "but it does the trick."

"I'm surprised you have any rooms to spare." Sarah is thinking of all the children who might be able to use this space.

"We always keep an extra room or two for visitors. When we can, we like to get a traveling doctor to stay, and short-term missionaries often stop by. Well, dinner will be at seven. Do you need anything before then? No? I will leave you to yourself, then."

As the door closes behind Lucia, Sarah draws a deep breath before slowly releasing it, realizing this is the first time in days she's felt truly alone. She welcomes the solitude, slipping from her sandals without hurry, savoring the cool hardwood floor beneath her feet.

She stretches out on the smooth coverlet and shuts her eyes. She needs only a minute, maybe two …

Her eyes open and she sits up. A glance at the clock tells her fifteen minutes have passed since Lucia left her. A tap sounds on the door, an echo of the one she dimly recalls hearing in her sleep. "Come in," she calls, still groggy.

Rachael enters, carrying a short pile of towels and wearing fresh clothes, her hair damp from a recent shower. "Sorry, did I wake you?"

"No—I mean, yes, but it's fine. I didn't mean to fall asleep."

She smiles. "Bet you can't wait to sleep in your own bed again."

"Just a couple more days."

"We'll miss you."

"I'll miss you too." Surprised to realize how true it is.

"In the meantime—" Rachael holds out the towels. "Thought you might like a shower."

"You are my hero." Her skin tingles at the mere idea.

"Also wanted to let you know there's been a change in plans. Jonas will be traveling back to La Paz with you and Chase tomorrow."

"Oh?" The plan had been for Jonas to return to the States from here. Today was to have been their last day together. "Why?"

"Marcos asked to see him."

"Marcos?"

"Aliguerra. The attorney. He wants to get Jonas's deposition before he leaves the country. Apparently, several of the victims' families are now bringing wrongful death suits against the driver."

"Does Jonas want that?" It doesn't seem like him.

Rachael shrugs. "I don't think he knows what he wants, to tell you the truth. But Rand insists he at least talk with Marcos before making that decision."

"Where is Jonas now?"

"On a walk."

"How do you think he's doing?" He's been so withdrawn since the memorial service. All but unreachable.

"I'm not sure. But I just got off the phone with Abby. She's going to go with him tomorrow to this meeting. She'll be there to help if he needs it."

A shout from the courtyard causes both women to glance toward the window. Rachael lifts the bleached muslin curtain and smiles at whatever she sees outside. Sarah moves to join her at the window.

Chase has returned. With him is a small boy of about eight with a mop of curly black hair, snapping eyes, and a snaggletoothed grin. "That must be Mowgli," Sarah says.

"Oh, yes." Affection laces Rachael's voice. "That's Mowgli."

There can be no other name for the boy. Even from here, Sarah can sense the wildness that practically seeps from his skin. The energy he exudes. His mouth moves in a constant stream of Spanish while Chase keeps a hand on his tousled curls, as if afraid the boy will slip away again should he let go.

"Has Mowgli been here long?" Sarah asks.

"Couple of years. His mom died in childbirth, his dad of Chagas disease when Mowgli was five. At first, he was sent to Santa Cruz to live with his uncle, but his family already had seven kids. Mowgli was more or less left to fend for himself. He dropped out of school and fell in with the shoeshine boys."

"Sounds like a boy band."

"Yeah, well, some people do consider them to be part of the local charm, but it's really another form of child labor. It's becoming more of a problem, too, as the boys drop out of school in order to run their businesses. If they're not orphans, their parents usually force them to turn over every cent they earn to support the family. A lot of them end up homeless, sniffing glue to get high and sleeping on the streets."

"And that's how Chase found Mowgli?"

She nods. "While most of the time Mowgli's content here, sometimes he hears the sirens' song of his old way of life. The lure of his old community. The boys become like family to each other. Hard to break those ties."

By now, a half-dozen other boys have gathered around Chase and Mowgli, gesticulating and shouting. Someone runs and grabs a leather ball, two teams form, and the ball begins moving from one end of the courtyard to the other. Sarah tries to follow the ball and pick out the rules, but after five minutes, she gives up. "What game are they playing? Not soccer." Or if it is, it's like no soccer game she's ever seen.

Rachael laughs. "It's called *ulama*, though I'm not sure it's strictly that, either. They kind of make up their own rules." Shoulder to shoulder, the women watch as the game unfolds. Every minute or so, the boys cheer as one of them scores a point or smoothly maneuvers around an opponent. Chase strips off his shirt, the lowering sun glistening off his skin as he glides from one end of the courtyard to the other. Sarah's eyes follow him, observing the way his muscles tense and release, his effortless grace.

A minute or two spins out, until she becomes aware that Rachael's attention has left the game. She's watching Sarah watch Chase. When Sarah catches her eye, Rachael raises a questioning eyebrow, a teasing smile tugging her lips.

Feeling caught, Sarah turns from the window and snatches up the pile of towels. "Think I'd better grab that shower while I can."

"Sure thing. Down the hall, last door on the right." Her knowing tone hastens Sarah's exit from the room.

~ ᗡ ᗡ ~

She returns twenty minutes later, wet hair wrapped in a towel and feeling far more human again. Rachael has disappeared and the courtyard below is oddly silent, making Sarah wonder if the game has gone elsewhere.

The bed squeaks as she sits. Taking advantage of the quiet, she calls home, a bit surprised to get voicemail for both Dad and Shane. She leaves them the same message, saying she'll try calling again once she's in La Paz.

The purple aguayo, her gift from Luz, lies where she dropped it, vivid against the white coverlet. She picks it up, smooths it across her lap. Chase told her the different animal motifs and colors marked the various regions of the weavers. At the Cortadera market, she'd seen designs in the form of llamas, birds, horses, even dragons, overlaying textiles in deep hues of green, crimson, blue and copper. While she was attracted to the individualistic artistry of each piece, Jenna would have been drawn to their stories: which region or people-group the motifs and colors represented. What the designs meant to the maker. And the woman whose fingers had woven this jewel of beauty, this piece of art, a form of which had been taught to her mother before her, and her mother, and on and on for centuries.

As she fingers the graceful gazelle woven into the aguayo's fabric, Sarah recalls a weekend her family spent in Seattle when Jenna was fourteen, Sarah twelve. They'd visited the Seattle Art Museum, seen the four-hundred-year-old portrait of Pomponne II de Bellievre, once the French ambassador to England. While Sarah and Mom studied the artist's use of color and texture and lines, Jenna had been fascinated by the picture's story. How for years the subject was anonymous and the painter assumed to have been a lesser Dutch artist. Only in 1994, when it was restored, was it discovered to be a van Dyck and its sitter identified.

The story always drew Jenna. Drove her, too. How, then, could she have given up on her dream to become a journalist? Luz and Matilde have both given Sarah a glimpse of the storytelling nature of the Bolivian people. Is this what Jenna loved about living here? The people's passion for story? Or was it the chance to help these women rewrite the endings to their own stories? Was this, ultimately, what Jenna found so fulfilling about her new life? Sarah will never know for certain.

And what of Jonas's story? How will it continue without Jenna by his side? Sarah thinks of his tears as he upended the urn of Jenna's ashes, spilling them into the river. Of his absolute silence on the long drive from Magdalena. Of the still-unanswered questions about his health and, ultimately, his future.

Rachael said he'd gone for a walk. Sarah reaches for her phone and punches in the number Jonas gave her before they left Magdalena. When he doesn't answer, she shoots him a text. *R u ok?*

While she waits for his response, she pulls her damp hair into a topknot and swipes lip balm across her lips. Then, impatient, she tries a second text. *Where r u?*

When Jonas still has not replied five minutes later, she scoops up a light wrap and her aguayo and leaves the room.

"Señorita, where are you going?"

Lucia's question, called from the dining room, makes Sarah pause on her way out the front door. "Has Jonas returned?"

"Not that I have seen, señorita."

"He's been gone a while now. I'll try to find him."

Lucia's gaze takes in the sweater, the serape sling. "You will not go far? Dinner is soon."

"I won't, I promise."

CHAPTER 33

A t the orphanage's front gate, Sarah hesitates, unsure which direction to go. The evening light has turned to liquid gold that spills across the tiled rooftops. Rising above the trees on her right, she spies the tips of two towers. Basilica Menor de San Lorenzo? She recalls Jenna saying Santa Cruz's iconic Baroque cathedral had become one of her favorite spots. One of Jonas's too? Seems likely. She heads in that direction.

She puts several city blocks behind her before turning at another corner, always keeping what she can see of the basilica in front of her. Once, after rounding a bend, she thinks she's lost her way, but then she catches sight of a sign that points her in the right direction again. As she makes the final turn, the landmark looms in front of her. Three sets of massive, sienna-painted doors are set into golden bricks which seem to glow in the fading daylight. Street vendors peddle salteñas and other snacks around the rim of the courtyard, their delectable aromas making Sarah's mouth flood with saliva.

She scans the palm-tree shaded area and quickly realizes Jonas is not among the tourists. She looks up at the enormous clock set into one of the towers. Inside maybe?

"Will I ever convince you that running off alone around here is never a good idea?"

She whirls around. "Chase." Her pulse flutters—whether because of his sudden appearance or because of the way he looks—freshly showered and wearing a clean, black bowling shirt—she's unsure. The image of him running shirtless in the courtyard flashes across her mind. Remembering Rachael's knowing look, she feels herself flushing. "What are you doing here?"

"Looking for you. Lucia said you headed out." He crosses his arms, the grooves between his eyes telling her he's less than happy with her decision.

Her stomach plummets. "How'd you know where to find me?"

"Jenna liked to come here. Figured you might know that."

"I came looking for Jonas." Obliquely, she notices his face has lost its pallor, his eyes seem more alert. The impromptu game must have restored him a bit.

"My concern is keeping you safe, Sarah. I can't do that when you go wandering off."

"Here?" She glances around. "This place isn't dangerous. You weren't really worried about me, were you?"

"It's my job to worry."

"Not about me, surely."

His eyes flick away, a shadow crossing his face. "Jonas returned to Zapatitos a few minutes after you left. He was never lost."

"Oh." Suddenly she feels foolish. "Why didn't someone call me?"

"I tried." His eyes flick to her serape bag. "It went to voicemail."

Her hand goes to the aguayo. Its limp folds inform her that in her haste to leave her room, she left her phone behind. Her heart spirals downward. "I'm sorry."

He rubs a hand on the back of his neck, the tension seeming to leave him. "I'm just glad I found you, okay? But, please, don't do it again."

"Okay. Sorry." She has to look away from the sharp focus of his gaze. "How's Mowgli?" Her fingers twist the straps of her aguayo.

He smiles reluctantly. "Happy and well-fed, I imagine. Probably reaching for seconds of Lucia's *picante de pollo*, which is exactly what we should be doing. Aren't you hungry?"

"Not really. Well, maybe a little."

He casts an appraising glance at the basilica. "Have you gone inside? You should at least go up the bell tower. Great view of the city. Well worth the climb." He captures her hand and heads for the massive church. She lets herself be pulled along. Inside, the building's dim layers enfold them, scents of incense and sandalwood tickling her nose. Stone steps on the left beckon them upward. Five minutes later, slightly out of breath, they stand side-by-side in the belfry, gazing out over the rooftops.

Sarah leans her forearms on the railing, inhaling long and slow as she absorbs the panoramic view: block after block of tidy stucco dwellings, ancient stone structures nestled among tree-lined boulevards, the setting sun glazing the entire scene in amber. *The gloaming.* She's never thought to use that word to describe something, until now. "The colors seem so much more vivid here," she says. "Why is that? Is it the light?"

"I don't know." He gives her a sideways glance. "I always thought it was just me."

"I don't think so. It's beautiful."

"Maybe it does come down to something as ordinary as the angle of the sun, but back home in the States, the colors don't pop the same way. Not for me, anyway. I never feel as alive anywhere else as I do when I'm here." He shrugs. "It wasn't always that way, but Bolivia is a weird country. It changes people. Changes the way you see things. I don't know what it is, but even with all we have to deal with here, I wouldn't trade this life. It's like the difference between living in a black-and-white and a Technicolor world."

Lines of poetry from one of Jenna's books come to her. "God fills His earth with heavenly wonder / but only she who lifts her head beholds it."

Chase's shoulder brushes hers. When he doesn't speak, she turns her head to find him studying her. The air between them shifts, crackles. The hairs on her arms stand up.

"You're a very unusual woman, you know that?"

"Me?" Heart hammering, she looks away from his intense gaze.

"Yes, you, Sarah Lanning." One gentle hand rests on her shoulder, pulling her to face him. She can't look away from those amazing eyes. "I've never met anyone like you." The huskiness in his voice pulls her toward him. "I can't stop thinking about you."

She can practically feel the heat from his chest as only inches separate them. Her gaze drops to his perfect lips, and she wonders how it would feel to kiss them. She glances up and her breath catches. He seems to have read her thoughts. His gaze shifts to her mouth and heat flames across her cheeks.

In the recesses of her mind, a warning bell jangles—faint at first, then crescendoing until at last it breaks through. *What am I doing?* She pulls back, pressing a hand to her stomach. *I hardly know this man. And in two days, I'm leaving Bolivia for good.*

She risks a glance at Chase, who narrows his eyes and starts to speak but abruptly stops. He edges away, exhaling sharply, his grip tightening on the railing.

Another moment passes, every part of her seeming to hold its breath, before he points to a leafy canopy of a city park several blocks away. "See that area over there?"

Breath rushes from her as she recognizes the olive branch, and she grabs it. "Where all the trees are?" Her voice sounds thin. She clears her throat and tries again. "On the other side of that fountain?"

He nods, not looking at her, one hand rubbing the back of his neck. "Used to be giant sloths living in those trees. Ginormous beasts existing their entire lives in the branches over people's heads."

She swallows, playing along. "Right here in the city?"

He nods. "When I first moved to Santa Cruz, I lived not far from there. With Jonas, actually. Before Jenna, and before I got involved with Los Zapatitos. Sometimes after dinner, we'd go out and grab a couple of *cervezas*, find a park bench and just watch the sloths move."

"And where are they now? The sloths, I mean."

"Few years back, the city made some improvements. The sloths were temporarily relocated to the zoo, then the city decided to keep them there permanently." His voice dips to a low note, resigned. "For their own safety. Said it was a sign of progress."

"Doesn't sound much like progress to me." A beat plays out. She draws a trembling breath. "Chase—"

He angles toward her, arms crossed in front of himself like a shield. "Sarah."

"Speaking of Jonas … "

His shoulders relax a bit. "Yes?"

"I'm worried about him." She can't quite meet his gaze, so she looks out over the city again. "I don't know how to help him." Her voice catches.

He blows out a breath. "You know he's going back with us tomorrow, right?"

"I heard."

"Think you'll stay in touch with him once you get home?"

"I plan to. Washington is a long way from So Cal, but we can at least talk on the phone."

"Good. He's going to need support when he gets back. I'm afraid that's when it's going to get really real for him."

She winces and rubs her arms, knowing he's right. "How do you think he'll manage? I mean, I know he's going back to live with his sister for a while, but that can't last forever." She hesitates. "What's he going to live on?"

"Jonas doesn't want your money, Sarah." In her periphery, she sees him reach out a hand, as if to touch her, before shoving both hands into his front pockets. "I know it bothers you that Jenna left her money to you instead of to Jonas, but it's really not something you need to worry about."

"Did she talk to you?"

"No, but I'm pretty sure she left it to you because whether you keep the money or give it away, it's a decision she wanted you to make from your heart. To be happy with your choice, no matter what."

"If she thought I'd see it as a gift, she was mistaken." She wants to say more, but at that moment, her stomach lets out a low gurgle. She wraps an arm around her middle, hoping Chase didn't hear.

But of course he did. "Thought you said you weren't hungry." She darts him a look and he feigns a frown. But a smile tugs at his mouth as he gestures for her to precede him, careful not to touch her. "Come on, let's go. You really don't want to miss Lucia's *manjar blanco*."

CHAPTER 34

"Good morning, Sarah." Chase is the first person she encounters the next day when she descends from her room, bleary-eyed, for breakfast. Rachael, in cargo shorts and a white tee, has already served herself and sits at the table, a local newspaper spread in front of her. Wearing a blue bowling shirt, Chase stands at the long buffet station, carafe in hand. "Coffee?"

"Please." Unable to hold his gaze, her glance skitters to the bounty Lucia has laid out for them. Eggs scrambled with chorizo sausage, grilled tomatoes and mushrooms, cinnamon-dusted flour tortillas, and a bowl of sliced star fruit and açai berries.

He hands her the fragrant cup. "Sleep okay?"

"Not as well as I'd hoped." She takes the mug between both hands, absorbing its heat into her palms. Last night, despite the comfort of the soft, white sheets, she lay awake far too long, feeling surprisingly unsettled with her time in Bolivia coming to an end. "You?"

"Same." His eyes find hers as he raises his mug and sips. "I kept thinking about our conversation last night. In the bell tower."

"Oh?" The sugar spoon she's holding slips from her fingers and clatters to the buffet table. She scoops it up and, deciding to skip the sweetener this morning, lifts the cream pitcher instead. "I mean—sorry. What were you saying?"

"Just that I was thinking about Jonas, how you might help him once you're home."

"Oh. Of course." From the corner of her eye, she sees Rachael look up from her paper, a bite of jam-slathered toast poised halfway to her mouth. How much has she guessed about what—*almost*—happened between them in the bell tower? Her cheeks warming, Sarah turns toward the buffet table and loads a plate with food she's barely hungry for. "And what did you decide?"

"Well, not a decision so much as a realization. I think it would be a comfort if you stayed in touch as much as possible." He pauses for so long she's forced to look at him. "I know it would mean a lot to me. If I were Jonas, I mean."

Sarah opens her mouth to respond, but at that moment, the object of their discussion joins them. Jonas mutters a greeting. Relieved to let the conversation drop, Sarah slips into her seat at the far end of the table. Except for a few desultory comments, everyone falls silent. No one, apparently, much in the mood for conversation.

⁓ ᴐ ᴄ ⁓

An hour later, Rachael hugs her tightly as they say goodbye at the airport. "Promise to keep me in the loop?"

Sarah nods. "Of course."

Rachael glances toward Chase as he strides toward the waiting Kodiak. "About everything."

Pretending not to understand, Sarah gives her one last hug and joins the men already aboard the plane.

The flight to La Paz is uneventful. Abby meets them at the airport, where they grab a quick lunch before Chase drives them to La Fuente headquarters for Abby and Jonas's one o'clock appointment with Marcos Aliguerra.

"Sofia should get back to the house around the same time you do," Abby says as Chase pulls up to the building. "She's at the market right now."

"All by herself?" Chase asks.

"Oh my, yes. She's a devil of a haggler. I don't know how she does it using only sign language, but I swear the vendors blanch when they see her coming."

He chuckles, the first note of levity Sarah's heard in a while. "So, when would you like me to come get you?"

"Don't worry about us. We'll flag down a *trufi* and find our own way home."

At Abby's house, Chase unlocks the back door with his borrowed key, sending up a frenzy of barking from Jake. When the door swings wide, Jake trades barking for dancing around Sarah's ankles as she pulls her carry-on over the threshold and into the kitchen while Chase closes the door.

"Someone missed us." He drops his backpack to the floor and bends to the dog's level. Jake rolls over in ecstasy, exposing his belly to be scratched.

Sarah welcomes the distraction, feeling suddenly shy at finding herself alone with Chase. "I'm missing Miski already." Jonas made the hard decision to leave Jenna's dog behind at Los Zapatitos. "He'll be okay, won't he?"

"We'll take good care of him, I promise." Maybe Chase senses her unease, because he seems careful not to catch her eye, lending his face a shuttered look. Because of his concern for Jonas—or their near-kiss in the bell tower? She herself is not sure which disquiets her more. "Jonas did the right thing. He's going to have other things to think about for a while without having to worry about nursing an injured puppy back to health."

Sarah straightens with a sigh, looking around Abby's tidy kitchen. A stainless steel carafe sits on the counter with an attached sticky note inviting them to help themselves. "Abby's left us tea. Want some?"

"Later. Got calls to make, but you go ahead." His step quickens as he leaves the room. She bites her lip as she watches him go, uncertainty plucking at her spirit.

Then she squares her shoulders. *I'm tired*, she decides. *Missing home and everything familiar. That's why I'm losing my grounding.* Her gaze settles on the carafe again. Maybe some tea and time in Abby's serene home will help reset her anchor. And a phone call to Shane.

She takes her bag back to the guest room to get settled before relaxing with tea. While digging in her bag for her phone, the scraping of the garden gate causes her to look out the window. Sofia trudges up the path to the house, her small form hunched beneath the weight of a mesh grocery bag that must weigh nearly as much as she.

Wearing a clean, yellow dress and brown, laced-up boots, the girl is still yards from the house when Sarah hears the slap of the kitchen screen door, sees Chase bounding to meet her. Sofia's head comes up and her lovely brown eyes light with pleasure, her bag landing on the stone walkway with a thunk as she hurls herself into his embrace.

A lump swells in Sarah's throat as she stands, riveted, watching their reunion. Chase's delight in Sofia is infectious, and Sarah's heart lifts of its own accord. After a moment, he stands and, taking the bag of groceries in one hand and Sofia's hand in the other, they make their way inside the kitchen.

Sarah withdraws from the window, wiping away tears. *What is wrong with me?* She closes her eyes. More than the weight of Jonas's grief or her memory of the now-empty sod house left behind, this man's kindness stirs something in her, touches her spirit in a way she hasn't felt in years. He has a way of really seeing those he cares about. And she is beginning to suspect that includes her.

But I'm leaving. Tomorrow.

Forty-eight hours from now, she will be home again, on the vineyard, digging out from beneath the pile of paperwork that surely awaits her. Dad will be there, and Shane.

Shane. Is she really ready to turn her back on their budding relationship for a long-distance one with a man she's known only a week? Who would do that?

Jenna would. The answer pops into her mind, faintly taunting.

With a lift of her chin, she brushes the thought aside. *I'm not Jenna.*

Deciding her phone call can wait, Sarah lingers in her room until she no longer hears Chase chatting with Sofia. She cautiously emerges and approaches the kitchen, but he's gone, probably to make his calls. Some of the tension leaves her body. Sofia stands at the open pantry, putting away her market purchases.

"Hello, Sofia," Sarah says softly in Spanish. The child whirls around, looking so startled Sarah wonders if she forgot Sarah was staying at Abby's too. "It's nice to see you again." The girl ducks her head and begins to turn away, but Sarah stops her. "Look, I brought you something." She digs into her shorts pocket. "But first you have to close your eyes. Now hold out your hand." With her eyes pinched shut, Sofia submits her palm. Sarah drops into it the small, carved dog she bought at the Cortadera market. "Now look."

Sofia opens her eyes. Her face glows as she examines the trinket, turning it over and over with her fingers. *Gracias*, she signs, her eyes crinkling with delight.

Sarah presses a kiss to the top of Sofia's warm head, which smells of lemons and sunshine. "*De nada.*"

Then she crosses to the counter to pour herself some tea. By the time she turns around again, Sofia has finished putting away her groceries and has splayed a length of rolled butcher paper across the table. After gathering a handful of charcoal pencils, she sits down at the table and begins to sketch. Sarah edges closer, looking on for a few minutes before pulling out a chair and sitting beside her. She watches for several more minutes as a mountainous landscape begins to take shape beneath the child's skillful hand. Sarah takes a sip of tea, the movement causing the charms of Jenna's silver bracelet to tinkle.

Sofia's pencil stills. She catches Sarah's wrist in her grip, staring at the jewelry before quizzically raising her eyes. "Sí, it's Jenna's. Would you like to see it?"

Sofia nods. Sarah unclasps the bracelet and slips it into the girl's open hand. Sofia fingers each of the charms in turn. A tiny bunch of purple grapes. A llama. A cross, a book, a key in the shape of a figure eight. "Did she ever tell you about these? Jenna collected them over the years. Each one meant something to her. Some our father gave her, some she chose for herself. I remember this one, especially." She points to the charm in the shape of a tiny, old-fashioned typewriter. "Our mother gave it to her shortly before she died. Back then, Jenna thought she might be a journalist or a writer."

She pauses for a moment, considering how much more to share, then decides that telling the rest might help this girl feel connected to Jenna's life in Magdalena. "When Chase and I were in Magdalena, a baby was born to a woman who was a good friend of Jenna's. Her name is Matilde. Like you, she misses Jenna very, very much." When Sofia drops her gaze, Sarah touches her hand. "I was wearing this bracelet when the baby was born. Jenna told Matilde that each charm was like a piece of her heart. For Matilde, it was a special reminder of how much Jenna cared for her, something she especially needed to remember when she was in so much pain." She reaches for Sofia's hand and joins the eye and clasp around Sofia's slim, brown wrist. "There. Beautiful, no?"

Sofia turns her hand this way and that, setting the charms jingling.

"I want you to have it."

The girl looks up, eyes wide, shakes her head, *no*. But Sarah nods, smiling. "Sí, Sofia, this is for you. I want you to have it. Jenna would want that too. She cared for you very much. It would please her to know you had something that was precious to her. As you were."

Sofia grows very still. Sarah hopes she hasn't opened a Pandora's box she has no way of closing. But after a moment, when Sofia reaches for her pencil, Sarah knows the girl has accepted the gift.

On impulse, Sarah grabs a pencil, too, and scribbles a shape that looks something like a sideways capital B into a corner of the butcher paper. Then she sits back and looks at Sofia expectantly.

Sofia's eyebrows draw downward, not comprehending.

"What does that look like to you?" Sarah prods. "Or what *could* it look like, with a little help from your pencil?"

Sofia looks again at the squiggle. After a moment her expression clears. She adds additional strokes until a smiling woman in a beehive hairstyle wearing an over-sized pair of shades emerges beneath her pencil. "Nice," Sarah approves. "Now your turn."

Nodding, Sofia sketches an open-ended triangle. Sarah narrows her eyes at the doodle, then with a few deft movements, transforms it into an overflowing picnic basket.

A floorboard creaks beneath Chase's footfall as he enters the room. "What game is this?"

The muscles across her shoulders tighten. As he bends closer to observe the drawing, she again catches his masculine scent, one that reminds her of cedar shavings.

"Something my mom and I used to play." She quickly scribbles a new shape for Sofia. "I haven't done this for a very long time." A quick glance up shows him staring at her, his brow creased. He tilts his head as if to speak, but then Sofia pulls on his arm to show off her picture. He leans in, his bicep brushing Sarah's shoulder.

At his touch, she drops her pencil, and it rolls off the table and onto the floor with a ping. Chase bends and returns it to her.

Sarah takes it without looking at him, attempting an encouraging smile while motioning for Sofia to complete her turn.

Chase pours himself tea from the carafe as Sofia forms a caricature of a screeching cat. Then it's Sarah's turn again. "You're very good at this." His voice softens as he studies the quick lines she lays down on the paper. "Why did you quit?"

"Because I had no one to play with."

"Not the game. Your art."

She raises her gaze. "How do you know I quit?"

"Jenna told me. And I got the sense she wasn't very happy about it."

A hollow sphere seems to expand behind her breastbone, reminding her that this trip has raised more questions about her sister than answers. "Jenna wasn't happy about a lot of things I did."

"Now that I see what you're capable of, I can understand why."

Sarah drops her head back over the paper, feeling an unexpected splinter in his words, though she can't say why. She gave up her art following the accident, when her grief, the grueling PT, and the complete loss of normalcy all became overwhelming. A necessary choice, but one she'd made of her own free will. Hadn't she? "I still keep my finger in it. I teach kids down at the community center once a month. It scratches the itch." Her breath hitches. Do her words sound as defensive to him as they do to her?

"Somehow, I don't think that's quite the same thing."

She looks up—she can't help it—and finds him smiling at her, green eyes soft and crinkled at the corners, what she'd taken as censure transforming into something sweet. It stirs emotions inside her she doesn't care to name, and she can't think what to say. She is spared a response as a key scrapes in the latch.

Jonas and Abby have returned.

CHAPTER 35

Jonas appears in the doorway, his eyes red, his skin gray-tinged. Sarah's smile of greeting dies on her lips. "Jonas?"

Abby comes in behind him, her own mouth compressed with worry. When Abby's eyes meet Sarah's, her skin frosts over. "What's wrong?" Instinctively, she stands, glancing between Abby and Jonas. He looks as if he's about to pass out. "What happened?"

Chase moves forward, resting a hand on Jonas's broad shoulder to guide him to Sarah's vacated chair. Jonas slumps forward, resting his forehead on the flat of his palm.

"Jonas spent the afternoon with the bus driver," Abby says quietly, in English.

"The—" Sarah's hand goes to her throat, the amorphous uneasiness she felt earlier congealing into a hard lump of dread. "The one who was driving when they had the accident?"

"Yes."

"Jonas even had to ride in a *trufi* with him while they went to speak to another lawyer." Abby's brow furrows as she watches Jonas.

Sofia, understanding something is wrong, creeps over to Chase and takes his hand. "Marcos should have warned him."

"He didn't know, Abby," Jonas says flatly, not looking up.

"He had to have known it was at least a possibility."

"What happened?" Sarah pulls out another chair and sinks into it.

Abby does the same. "We thought we were meeting with Marcos and Rand so they could get Jonas's deposition on file. Even when Marcos said we needed to go to the courthouse, we didn't think much of it. Marcos took us to a room to wait while he went off to talk to someone else. Three other men in business suits were sitting there with some other people, all Bolivians. The families, we assumed, of those who had been killed.

"Around this point, I began to realize this wasn't just about Jonas, but I still assumed it was going to be the victims' families gathered together for the attorneys to address all at once. We were sitting there, waiting for something to happen, when the door opened. Marcos walked in with a couple other attorneys. And right behind them was this little middle-aged man."

Jonas raises his head, his red-rimmed eyes meeting Sarah's. The torment she reads there makes the hairs on the back of her neck stand up. "As soon as I saw him, it all came rushing back."

"What—" Fear causes her voice to catch. "What are you saying? You remembered him?"

"Not just him." He swallows. "Everything."

Sarah's mouth goes dry. "You remember the accident?"

"Everything," Jonas repeats flatly. "The accident, why Jenna was leaving. I remember it all."

Why should those words make her heart pound against her ribs? Perhaps it was the way his features pinched together, twisted out of shape as if by an unseen hand.

Jonas swipes a hand over his face. "It's so strange. I'd thought it would keep coming back to me in bits, like pieces of a jigsaw puzzle. Instead, it's like everything that happened was hidden behind a curtain, and that curtain was suddenly swept aside so I could see it all."

He splays his big hand on the table, staring at it as if his script is written on his skin. "My first thought was that this man, the driver, looked so different than the night of the accident. That night, he seemed a lot younger. Confident. Almost cocky. I remembered Miski falling over his feet and him laughing about it. I *liked* him."

Sarah is dimly aware of Abby leading Sofia from the room, of Chase moving to the refrigerator and returning with two glasses of water. Jonas drinks half of his. Though her mouth is dry as cotton, Sarah ignores her glass. Chase sets it aside and comes to stand at her shoulder.

"This guy today, though," Jonas goes on. "He had a paunch and gray hair, and he walked with a limp. He wouldn't look at any of us. The picture I'd been keeping of him inside my head was of some kind of a monster. This poor wretch was nothing like that. He was … pathetic." He frowns, shakes his head. "His wife was there too, shaking, scared to death. Marcos said they have six children, and this poor guy won't ever find work as a driver again. He'll have to find a new way to earn money for his family." He pauses to finish off his water.

"His name?" Sarah asks. "What's his name?"

"Arturo Estobol. Until today, I didn't even know that. I wish I didn't know it now. It makes him so … human."

"What else do you remember?"

"That I prayed for us." Jonas looks down at his fists, clenched between his knees. "Before we left Cortadera, I put my hands on the micro and asked for protection for our journey, for God to send His angels to fly at each of the four corners of the bus, so we would be safe." Jonas raises his head, his eyes meeting hers. "But that's not all, Sarah."

The dread she felt from the moment Jonas walked through the door gathers itself into a stone beneath her heart. "What?"

"I know why Jenna was leaving. Why she was flying home."

She licks her lips. "Why?"

"To see you."

"Me?" Her breath labors as if the air has been sucked from the room. "Why?"

"Because of the notes."

"Notes?"

Jonas reaches across the table and takes her hand. "She'd been getting anonymous notes from someone back home, postmarked from different cities in Washington. Threatening her. Notes like the one you brought me."

Her stomach sours, and she pulls her hand free. "And she thought I sent them."

"No, no. But they were about your accident. They scared her."

Her mind spins, trying to fit these pieces into a whole that makes sense. The letter postmarked Chelan was odd, sure. But not specific. "What did the other notes say?"

"They threatened to tell the truth about what happened on the mountain the day that TJ died—and you were so hurt."

"The truth? We know what happened."

"This person claimed he—or she—knew the part Jenna played in your accident."

"We already know that. She saved me. She tried to save TJ. It wasn't her fault she couldn't get to him in time."

"That's not what the notes said." Jonas's tone is flat, two-dimensional, as if this will somehow make his story easier for her to hear. "They claimed that what happened was Jenna's fault, that she'd kept the truth from you all these years. And whoever sent them said he was going to go public with what he knew."

A long silence stretches to the breaking point. "Are you saying someone was blackmailing my sister?" Incredulity edges her tone. The accident was caused by her own foolishness. "Why would anyone do that to Jenna?"

Jonas hesitates before answering with a question of his own. "What do you remember of that day?"

"Nothing. I told you that. After I came out of my coma, my memory was wiped clean."

"But Jenna remembered."

"Of course she did, she was there. She even tried to stop me when I was being stupid. And when she couldn't, she risked her own life to save mine."

"That's the story she told you. It's what she told everyone." He stops, swallows. "But a week before she died, she told me it was a lie."

A lie? The stone beneath her heart begins to crack. She shakes her head, hoping to stop the fear squeezing the breath from her lungs. If what she has believed—what they have all believed—is a lie, what then is the truth?

An ugly possibility unfurls, slithering and poisonous. "That can't be."

Jonas closes his eyes. "But it is."

CHAPTER 36

JENNA
Age 22
Washington backcountry

If I'd known Sarah was cross-country skiing that day, I'd have never gone, too. But I was bored and edgy and sick of my own company, having been cooped up inside with a bad cold for the last week of Christmas break. Classes at Eastern resumed in two days, and it had snowed six inches the night before, so when Tomaso suggested it, I agreed that good, hard skiing in the backcountry would be just the thing to brush out the cobwebs before buckling down to the books again.

Later, I wondered if Tomaso had planned it. He must have known, after all, that his grandson and my sister were heading out to the same favorite trail head, probably gave them the same warnings about avalanches. An unusually warm spell over Christmas, followed by a hard snow, primed untended slopes for slides. But having grown up skiing in the backcountry, we were all well-versed in mitigating the risk. Did Tomaso hope we would run into each other? And that in the crystal beauty of creation, something good would come of it? Probably. Dad was blind to my foul moods lately—either that or he was choosing to ignore them. But Tomaso was all too aware and had scolded me, in his gentle way, of course, about the danger of putting up walls between those we loved.

I considered inviting Samantha or another friend but thought better of it. Though I wasn't the daredevil Sarah was, I'd skied since I could walk and was perfectly comfortable setting out alone. Tired as I was of my own self, I sensed that being outside in the crisp, wintry sunshine would make a difference. Who knew, maybe I'd even find some of the peace I craved.

Of course I was hardly alone. Even with acres and acres to choose from, I encountered dozens of skiers, half of them college kids like me relishing their last day of freedom before the new semester began.

I made a wide circuit along a well-traveled trail and was coming to the rise of a knoll when I first saw them. Sarah's cherry-red ski suit was hard to miss. I angled away, hoping they hadn't spotted me. But—"Jenna!" My sister's call rang, bell-like, across the frosty air.

Reluctantly, I turned and coasted over to them as firs cast their lengthening shadows across the blue-tinged snow. A yellow avalanche warning sign stood beyond where Sarah and TJ waited. Close up, I saw Sarah's lips had that swollen look belonging to a girl who's just been thoroughly kissed. Her cheeks were flushed, making her unusually pretty, and TJ himself wore a self-satisfied air. Seeing them like this, together, sent a shard of envy shafting through my soul.

"What are you doing here?" At my tone, hurt flashed on Sarah's face. I hated myself for putting it there. But I couldn't help it. Jealousy twisted inside my gut, a living thing. A demon turning me into someone I despised.

And then there was TJ. His thickly fringed, black eyes caught mine. For one unguarded moment, I sensed him peering into my soul, the way he did back in the days when we were inseparable friends. Before he belonged to Sarah. Though it had been a decade since he'd been my confidante, he still knew me. And though he couldn't have had a clue as to what troubled me, he understood there was something. In the way his gaze held mine, he let me know he was sorry for whatever it was.

Still, he wasn't going to let me hurt his girlfriend. Though he did nothing more than touch Sarah's back, it was enough to tighten the knot inside me. His very presence a visible reminder that Sarah had the guts to do something I never could. To stand up to Dad. My weak backbone had cost me Mike. I'd failed myself. But worse, I'd failed someone I cared about.

I pictured my carved mahogany box and the secret it contained. Did anyone else know? Testing the waters once or twice, I concluded Dad didn't. The one who knew for sure was dead. But there was one other. Sometimes I suspected he knew by the way he watched me. Besides, wasn't the truth obvious on his face? On mine? But I was too much of a coward to find out for sure.

That was the reality of it. I was a coward, in every way. I felt, sometimes, that I could drown in the shame of it. And piling insult on injury, I saw how Sarah's determination to stand up to Dad had changed their relationship. He was beginning to look at her in a way he used to save for me. He respected her. The way one kindred spirit did another.

If I'd made different choices, would that kind of respect have been mine, too?

Stuffing the swirling questions back inside the dark pit of my mind, I mumbled a stiff goodbye before pivoting and gliding away. I told myself not to let Sarah's presence bother me. Backcountry was a big place, after all, with plenty of room for everyone. I made a few more runs before encountering someone else I hadn't counted on seeing.

Shane.

I'd been the one to break off our relationship months earlier. He was a nice enough guy, didn't do anything wrong. But since the day I was stupid enough to let Mike go, I'd never found another guy to measure up. It wasn't fair to keep Shane on a line I had no intention of reeling in.

Though the sight of him now made my insides squeeze painfully, it was too late to dodge him. He'd spotted me. To my surprise, he invited me to join him for a run or two. I didn't see the harm, so I did, even posing with him for a selfie. But then the buckle on his ski boot broke, and he had to hobble back to the spot where he'd left his car. I probably should have gone with him, but I didn't want him to misread the gesture.

Sunlight was beginning to fade when I decided to make one more run down a slope rated D17 for difficulty, R3 for risk, by far the most challenging slope in the area. When I circled back around to the top again, panting, I knew I had an hour of daylight left, at best. Still feeling the exhilaration of my run, I'd all but forgotten Sarah and TJ were anywhere around. But then, there they were, sharing that look of young lovers. The look that said no one else on the planet had things as good as they did.

They'd come straight from the bowl flagged for avalanche hazard. "How was it?" I asked, trying to act as if I cared.

The two of them exchanged guilty looks. "Amazing," Sarah admitted. Though the slope wasn't marked, I guessed it might rate a D18 or 19, delivering a major thrill if you had the chops to make it down in one piece.

I lifted my chin a notch. "Maybe I'll try it next."

Sarah and TJ shared another glance. "You better not, Jen. We were pushing our luck doing it once. We could hear things loosening up above us."

"Are you kidding me? And let you have all the fun?" Without giving them time to protest, I started down the slope.

Sarah's and TJ's cries faded behind me as I went racing downhill, relishing the icy wind nipping at my cheeks.

Then the rumble began.

I glanced back to see TJ and Sarah tearing after me. Then a great, white tidal wave swooped them up, and they disappeared.

Horrified, I pulled to a stop and scrambled out of my skis. Screaming their names, I fought my way back as fast as I could, aiming for the places I'd last seen their cartwheeling bodies.

After what felt like hours, I saw a glimmer of red fabric against the snow. I dug frantically until I found Sarah, unconscious, but breathing.

Breathing, thank God.

It was the last time I thanked Him for a very long time.

CHAPTER 37

SARAH
La Paz, Bolivia
Present day

Sarah closes her eyes, absorbing Jonas's words, hoping they will ignite something inside her, spark a memory. But it all remains as cold and white as if her brain remained buried beneath that avalanche.

When Jonas falls silent, she opens her eyes. Somewhere along the way, Chase has taken her hand. He holds it now, his grip like a lifeline. She's obliquely glad for it, even though her heart is numb to his touch. In that moment, she feels weightless, untethered, certain if Chase were to let go, she would float off into space, gravity having lost its power over her.

"She never meant to lie," Jonas is saying. "It began as a sin of omission. She simply left out the part about her skiing ahead and you chasing after her. Everyone assumed it was the other way around because you were the risk-taker. She never corrected the assumption. And then, when you came out of your coma, she thought you'd remember, set the record straight. Only you never did. She felt trapped. She was afraid of what your dad would do. She didn't know how to tell the truth."

"Until someone threatened to tell it for her." Sarah hardly recognizes her own voice, as tight as if someone is pinching her windpipe. Chase's fingers gently squeeze hers.

"Jenna knew she had to come clean, but not just because of the notes. She wanted to make it right, Sarah." He leans forward, so close she can see the tiny veins radiating from his irises. "It had been haunting her for so long. She had to tell you."

She stares at him, a bubbling cauldron churning in her heart. That Shane had been around that day came as a shock, but it faded beneath the impact of what mattered. For all these years, Jenna had allowed the blame of what happened to rest on Sarah's shoulders. And it was a lie.

Questions swirl through her mind until one jumps out: Why had she chased after Jenna, anyway? Why put her own life—and TJ's—at risk? She must have known they had no hope of outrunning an avalanche. Some instinct must have propelled her forward, a need to be with her sister even as disaster struck.

But what did that matter? Jenna had let everyone believe Sarah's recklessness had cost TJ his life. When, in fact, it had been her own.

Slipping her hand from Chase's, the old hurts gather, encasing in ice the rock-hard knot inside her chest. Then she stands, swaying slightly, ignoring both men when they ask her to sit. Leaving the room, she moves blindly down the hall, vaguely aware of passing Sofia before closing herself inside the guest room. There she sags against the door, its knob biting into her spine, and raises her eyes to the ceiling. *Dear Jesus, what do I do now?*

CHAPTER 38

"Don't think this is the end, Sarah." Chase clasps her cold hand between his warm ones as they stand together in Abby's kitchen the following morning. "Whatever else you think it may be, it's not that."

His touch might be the only thing keeping her upright. She's dizzy with exhaustion after a miserable, sleepless night. Abby is already in the car, loaded for the airport, with Jonas, who can barely meet Sarah's eye whenever they're in the same room. Chase has come back inside to help her carry the last of her things.

She shakes her head, dry-eyed, having cried all her tears into her pillow. "It is the end, Chase." Of so many things. She can't even begin to catalog them. But most of all, it's the end of whatever goodness she believed existed between her and her sister.

"Not everything is what it seems." His face gives evidence to a sleepless night of his own, his skin taut and colorless, like a canvas stretched too tightly over its frame. But his eyes ... those green eyes search hers, trying to tell her something she can't fathom. Probing in a way that would have melted her twenty-four hours earlier. Now her heart is too wrung out to care.

He moves a step closer. "What appears dead may only be sleeping. I know what Jenna did doesn't make sense to you now. But she was the real deal. You saw that yourself, didn't you? There's no way to counterfeit love like hers. Which tells me there is a reason Jenna kept silent. You just have to find it. I hope you'll have faith enough to keep looking for the truth."

She can only stare at him, wondering how he can be so blind. Finally, she tugs her hand free and hoists her leather tote to her shoulder, Luz's purple aguayo now packed away, along with everything else that might trigger unwanted memories of her sister. "We'd better go."

Chase grips her arm, his fingers surprisingly firm, turning her to face him. With a knuckle, he lifts her chin. "Sarah." The deep grooves etched alongside his mouth make her heart ache even more. How is that possible? She has to get out of here, or she'll never hold the pieces together.

"Please, Chase." Gently pulling her arm away, she shakes her head. "Please, just let me go."

"I don't know if I can," he says, his voice husky.

"I don't think either of us really has a choice." She tilts her head, heart squeezing as she holds his gaze. "Do you?"

"We always have a choice, Sarah." His eyes bore into hers, as if willing her to see things his way.

"Well, then, this is the choice I'm making." As the hurt slashes across his face, she almost wishes she could take back the words. Almost. Because in the end, maybe it's better this way, to leave him like this. Less complicated. And right now, with what she believed to be the truth lying in tatters at her feet, uncomplicated is what she wants most.

"Come on." Her fingers brush his cheek, a touch she wouldn't have dared before, then lets her hand fall to her side. "I can't afford to miss my plane."

⁓ ⌒ ⁓

Shane awaits her at Sea-Tac, pacing in baggage claim. He's wearing a sky-blue polo shirt and boot-cut jeans. His eyes light up when he sees her. "I've missed you!" She returns his hug, welcoming the feel of his arms around her, but when he tries to kiss her, she turns her face aside. "Sarah?"

"Sorry, it's—" She fiddles with the cotton sweater tied around her waist. "Can we just go home?" What is wrong with her? She's been waiting for this moment for the last twenty-four hours, longing to have her feet back on home ground, to settle into Shane's familiar presence again. So why does she want to rush through these minutes and get on with it?

"Sure, we can go home." He gives her a quizzical smile. "I'm just glad to have you back."

"I know, I'm just—sorry." She sighs. "Exhausted."

"Of course." He takes her carry-on and starts for the exit.

"Wait." She grabs his arm, remembering what she's wanted to ask him since first learning of it. "You were there that day. Why did you never tell me?"

"There?"

"The day we lost TJ. In the backcountry. Why did you never say?"

Bewilderment and something else—displeasure?—flash across his face before his features relax. "I never knew how to tell you." Sounding almost relieved, he speaks quickly. "I wanted to, but I was afraid. I didn't want to remind you of what you wanted to forget. And then, when things started happening between us, I didn't want you to think … well, that my interest had anything to do with Jenna. She and I had both moved on by then anyway, so it didn't even matter that I saw her." Perspiration dots his broad brow. "How did you know?"

"You were mentioned in something someone said about Jenna. I put it together."

His gaze probes hers. "Is there anything else?"

"What do you mean?"

"That we should talk about."

"No." It was the truth. For now.

He nods, apparently satisfied. They resume their way through the airport.

"Where's Dad?" She had thought—hoped—he would be here to pick her up. When they spoke before her flight out of La Paz, he said he would if he could.

"I convinced him to let me come. He wanted to, though." Taking her hand, he gives it a squeeze. He can't seem to stop looking at her. "You look wonderful."

She musters a small smile. It's a lie, but he means well. She's a wreck, not having brushed her teeth or hair since leaving Abby's house—was it only yesterday? Already all that happened there seems so distant. Like a movie she once watched, not something she actually lived through.

The only good thing about being so utterly exhausted is she finally slept—for almost the entirety of both long flights. Even now, the dregs of fatigue keep her brain shrouded in a welcome fog.

As she follows Shane to his Blazer, and later, as they're on I-90 heading east, she allows him to talk, his words like cotton wool she stuffs inside her mind to keep it from filling with anything else. During a lull, she dozes off, her head against the backrest, but rouses again as he asks her a question about Jonas. "Jonas?" She frowns. "Why would you ask about him?"

He shrugs. "No particular reason, I guess. Only that the last time we talked, you hadn't yet met him. I'm curious what he's like."

She looks down at her hands, fingers splayed across her denim-clad knees. Her eyes pinch closed as the memory of her last minutes with Jonas floods in.

They shared the same flight out of La Paz to Orlando, but with seats on opposite sides of the plane. Once onboard, she didn't see him until they deplaned in Orlando. After clearing Customs, they had separate flights to catch—he to L.A., she to Seattle. They faced each other beneath the digital kiosk displaying departure times.

Jonas lifted his carry-on to his good shoulder. "I guess this is goodbye."

"I guess it is." She offered a tepid, one-armed hug, intending to keep their parting as emotionless as possible. "Goodbye."

Jonas must have felt the same because he barely accepted her gesture before stepping back, away from her. Without another word, he turned and shuffled down the concourse that would take him to his flight. She stood there, her heavy tote making her neck ache, her eyes on the defeated slope of his broad shoulders. And something inside her cracked.

"Jonas!" She ran, ignoring the startled faces turning in her direction. She flung herself at him. Clung to him, mindful of his injured shoulder. Though from the way he hugged her back, he seemed to feel no pain. Physical pain, anyway. Tears slid down his face. She wished she had a spare Kleenex to wipe them away. "It's not your fault," she whispered.

"I'm sorry." The choked-out words fell to the ground between them.

"I know." Whatever else, she couldn't blame Jonas for what Jenna had done. He would have enough grief to work through without her adding to his pain.

She last saw Jonas standing beneath the Delta departure sign, lifting one big hand in a wave as she walked away.

"He's a good man," she says to Shane now. "Jenna was lucky to have him."

He nods once, his eyes never leaving the road, and asks no more questions for the duration of the drive. When they pull into Silverwood's long lane leading to the house, her stomach sinks at the sight of row after row of grapevines divested of their treasure. A shock, for not having been here to witness it.

Dad emerges from the house before Sarah even opens her door. As soon as both feet touch the ground, he wraps her in his arms. "Welcome home, Sarah." She feels his kiss against her hair. "You did good."

Her heart swells at his words even as she presses her cheek against his shirt, not wanting him to see her face. Afraid he'd read the secrets that might be written there.

CHAPTER 39

An icy north wind swirls Sarah's hair across her face as she hurries across the street while pressing the key fob to unlock the pickup truck. She hastens to the back end and deposits her box of art supplies with a *thunk*. Shivering in her light coat, she starts to slide behind the wheel, but a voice calls her name. She recognizes Angelica Garcia, the mom of one of her students, striding across the adjacent parking lot toward her.

Pinching back a sigh, Sarah pastes on a smile. "Angelica, hi. Conner did good work this afternoon; did he show you?" Today, their last day of class before the holiday break, she'd shown her students how to watercolor a wintry landscape, a good choice for easing back into teaching. Unlike other mediums, watercolors are so forgiving.

"It's lovely, yes. I am so thankful for what he accomplishes when he is with you. Few of his teachers are able to coax him to create beauty the way you can."

"Thank you." Conner has autism. Her painting class has become a kind of therapy for him, a means of self-expression when words fail. "I appreciate hearing that."

Angelica nods, her eyes darting, a hand fluttering at her throat. A slight woman with wispy, shoulder-length dark hair, which Sarah has never seen in anything but a ponytail. Sensing her nervousness, Sarah lays a hand on the woman's arm, bird-thin through the fabric of her coat. "Angelica, is everything okay?"

"With us, yes. I mean, we're fine. Conner's fine." She draws a breath. "I just wanted to say Conner's dad and I were so sorry we weren't able to speak to you at your sister's service."

Sarah stiffens, her hand dropping to her side. "I'm sorry, I didn't realize you were there or I would have said hello." Though the memorial service took place soon after her return from Bolivia, over a month ago, she continues to be confronted by this sort of conversation.

"No, no, you have nothing to be sorry for," Angelica insists. "There were so many people. We sat in the back. You couldn't possibly have known we were there. We had wanted to stay for the reception, to tell you and your dad how sorry we are for your loss, but our sitter canceled at the last minute so we had to bring Conner with us. He was getting very antsy, so—"

"Please." Sarah tugs at her scarf, snugging it around her neck. "I completely understand. It means so much you were there at all."

Angelica meets her gaze then, her eyes swimming with tears. "I lost my sister when she was very young. Drunk driver. So I wanted to say that, well, I—I know something of what you're going through."

Sarah presses out a thin smile and nods.

"We didn't know Jenna well," Angelica goes on, "but we were always so impressed with her. I remember reading her articles in the paper years ago. She seemed like a very good person. I'm sure there must be a certain amount of peace in knowing she died while doing something worthwhile in the world."

A thump from behind them makes them both turn. Conner is banging his head against the minivan window. "I'd better go before he melts down." Angelica clasps Sarah's fingers tightly in hers. "But please, accept our condolences. Tell your father, too, how very sorry we are for your loss."

Angelica skitters back across the parking lot while Sarah eases herself into the truck. Locking the doors automatically, she leans her head back, closes her eyes. She's been home for six weeks now. Shouldn't these encounters be getting easier?

She'd hoped today's art class would help. She loves working with the kids, loves learning what motivates them, using their idiosyncrasies to help them rather than hinder. And the creative process always feels like something akin to magic—*ex nihilo*, making something out of nothing.

But today the magic was missing.

Being back in front of her art class again makes her think of Mom. Mom started teaching special-needs kids at the community center nearly twenty years ago. After she died, the local high school art teacher had carried on until she married and left the area. After that, Sarah took up the mantle.

She considers what Mom would say in response to what she's learned about Jenna. About what Jenna did. *She would invite me to offer grace, to forgive, to assume the best. Or at least not the worst.*

Opening her eyes again, she shakes her head. If she only understood *why*. Why had her sister never owned up to her role in what happened? Did it have anything to do with the tension growing between them in the years before? But she knew Sarah blamed herself, so her silence feels like a betrayal. A far cry from *Lannings take care of their own*. Though Jonas said Jenna was afraid of Dad's reaction, Sarah doesn't buy it. Dad would have been upset, sure, even angry, but Jenna had to have known nothing would change how much he loved his number-one daughter.

A sigh escapes her lips. If not for the temperature falling along with the dusk, she would love to sit here for another hour or more, emptying her mind of everything. She certainly has no desire to return to Silverwood, where at every turn there are tangible reminders of Jenna. But she has to take a shift in the tasting room in half an hour, relieving Ana, whom Vina needs in the dining room.

Inserting the key into the ignition, she is about to start the engine when she catches the ripple of a woman's laughter. Turning toward the sound, she sees Shane emerge from the Wells Fargo Bank across the street. With him is Kellie, whom he hired while Sarah was in Bolivia. Kellie laughs at something Shane shows her on his phone.

Sarah watches the pair as they pause at the corner, waiting for the light to change. Shane, wearing only a windbreaker over his polo and jeans, appears oblivious to the cold whisking across the valley, giving his full attention to Kellie, who looks sleek and sophisticated in her stiletto boots and red, belted coat. She's talking, not paying attention to the traffic, and starts to step into the street as a car approaches. Shane takes her arm, pulling her gently back, then smiles down at her as they cross a moment later.

Longing swells like a balloon inside Sarah's chest, a wish to feel that happy and at ease with life again. So carefree. She frowns and twists the key in the ignition.

The rumble of the truck's engine must snag Shane's attention because he glances her way, catching her gaze. Swiftly, he bends his sandy head to Kellie's dark one, saying something that causes her to look at Sarah, too. Kellie smiles, giving a breezy wave before moving on down the street, while Shane heads in Sarah's direction.

She rolls down the window as he approaches, a smile lighting his ruddy face. "Hey, didn't expect to see you here."

She fakes an answering smile as she stills the engine. Then, as if remembering, he glances across the street at the community center as the street lamps flicker on. "That's right, Harrison mentioned you had art class today. How'd that go?"

"Fine." She shivers at the cold air cascading into the car. "Good to be back with the kids again."

He tips his head, alerted by something in her tone. "But?"

"But nothing." She thinks of the exchange with Angelica, knows she can't tell him about that. "It was good. I enjoyed it."

He strokes her arm propped on the open window, the crease marring his freckled forehead tells her he isn't buying it. "Sarah, are you doing okay?"

Suddenly she's tired of the pretense. "Not really." She massages her forehead, a dime-sized patch of tension burning at each temple, but manages a smile. "Been a long day."

He leans down, his forehead still puckered. "You sure that's it?" Though the gathering darkness shadows his face, his worry is unmistakable. "It's Jenna, isn't it?"

"Yes." Safe enough to admit that much.

"I'm sorry, Sarah." His voice deepens. "I wish there was something I could do."

"I know." She looks into his blue eyes, grateful he cares, wishing the ice encasing her heart since the discovery of Jenna's secret would thaw far enough for her to show her gratitude. "Thanks."

"Why don't we go somewhere and grab dinner tonight. Relax a bit. It's been a while."

For one fleeting moment, her spirits lift. It does sound nice, and he's right, it's been too long. But— "Wish I could, but I've got to get back. I'm scheduled for the tasting room."

"Bummer." He really does look disappointed.

She touches his hand as it rests on her arm. "Rain check?"

He shrugs, about to say something more when Sarah's cell phone buzzes on the passenger seat. She withdraws her arm and reads the new text. *Can we talk?*

In a bit, she types, then tosses the phone back on the seat, looking up to find Shane watching her curiously. "Jonas," she says, answering his unspoken question.

"Ah." His lip curls faintly. Ever since Jonas decided not to fly up for Jenna's memorial service, Shane has projected an unsettling hostility toward him. Sarah finds it odd, considering he's never met the man.

The silence stretches thin. "Guess I'd better get back."

"Guess you'd better." He reaches in, squeezes her hand. "We're still okay, aren't we?" He searches her eyes.

"Of course we are."

"It's just, you've not been yourself since you came home. And it seems like it's something more than just grief." She looks away, unwilling to follow that thread where it would lead. "It seems like you're upset with me, actually."

She meets his eyes. "I'm not upset with you. I'm just … upset."

"Because I didn't tell you I was there that day—on the slopes? That I saw Jenna?"

"No. It's not that."

"Then will you tell me what it is?"

"Someday, maybe." She reaches for the ignition. "I've really got to get back."

"Okay." A pinch of concern still creases his brow. "Catch you later."

She gives him a small wave and pulls forward. As she looks in the rearview, he's still there, shoulders hunched, hands shoved deep inside his pockets, watching her drive away.

CHAPTER 40

Sarah turns up the long, winding drive to the house, rolling through the acres of her father's vines. Stripped of grapes, their leaves turning brown, these same plants will look positively dead, limbs bare and shriveled within two months. Yet just a season past that, they'll be shooting out new growth, ready to begin producing luscious fruit once more. It always shocks her how life can spring again from something so seemingly wasted.

Inside the house, Cork greets her at the door, then pads behind her as she climbs the stairs to her room. A glance at her bedside clock tells her she has enough time to change out of her paint-speckled clothing before taking over for Ana.

In fresh jeans, she's about to tuck her phone into her rear pocket when she hesitates. Before leaving Bolivia, she promised Chase she'd keep in touch with Jonas once they were back home, but keeping her word is harder than she imagined. It's bad enough the way her conversations with Jonas take awful twists and turns around the subject of her sister's deception, ignoring it as if it doesn't exist. But even worse is her niggling sense of self-betrayal. It feels as if maintaining ties with Jonas erases what Jenna did. Makes it okay, somehow.

But it isn't okay. *She* isn't okay. Not even close.

She wishes she could ask Chase whether he would actually hold her to a promise made before either of them knew Jenna's secrets. She checked her phone frequently those first several days after returning home, part of her hoping to see Chase's name. But in all these weeks, he hasn't sent a word, and she can't bring herself to make the first move. Abby never mentions him in her periodic updates, believing, perhaps, that he is communicating with Sarah on his own. It shouldn't bother her that he isn't. In fact, given how unsettled he made her feel, she should find it a relief. But she doesn't.

Sighing, she dials Jonas's number. He answers on the first ring. "Sarah." He sounds relieved to hear her voice, the way he always does. "Thanks for calling."

Despite her resolve to stay at arm's length, the hard knot inside her chest softens. "How are you, Jonas?"

"Not great."

She sinks down onto the edge of the bed as Cork settles on the floor beside her feet. She absently runs his satiny ears through her fingers. "Tough day?" Every day is tough. She knows this, but she also knows he knows what she means.

"Yeah." His sigh travels the miles to reach her ear. "Today would have been one year."

A beat passes as she absorbs his meaning. Then it hits. "Today is your anniversary?"

"Would have been."

"I'm sorry. I didn't know."

"I know. Another regret."

"What do you mean?"

"Our families didn't know that we got married. And now I feel we short-changed everyone—ourselves, too—by not letting anyone into our happiness."

"Why didn't we know?" It's a question she's wanted to ask many times since discovering her sister's secret marriage.

"It all happened so fast, I guess. It seemed like such a fantastic secret. Though I wouldn't have minded telling when we got engaged, she didn't want to. She wanted to wait until we got married. And then there never seemed a good way to say it. At that point, it seemed like an insult or something."

"But she was coming home. Wouldn't she have said something then?"

"I think so." His voice drops. "I was sure I had won the lottery when I married her." He pauses. "You probably don't want to hear this, but she was honestly the most loving person I'd ever met. Beautiful, inside and out. She was like a light. People were drawn to her. They couldn't help themselves."

Her chest tightens as she thinks of Angelica's gushing praise. "I know. I still get stopped by people who have to sing about Jenna's goodness." She lets a beat of silence pass. "Even people who didn't know her well can't help but tell me how wonderful she was."

"Sarah." His voice sounds stretched. "I'm sorry. I shouldn't have brought this up. Just, please, don't do that."

"Do what?"

"You're angry."

"Don't you think I'm a wee bit entitled, after what Jenna put me through?" She closes her eyes, hating herself for taking out her hurt on Jonas. But who else can she say these things to? She has no one. "I mean, don't you feel a little entitled to be mad at God for what He's putting you though? For letting Jenna die."

"I'm not mad at God."

"Really? Even though you specifically asked God for His protection on the night Jenna died? I mean, don't you feel betrayed?" Sarah stands, causing Cork to look up at her nervously and thump his tail. "I would."

"Yeah." He sighs. "I guess I do."

"Well, that's how I feel, Jonas. What she did was a betrayal. For her to let me go on for years believing I was responsible for TJ's death. All I can think is she must have really hated me to do that."

His breath hitches. "She didn't hate you."

"Then I'm missing something, because I can't imagine what else would make a person do what she did to her own sister, can you?"

"She paid for it, though."

"She paid for it?" Though she knows her sharp words slice into Jonas's tender spirit, they surge from her mouth like water through a breached dam. "Is that what she wanted me to see? Is that why she insisted I come to Bolivia, so I could see how she paid?"

"I don't understand what you're saying."

"I know Jenna wanted me to find something down there. To learn something. Was this it? To see that she had sacrificed herself and suffered for what she'd done? Did she want me to know so I wouldn't hold it against her?" Every night Sarah is tormented by dreams, only they aren't about TJ anymore. Now Jenna's shape-shifting form flickers across her shuttered eyelids. As if she's led to admire a beautiful painting, absorbing every fine detail, only to realize it is a fake, a forgery. Peeling back the veneer to see what lies beneath and finding something as ugly as it is disturbing.

"She wasn't that kind of person. I wish you could believe that." His voice catches again. "She loved you."

Her heart twists, his pain-filled voice leaching some of the heat from her body. "I wish I could believe that," she says, softly. "But I can't. Not anymore." He says nothing, and she sighs. "I better go.

Sorry, Jonas. Sorry I made this into something about me when you're the one hurting today."

"I don't deny you're suffering, too."

"I know. But—well, I'm sorry about your anniversary." She swallows. "I'm sorry about everything."

⌒⌒⌒

Disconnecting the call, she notices the time. *Shoot.* Now she's late to start her shift. After jamming her feet into leather boots, she hastens for the stairs, Cork scrambling to keep up. A minute later, she bursts into the dining room. "Sorry, sorry."

But Ana isn't there, only Tomaso, who smiles from behind the counter. "Nothing to be sorry about. You're fine. Ana called me when she couldn't reach you. Figured you got held up somewhere."

"I got caught on a call with Jonas."

His smile fades. "And how is Jonas?"

"Not good." She avoids his gaze as she moves behind the counter to check the wine supply.

"For a particular reason or just in general?"

"There's a reason." She doesn't want to elaborate, afraid of where it might lead. She's told no one what she learned about Jenna. Not Shane. Not Dad. Not even Tomaso. She might have told Tomaso, except knowing how he helped Jenna keep tabs on her, she now questions his loyalty. These days, she's far too fragile to test it. She glances at Cork as he circles his pad in the corner before plopping down in a chocolate-brown heap. Her dog is in on her secret, but only because he cannot tell.

When Tomaso continues to gaze at her in his patient way, she knows she has to tell him something. She chooses a fragment of truth. "We were talking about how hard it is for him to trust God after He failed to answer his prayer for protection that night."

"That's very natural." He pauses. "But I sometimes wonder, in cases like these, if we are failing to see the whole picture."

"What do you mean?"

"I mean maybe He did answer Jonas's prayer. He survived, didn't he?"

Sarah stares at him, feeling he's somehow missed the point.

"Do you think I didn't have a similar crisis of faith after your accident? After losing TJ? Do you think I didn't pray for your and TJ's protection that day? That I didn't wonder why God didn't answer my prayer? But you see, that's just it. He did answer my prayer. He saved you. As He saved Jonas. And others on that bus."

"Are you saying it could have been worse?"

"Well, couldn't it?"

She shrugs.

A pause stretches out. Then, "I wish you would tell me what really troubles you, *mijita*."

She should have known he would see right through her. "It's nothing. I mean, just what you would expect."

"You've changed since your trip."

"Bolivia is a weird country." Her heart tightens as she finds herself hijacking Chase's words. "It changes people."

Tomaso regards her in silence for several long seconds. "It changed Jenna, too," he says at last, softly.

She turns away so he cannot see her eyes flood with tears. This is Jenna's ultimate coup. She died practically perfect. Or so everyone thinks.

Sarah can do nothing but flail helplessly against this ghost. This saint.

How can I possibly hope to triumph over that?

CHAPTER 41

Sarah turns off the hose and wipes a forearm against her perspiring forehead. Though fresh snow from last night's storm lies on the ground outside, inside the cellar, with its enormous fermentation tanks, it's plenty warm. She looks around, pleased with what she's accomplished. With Christmas now two weeks behind them, they've entered the brief lull of relative inactivity before preparations for the new season begin. She's become an expert at the art of distraction. The cleaning of counters, the filling of supplies, the making of small talk with customers. While her hands are busy, her mind has less time to churn. Today, she spent the better part of the afternoon spraying down floors and equipment, leaving her jeans wine-splattered, her flannel shirt sweaty.

On her way to the house to shower, she passes through the restaurant—closed for the day—pausing to make sure they have enough bottles on hand for when they reopen tomorrow. January might be a slower time for winemakers, but the chilly weather doesn't seem to deter buyers.

As she turns from the counter, the mural that covers the wall behind it catches her eye. This mural, depicting Jesus' first miracle, His turning of water into wine at the wedding feast in Cana, represents some of Mom's best work. It's an interior scene, the viewer looking in as if through an enormous window. Behind the milling guests, the Galilean landscape is depicted in warm hues in the background. The bride and bridegroom have their heads bent toward each other in the corner, smiling as if they are sharing a great secret. Jesus and his disciples occupy most of the foreground, with Mary, His mother, at His right side. Mom captured the moment at which the new wine Jesus created is poured out and sampled by the ruler of the feast, his face a study of wonder and delight.

Sarah walks closer to the painting. Why did Mom choose this particular story for this wall? Other than the obvious connection to wine, it's an unusual choice. Many wineries use murals to tell their own personal stories or to sell their brand. Some depict Washington scenery, others, the history of a vineyard's family. Though she's never asked, she's certain that would have been her father's choice. Yet somehow, Mom got her way on this.

Though she thinks Mom became a believer sometime after she married Dad, Sarah doesn't know much about her mother's faith beyond what Tomaso has shared with her. What significance did this scene have for Mom? Sarah has always understood this story to be more about Jesus than the wine. A sign of Who He is. She's always loved that not only did Jesus make wine, he made very *good* wine. Showcasing His power to change the ordinary into something extraordinary.

She turns and leaves the tasting room, thoughts of Mom tugging her toward the stables, now shrouded in darkness. Only a single light over the double doors illuminates the building. From inside comes a faint rustling. She imagines Sassy Britches and Old Romeo sharing an easy camaraderie in the warmth and comfort of their adjoining stalls. Sarah pauses, the chill evening air nipping at her nose. She's tempted to go inside. For days, she's kept herself too busy to visit Sassy, and she misses her. But with a sigh, she moves on toward the house. She and Shane have plans to go out tonight, and she's nowhere near ready.

CHAPTER 42

In her room, she pulls off her socks and tosses them in the hamper inside her closet. Jenna's blue knapsack still rests on the floor where she threw it the night she returned from Bolivia. Since then, she hasn't been able to bring herself to touch the bag.

The sight of it takes her back to the Magdalena house, packing up Jenna's belongings, Jonas telling her about Jenna's plans for murals on the walls of a community center, showing her the thumbnails Jenna created. She remembers how Jenna had insinuated Sarah's image into each of her sketches. Though she hasn't allowed herself to think about it for weeks, she wonders afresh why her sister did this. She feels as certain now as she did then her sister was trying to tell her something. But what?

Another memory surfaces: Jonas mentioning another sketchpad, one Jenna had with her when she died. Could it be among her things?

Slowly, as if approaching one of Jenna's tarantulas that could easily turn on her, Sarah gathers the knapsack and takes it to her bed. Unzipping it, she roots through loose papers until she finds it.

Jenna's sketchpad. As she pulls it free, something shiny falls to the bed. Jenna's bracelet. A jolt runs through Sarah, finding it here. She assumed she'd never lay eyes on it again after giving it to Sofia. Then she recalls seeing Sofia outside her room that night after Jonas told her everything. Although the child wouldn't have understood what had happened, she was bright enough to have gathered it had something to do with her beloved Jenna. She must have thought Sarah would not want to part with an item that had belonged to her sister and had slipped it inside Jenna's bag.

Sarah closes her fist briefly over the links, cool against her palm, before placing the bracelet back inside the knapsack.

Sitting crossed-legged on the bed, her back against the headboard, she flips through Jenna's thumbnails. They are similar to the ones Sarah has already seen, some of them the same scenes with variations in characters or background. She imagines each sketch fleshed out to real-life proportions. Once upon a time, she would have loved a meaty project like this.

The knowledge it will never happen saddens her.

But something sparks. An impulse she chooses not to question.

She springs to her feet, goes to the jewelry box atop her dresser and rummages in the recesses of the bottom drawer. When she comes up with a small object, she tucks it into her palm. Then she slips her bare feet into a pair of soft, warm boots and, sketchpad in hand, heads back outside.

The frosty evening air raises goosebumps on her arms as she hastens to the door of an outbuilding she hasn't been inside for years. The last time was several months after TJ's death, when she hid her art supplies with Mom's.

It remains a kind of time-capsule, enshrining Mom's memory. To her knowledge, neither Vina nor Ana enters it to clean. And though she's never seen him do it, she suspects Dad comes here on occasion.

Despite his determination to leave the past behind, even he needs to remember sometimes. Why else would he let it remain?

After years of non-use, the place smells closed up, faintly musty but not unpleasant. In the daytime, natural daylight streams through the enormous picture windows that make up the entire south wall. Since night fell hours ago, Sarah hits the switch, flooding the room with a soft, white light.

The room is pretty much how Mom left it before riding out on Sassy that last time. Brushes have been cleaned and put away, but Mom's work-in-progress, a Palouse landscape, still rests on its giant easel in the far corner. Sarah has seen it many times. Before her accident, she often crept in here to practice her own art, her mother's spirit as her muse.

What snags her attention now is the small, framed still life on the wall, the first oil on canvas she ever attempted, painted under her mother's tutelage. How vividly she recalls standing with Mom in this very room. *Remember, Sarah, shadow is as important as light. We need them both or we're left with something flat and two-dimensional. Dull. But when we bring them together, shadow and light add depth. Interest. Life!*

Sarah smiles as she walks a wide circle around the studio, looking, absorbing. Then she turns to the first of Jenna's sketches, one depicting the woman with Jesus at the well. Sarah closes her eyes, imagining how she might flesh it out. Figures outlined fluidly, sparely, in soft colors. Almost monochromatic, with light blending so gradually into shadow that the longer one looks, the more one sees.

Moving quickly now, Sarah goes to the great, white desk sprawled along one wall. From one of its drawers, she extracts a pad of paper and from memory begins to draw. Ideas flow, her hand scarcely quick enough to keep up.

Finishing one, she turns to another and begins again.

She has made her way through half a dozen of Jenna's thumbnails, transforming them into solid sketches, when she startles at the buzzing of her cell phone. Shane, texting: *I'm here. Where r u?*

Shocked, she realizes nearly an hour has passed. She types a quick message—*Coming*—then shoves the sketchpads into a drawer, turns off the lights, and hurries back to the house.

Shane is in the living room with her father when she enters through the front door. A hearth fire warms the room with heat and light. Dad leans against the mantel holding a glass of red wine.

Shane's eyebrows rise as she comes bursting in, and no wonder. She's still a mess from her work earlier that day. "I thought you were upstairs changing." He takes in her untidy ponytail and sloppy boots.

"Sorry, sorry. On my way."

"Shane expected you thirty minutes ago." Dad's forehead pinches into a frown. For him, promptness resides next to godliness. "What have you been doing?"

"Nothing, I just lost track of the clock."

Dad's glance travels to her right hand, which holds the key to Mom's studio. The one he doesn't know she has. She wraps her fingers around it, feels its teeth bite into her palm. "What time are we meeting Tyler and Mia?" she asks Shane.

He glances at his phone. "Um, twelve minutes ago?"

"I'll be quick." She's already heading for the stairs.

CHAPTER 43

"Thanks for coming in." Sarah smiles as she herds a straggling couple out the door. The rest of the tour group boarded their bus ten minutes earlier while this couple debated whether to add a case of cab sauv or cab franc to their purchase. They finally chose the franc and arranged for shipping to their home in Coeur d'Alene. Now Cork brings up the caboose as she leads them from the building, waving to the driver to let him know she appreciates his patience. She waits while the husband helps his wife up the bus steps and both disappear inside. The pneumatic doors hiss closed. Finally, they are off.

It is a crisp, wintry day, snow still dusting the ground where sunlight hasn't melted it away. Sarah lifts closed eyes to the sun, then turns to face the distant foothills. Out there somewhere she lost TJ—and much of herself as well. Sometimes, when she is alone, she can't help but dwell on Jonas's words as he told her the truth of that day. She replays them over and over, willing a snatch of memory to come to her.

But—nothing.

In the fields near the house, the vines are at their shriveled worst, a mass of dead-looking twigs. She feels an odd kind of kinship to the landscape, so scraped and raw. The way she feels inside.

A flash of crimson startles her as a male cardinal darts into the sky. A small plane cuts across its crystalline azure. When she recognizes the silhouette of a Kodiak, her stomach flip-flops, her mind spinning back to Chase.

In the months since she left Bolivia, after the shock of Jonas's revelation faded, she's regretted being so quick to push Chase away, wished she could now share with him her sense of isolation and loss. From their first connection over Sofia, she saw a depth in him that went beyond physical attraction. At times, she longs for his company in a way that rumples her spirit and leaves her irritated. Why can't she share that kind of connection with Shane?

She thinks back to last night's dinner out, their double date with Tyler and Mia. Six-foot-four Tyler, Shane's friend from college, married to diminutive Mia, who barely tops five feet. She doesn't know them well, but they both work in the wine business, so they share a lot of common ground. Conversation, for most of the meal, centered around the latest blends hitting the market, but after their dinner plates were cleared, as they waited for their dessert to arrive, Mia asked Sarah about her time in Bolivia.

She didn't want to talk about Bolivia, so she tried to answer briefly and change the subject. But Mia persisted. "I hear it's beautiful but very poor. Where did Jenna live, exactly?"

"In a remote village a couple of hours from Santa Cruz." In the end, she told them about Jenna and Jonas's work in Magdalena, as well as what Chase and Rachael do for the orphans at Los Zapatitos. She talked about Abby, Sixto, and Matilde, even about her encounter with Sixto's friends as she walked back to Magdalena. Somewhere along the way, she became aware of Shane's arm slipping from around her shoulders, and she registered his expression—bemused bordering on hurt, maybe even annoyed. No doubt wondering why, despite his attempts to get her to talk, he'd never heard any of this until now. At the same time, she felt pleased to be able to tell the story with some emotional neutrality, making her believe maybe she was starting to put some of what had happened behind her.

When she finished, Mia's glance traveled between her and Shane, probably trying to puzzle out why Shane seemed to have withdrawn. "Well, I'm awfully glad you made it home safely after all that. Right, Shane?"

"For sure." He pulled his wallet out in preparation for paying the bill. "I also think we need to get together with you and Ty more often. This is the most I've heard her talk since she's been home." He gave a short laugh that ended in a frown.

Now, wrapping her arms around her middle, Sarah watches the Kodiak until it disappears against the white horizon. It strikes her that this is what bothers her: she can't bring herself to tell Shane everything. A part of her knows she'll feel so much better if she shares her burden. At times, she feels herself approaching the edge, the very jumping off place, about to tell him.

And then she pulls back.

Why? She doesn't understand her own heart.

In time, she promises herself. *In time, I'll tell him everything.*

Sighing, she shuts the door on memories. "Come on, Cork, let's get back inside where it's warm."

While Cork circles onto his pillow in the corner and settles, she picks up her phone from the counter, checking for messages, hoping for one from Abby. She's not disappointed. Though she still speaks weekly with Jonas, it's Abby who keeps her tuned into all that is going on with La Fuente. News that, despite everything, she still craves.

She leans against the counter to read Abby's most recent update, telling of her latest trip to Magdalena to care for the community's medical needs. Matilde's baby boy has put on five pounds since her last visit, and the women's co-op is thriving, thanks largely to Matilde's work. "I can't understate the marvel of this," Abby has written. "It is perhaps Jenna's most enduring legacy. She helped these women to see God calling them away from smallness, from invisibility, toward a bigger sense of who they really are. And from there, to speak their truth into the world."

Sarah skims past this part—praise for Jenna still pricks like a thorn—but smiles when she reaches the P.S.—a scanned watercolor of Lake Titicaca from Sofia.

Pocketing her phone, Sarah surveys the mess of crumbs and wine spatters left by the tour group and sets to work. She places used wine glasses in the dishwasher, refills the cracker bowls, and is in the process of restocking wine beneath the counter when Shane comes in carrying a tumbler of rosé. He's been working next door all afternoon, preparing to take the wine off cold stabilization prior to bottling.

"Hey." His eyes capture hers. In them she reads uncertainty, as if he's not sure of his welcome.

"Hey, yourself." She smiles—not exactly happy to see him, because happy doesn't seem to be in her emotional wardrobe these days—but relieved, perhaps, that he's sought her out again so soon after last night. She knows her company wasn't all it might have been and is half-glad for the chance to make it up. She nods at the beaker in his hand. "Watcha got there?"

"Something for you to try." His expression lightens as he moves behind the counter, evidently sensing the peace offering. He reaches for a pair of goblets. "I'd like to know what you think." He empties the tumbler into both glasses and hands her one.

She brings the sample to her nose and sniffs. The rosé is new for Silverwood, something Shane talked Dad into trying. This one has an ether of rose with low notes of vanilla and strawberries. "I like the bouquet." She sips, the flavor hitting her palate with an intensity of fruit. "Nice texture." Another sip. "Pretty in the mouth, too."

"I thought so." Shane swills the amber-pink liquid in his glass. "I don't think it wants any more barrel aging, do you?"

"No, I really don't think it does." She sips again, smiling at him over the rim, knowing he doesn't really need her palate to tell him when a wine is ready for bottling. That is his forte, not hers. "I'd say it's perfect."

"So would I." He swirls the liquid again, looking down at it. "Harrison and I were discussing a name for it."

"Oh?" She tenses, the vibe she was enjoying vanishing as she senses where this is going.

"We thought we would name it after Jenna."

A heartbeat. "Whose idea was that, yours or Dad's?"

"Does it matter?"

She shrugs. "I guess not. But why are you telling me? Surely you're not asking my opinion." She pours the rest of the wine into the dump bucket.

"We're trying to involve you, Sarah—" His voice hardens as his eyes flick to the dump bucket, color rising from his neck and creeping into his cheeks. "But you're not making it easy. We have plans for this place. Dreams. Decisions to make. We want you to be a part of that. But ever since you came back from Bolivia, it's like you're on lockdown or something." He paces two steps away, then pivots, a muscle jumping in his jaw. She freezes in the glare of his stare.

He must see the effect he's having because he closes his eyes briefly and blows out a measured breath. "Sometimes I think I'm getting through," he continues in a milder tone, "but then I don't know. Because I get—" With a hand, he fans the space dividing them. "This."

She can't meet his eyes, shaken by his words, though unable to deny what he says. Despite her desire to connect with him, she knows she's failing. She still holds herself apart from everyone. She feels she has to in order to hang onto what shreds of her identity she can still claim.

He chances a step toward her. When she doesn't back away, he touches her arm, approaching her as a hunter might approach a deer he doesn't want to startle. "Tell you the truth, I'd like to involve you in more of my life, too. If you'll let me." His tone softens even more. "Will you, Sarah? I'd like to think my future includes you. Before you left for Bolivia, I thought we were on the same page." Again that tightening in his jaw. "But you've changed since you've been home. You don't seem to want me around much, and you're sure not telling me whatever's really going on with you. So if you want to call it off—whatever we might have had, you and me—I wish you'd tell me now. Put me out of my misery."

She stiffens. He's pushing too hard, too fast—surely he knows that?—but when she looks into his eyes, she sees something that makes her pause. Hurt? No, something harder. Anger, maybe. Or frustration. Because she's not letting him in? What else would prompt that look?

If I go on keeping him at arm's length, one of these days he's going to give up. Am I willing to let that happen? Only a few months ago, she saw Shane as an answer to some kind of unvoiced prayer. A man who sought her out. Someone her father respected and treated as his own. Who reminded her what it felt like to belong to someone.

But that was before Chase. The thought arrives unbidden. She pushes it impatiently aside. Whatever may or may not have been happening between her and Chase is behind her. Shane is the man who stands before her now. And no man will keep pursuing a woman who's turned herself into an icicle. Afraid to trust. Afraid to let anyone near.

Her heart pulses in her throat. Yes. It is time to put Jenna's betrayal behind her. Dwelling on it, letting it poison her life, her relationships, will change nothing. "The future sounds awfully big to me, Shane." She manages a smile, though she feels it tremble. "But maybe we can start with tonight? Just the two of us this time? And I'll try to remember I have to contribute to make this work. I can't let you do all the heavy lifting. Can we start there?"

Though it seems like a small offer, apparently it's enough. Relief floods Shane's ruddy features, and he pulls her close as Cork scampers for the door. She and Shane pull apart as a woman in her late twenties steps across the threshold.

Moving farther from Shane, Sarah gathers a smile. "Welcome to Silverwood. Here for a tasting?"

"No, I'm here to see you, actually. You are Sarah, right? Sarah Lanning?"

She studies the woman, pretty, with soft brown hair and clear, smooth skin. And then it clicks. "Samantha?"

CHAPTER 44

"You remember." Samantha smiles.

"Of course I do." Sarah comes around the counter to give her a hug. "It's so good to see you again." Jenna's favorite college roommate has filled out some since the last time Sarah saw her, but the smile lines around her mouth and eyes say she's happy. Content.

"I only wish I'd come under happier circumstances." Samantha steps back, her brown eyes soft. "I can't tell you how sorry I was to hear about Jenna."

"Thank you." Then, aware of Shane behind her, she turns to introduce him. "Samantha, this is Shane."

Her eyes widen. "Shane?"

"Hello, Sam." Color climbs his neck.

"Wow, this is a surprise. I—I have to say, I never expected to find you here."

"Life is full of surprises, isn't it?"

Sarah darts him a look, wondering at the defensive edge that has entered his tone, but she doesn't have time to wonder long.

"Listen, I'd like to stay and chat, but I've got to get back to the vats. Nice seeing you again, Sam." He gives Sarah's hand a quick squeeze. "I'll see *you* tonight." He's out the door as soon as he finishes his sentence.

Sarah faces Sam again, left puzzled and a little off-center by Shane's abrupt departure. "I'm sorry he couldn't stay longer, but he's very busy."

"He works here now?"

"He's our winemaker."

"It's just so … wow. I met him when he hooked up with Jenna our last year at college, but after they broke up, I hardly saw him again."

Sarah's brows pull together. "I forgot you knew him back then." Something niggles at her, a faint bell at the back of her brain.

"I wouldn't say I knew him, but I certainly remember him. He and Jenna didn't last long, but he fell for her *hard*. Always hanging around, calling and texting. Honestly, I think it made her a little claustrophobic. He was crushed when she dumped him, so I'd never have thought he'd want to hang out here of all places."

"She'd been living in Bolivia four years by the time Shane started working for Dad. It wasn't like he needed to fear they'd cross paths."

"And once she left, she never came back?"

"Just that one summer, four years ago. Two years before Shane starting working here."

"That's right. I lost touch with her after that. Married an Army guy and lived overseas, mostly. I just got back in the States last week. We've been stationed in Germany, but after I heard about Jenna, I knew one of the first things I had to do when we returned was to come see you. To tell you in person how sorry I am. I was so shocked when I heard the news. Jenna's not one of those people you expect to die young, you know? She had so much to offer."

Sarah moves behind the counter. "Sure you wouldn't like some wine? I'll join you." Having a glass in her hands would give her an object to focus on.

"That sounds nice, thank you."

Sarah pulls out a bottle of this year's reserve red blend and pours them each a glass. As Samantha takes her first sip, her glance slides to the mural behind the counter. "Your mother painted that, didn't she?"

"Good memory."

"The first time I paid attention to it was the last time I was in here. I remember because I'd just turned twenty-one, and your dad finally let me sit at the tasting counter." She smiles at the memory, then her eyes swivel to Sarah's. "You used to paint."

"Used to, yes."

"Jenna said you had a talent for it."

Sarah cradles her glass in her hand as she allows Samantha's casual observation to wash over her. Though many people have said the same thing in recent months, somehow it's different coming from Samantha. Perhaps because it's spoken by someone who has known them both.

"Jenna left sketches for me," Sarah says, surprising herself. Besides Jonas, no one knows of the thumbnails. "She had dreams of opening a kind of community center in a village near where she worked in Bolivia. She wanted me to paint murals on the walls so even those who couldn't yet read could be encouraged by the stories of the paintings."

"What a beautiful idea. Sounds like something Jenna would dream up." She pauses. "Do you remember how she loved poetry? She had one poem pinned to the board above her desk. I still remember part of it. 'But one life you are given—just one precious, golden gift. How then will you give it before it is gone?' That seemed to be a driving force for her, even back then."

"Sometimes I envied Jenna for that," Sarah admits. "She always seemed to know what she wanted."

Samantha nods. "That's what I always thought, too. Most of the rest of us floundered around, kind of groping in the dark, hoping we'd end up doing what it was we were supposed to do." She pauses. "Which is why we couldn't understand it when she abandoned college with only a semester left. She was going to become a journalist and change the world. But then she went to Bolivia, not as a journalist but as a worker. An activist. Though I guess she did manage to change the world. Her world, at least. Maybe that's what really matters. When I heard Jenna had died, I found some comfort in believing at least she had found her calling and had died doing what she loved best: giving her one, precious golden gift."

CHAPTER 45

Soon after Samantha leaves, Ana comes in to relieve Sarah at the counter, allowing Sarah to return to her office to catch up on invoicing. Her mind, however, keeps wandering to her conversation with Sam, replaying parts of it. Sarah is certain Jenna would have considered Sam her greatest friend from home. Not only had they shared a dorm room for a couple of years, they'd shared their lives. For one summer, especially, Samantha had practically lived at the vineyard. And yet Jenna hadn't kept in touch with even her after that last visit home. Sarah supposes she should find some comfort in this, that she wasn't the only one Jenna cut off. But for some reason, it only adds to the mystery. Would she ever understand who Jenna really was?

The landline at her elbow rings. "Silverwood Cellars, this is Sarah."

"Sarah, Tim Roberts, calling for Shane."

"Sorry, he's not here right now." An hour earlier, she'd seen him take off in his truck. "May I take a message?"

"Sure. I did leave a message on his cell but thought I'd try to reach him at the office since I know he's in a bit of a hurry. Tell him the plans I've been working on are ready. He can stop by anytime to go over them."

"Plans?" she repeats, wondering why this guy's name rings a bell.

"For your new addition."

Then it clicks. Tim Roberts, junior partner of the new architectural firm in town. She met him briefly at a wine pairing dinner at Silverwood last year. In the back of her mind an unpleasant thought bumps around.

"Tell him I'm pleased with how these turned out," Tim continues. "Think he's gonna be real happy with them."

"Sure thing, I'll tell him—no, wait." She thinks quickly. "I'll be in town in about an hour. Why don't I stop by and pick them up myself."

Two hours later, Sarah stands in Dad's office, lamplight spilling onto the blueprints scrolled out across his massive desk. "So you knew about these?" she asks.

"Of course I did." Harrison Lanning runs a hand over the plans. In the last few weeks, he's started looking more like himself again, putting on the weight he lost in the months following Jenna's death. His thick, graying hair has been neatly trimmed, and his gaze holds some of its old resoluteness. "Not in all this detail, but I told Shane to go ahead, wouldn't hurt to at least get some ideas flowing."

"Ideas for expansion."

"That's right. We've been talking about that for a while."

"And how are you going to pay for it?" The plans Tim Roberts has drawn up are not for a simple expansion but a sizable one, and to more than the main building. When she asked Tim for an estimate of how much it would cost, the amount topped seven figures.

"Why are you asking me?" Her dad's brow furrows. "Don't you know?"

A tap sounds on the door. Shane pokes his head in. "Harrison, I'm just going to—" He breaks off when he sees Sarah then does a double-take when he realizes the focus of their attention. He frowns. "Where'd you get those?"

"From Tim Roberts. He called looking for you." The peace she felt only hours ago at their newfound understanding evaporates as she faces him. "But I'm guessing you know that by now. Thought I'd save you a trip." She taps the prints with her finger. "How exactly did you expect us to pay for this, Shane?" She keeps track of the winery's receipts, knows exactly what kind of a year they've had. A good one, but not that good. Not good enough to afford all this without going into debt. And after the hard time Dad had getting a bank loan twenty years ago, that's something he's sworn to never do again.

Though Shane says nothing, his earlier words come flooding back. *We have decisions to make.* "Is this what you meant by involving me? You're hoping I'll use Jenna's inheritance money to expand this place, aren't you?"

"I thought it might be worth discussing."

She looks to her father. "Dad?"

"Assumed you knew." He scratches his chin.

"No." She narrows her eyes at Shane as a new suspicion takes root. "Is this why you've been so interested in me? Why we've been an *us*? So you could get at the money?"

"Good grief, Sarah—" Dad starts, but Shane interrupts.

"You know it's not like that."

"*How* do I know?" She crosses her arms, suddenly feeling exposed as all the doubts she's tried to suppress come bubbling up again.

"Sarah." Shane steps forward, moving as if to take her hand, but she pulls away from the gesture. "I've tried to show you I care." He shrugs. "What more can I do to prove it?"

Words collide with questions and pile up on her tongue, but she can't put voice to any of them. When she doesn't respond immediately, Harrison takes off his half-glasses and drops them on top of the plans, rubbing the bridge of his nose the way he does when he's tamping down impatience. "So what's the problem, Sarah?"

She wheels toward him. "Don't you think I should have been asked about this?" She jabs a finger at the blueprints still sprawled across his desk.

"Yes, you probably should have been, but you would have been brought in on the discussion in due course. And we didn't really think there'd be an issue. Is there?"

At this, Shane's shoulders loosen and the faintest hint of a smile touches his lips, though he tries to stop it. Heat rises up inside her. "I have no idea if this is how I want to spend Jenna's money. I need time to think about it."

"How much time?" From Shane.

She plants her hands on her hips. "As much as it takes."

"Sarah." Her father touches her shoulder. "Shane's given this a lot of thought. It's not like he's charged into something rashly."

She frowns, shrugging away from his touch. "Why do you do that?"

"Do what?"

"Take his side. Why not take *mine*?"

"Aren't we all on the same side here?"

She ignores his question. "First Jenna. Now Shane."

"Why on earth are you dragging your sister into this?"

"Because she's still here! In the thick of things. Right here, right now. She's dead, and there's still barely enough room for me."

Her father's mouth firms. She knows she's crossed a line. "She was my daughter, Sarah."

"And what about me, Dad? What am I? I don't think—" Hurt closes her throat. Sparing him an answer, she lurches for the door, avoiding Shane's hand when he tries to stop her.

CHAPTER 46

She runs upstairs, catching the banister when her left leg buckles beneath her. Ahead, the door to Jenna's room stands closed, as usual. From downstairs, Shane calls her name as his footfall nears. Sarah surges up the remaining steps, hesitates, then darts inside Jenna's dim room, quietly closing the door behind her. Leaning her forehead against the door's cool wood paneling, she hears Shane pass down the hall. At her bedroom door, he knocks and speaks her name. In the pause that follows, the hinges creak as he opens the door. A moment later, he calls to her father as he passes back down the hallway. "Not up here."

"Well, when she resurfaces, we'll talk," Dad replies, his voice projecting up from downstairs. "In the meantime, try not to worry about ..."

As their voices fade, the adrenaline that fueled her flight drains away. Turning around, she faces the room and feels a sick jolt of surprise.

Jenna's belongings are gone. Every single one of them. Down to the last book. All that remain are the room's bare bones: the furniture, some lamps, the curtains, two of their mother's framed oils on the wall. Sarah reaches for the nearest lamp and flicks it on. The light reveals that even the bedspread has been changed from Nana's quilt to a fluffy, cream duvet. Very new. Very neutral.

On the desk is splayed an array of paint chips, all of them in muted grays and blues. She crosses to the walk-in closet and throws wide the door. Every item of Jenna's clothing has been removed from the rods and shelves. In their place, boxes are piled high to the ceiling, each neatly labeled in Ana's bubble script.

She backs up to the bed and sits heavily, feeling sucker-punched. Although it is Ana's handiwork, Dad is surely behind this. He did the same thing after Mom died. So quick to move on, to put the past behind, removing all trace of her color and life.

Suddenly drained, Sarah creeps beneath the pristine duvet, curls onto her side and pulls the covers to her chin. She doesn't want to feel the pain anymore. She doesn't want to think.

Closing her eyes, she consciously clears her mind, imagining an expanse of white. A fresh canvas, unspoiled.

Incredibly, she sleeps.

And she dreams. She dreams of Jenna, a mosaic of images: Crouched on a stool, book in hand, encircled by Magdalenan women, teaching them to read. Snuggling with Sofia, Jake stretched across their laps. Arguing with Sixto, fire flashing in her eyes. Haggling with Luz at market before bursting into a cascade of shared laughter. Jenna, a kaleidoscope of vivid hues, at ease in Chase's Technicolor world.

And then the lens changes. She sees herself running with Jenna through lavender fields.

"Mama, Sarah got hurt."

"And you brought her to me. Good big sister, looking out for baby girl."

"That's my girl." Dad crouching beside them both but touching Jenna's auburn tresses. *"Looking out for your sister. Blood is blood, right?"* Dad pulling Jenna to him, embracing her. *"My girls should know they're Lannings to the core."*

When Sarah opens her eyes, the light has become burnished, its violet shadows long. She must have slept clear through the night, missing dinner. Blinking a few times, she tries to clear her vision. Her eyes feel scorched, and she has a sudden, sharp wish for a steaming cup of Abby's maté de coca.

Sitting up, she runs her fingers through her tangled hair, remembering shards of her dreams. *She was the real deal,* Chase said once. *You can't counterfeit that.*

And yet, to do what she did. To construct such a deception, then to keep quiet about it for so many years. *It's like there were two of you, Jenna: one for me, one for everybody else. How can I possibly reconcile the two?*

Her heart stutters with a rush of grief that, suddenly, is pure and uncomplicated. Maybe here, in Jenna's childhood room, she feels close to her sister, despite its being stripped of everything personal. Her sister breathed and slept and dreamed inside these four walls. Her essence remains, no matter how thoroughly Ana has purged.

I miss you. I've always missed you, even when I tried not to care. Did you miss me too?

Sarah left the closet doors wide open before climbing into bed. Her gaze now falls on the corner of a picture frame jutting from a box. Getting up, she lifts out the photo. A family picture, one of the last that included Mom. Jenna was seventeen, Sarah was fifteen, with braces on her teeth. Mom had her arm tight around Sarah, both smiling into the camera. Beside them, Jenna and Dad were smiling too, but at each other, their faces turned nearly to profile as they shared some private joke.

It had always been like that. Dad and Jenna. Mom and Sarah. When Mom died, she had no one to cherish her the way Dad cherished Jenna. *And now just the two of us remain.* What will that mean for them? Can they find a way to become each other's favorites?

Replacing the photo, she notices Jenna's old mahogany treasure box. As she picks it up, she hears the familiar rattle of a loose object inside.

Curiosity springs to life. She *will* know what is inside. Now there is no one to stop her. She looks around for something to pry loose the lid, no longer caring if she damages the lock or the box because no one need ever know. She finds an old, tin ruler stashed with Jenna's desk supplies. Inserting it beneath the lid, she maneuvers the box to force it open.

That's when she notices the strange shape of the keyhole. Like a figure eight. She's seen that shape somewhere recently. Where?

Jenna's bracelet. *The key charm.* Sarah's body flushes hot, then cold as the answer comes to her. It isn't just a charm. It is an actual key. A key to this box.

Taking the box with her, Sarah creeps to the door and listens for noises beyond. All is silent, save for the occasional clank and rattle from Vina working in the kitchen below. Quickly, Sarah moves from Jenna's room into her own and shuts herself in. She sees Cork's vacant cushion on the floor and wonders where he spent the night. She goes to her closet. There, she drops to her knees and pulls Jenna's knapsack toward her, digging until her fingers close over the links of Jenna's charm bracelet.

Her hands shake as she grasps the key and inserts it into the lock. Holding her breath, she turns her wrist. With no effort at all, the lock opens with a tiny snap.

She lifts the lid. On top is what appears to be a handwritten letter on lined paper, the perforated kind torn from a spiral notebook. She unfolds it, checks the signature. Mike. A love letter, apparently, from the boyfriend Dad made Jenna break up with. She reads the first lines … *Whoa.* Feeling like a voyeur, she sets it aside.

Beneath this letter are papers. Documents, by the look of them, folded and placed one on top of another. A disappointed sigh slides through her lips. All that mystery for a bunch of paper?

Then the box shifts on her lap and she hears it again, the sound of a hard object sliding around inside. Removing the papers, she finds a snapshot nestled on the bottom. She recognizes this photo. She was the one who snapped it, years ago, with Mom's old camera. Jenna and Mike grinning at each other, he as drop-dead gorgeous as she remembers. Jenna had been nuts about him, maybe even in love. As Sarah lifts the snapshot to have a closer look, she sees what caused the rattling noise.

A locket. A gold, heart-shaped locket.

She picks it up, wonderingly, certain she's never seen it before. Where did Jenna get this, and why has she kept it hidden away? A gift from Mike, maybe?

Using a fingernail to undo the tiny clasp, she finds inside a minuscule photograph. But the faces that smile out at her do not belong to Jenna and her long-ago beau. The face on the right is her mother's, the one on the left, a man's. A handsome man, but not her father. Though his features are familiar. Yet the image is so tiny, and the photo is aged. She can't identify him.

She turns the pendant over in her hand. On the back, an etched inscription.

To M., love always. 1988

1988. The year her parents were married. So who is this man? And why did he give a locket to her mother when she was practically married to someone else?

Her curiosity piqued, she turns to the papers in Jenna's box. Jenna's birth certificate and their parents' marriage certificate. Why would Jenna have kept these in a locked box?

She remembers about a year after Mom died, toward the end of Jenna's senior year, Jenna asking if Sarah had gotten around to sorting through the rest of Mom's things, the few boxes Dad kept of her most personal belongings. He had left them for her daughters to take care of. Of course Sarah hadn't done any such thing. That was the kind of action for practical, responsible Jenna, not her. Though the subject never came up again, the job got done, so Sarah knew Jenna had organized everything, keeping and tossing things as she saw fit.

Soon after that, now that she thinks about it, Jenna started keeping her distance. She'd never made the connection before. Was there a reason for one to follow the other?

Toward the bottom of the pile of papers is an official looking letter in a long envelope, addressed to Jenna and bearing an ominous red stamp: CONFIDENTIAL.

The return address belongs to a medical lab in Seattle. Inside the envelope are two sheets of paper. The first is a letter explaining the enclosed document. The other looks like some kind of lab report. Puzzled, she skims the letter, and her heartbeat thuds with shock.

Based on the DNA samples provided, Harrison Lanning is not the biological father of Jenna Lanning.

CHAPTER 47

*J*enna was not a Lanning.

The astounding truth of it reverberates through Sarah's body. She and Jenna were half-sisters. They shared a mother, but not a father.

But if not Dad, then who?

Sarah picks up the locket, intuition telling her it provides a clue. *To M., love always ...*

Squinting, she studies the photo.

And then she knows.

It seems so obvious now. Jenna had his long, straight nose, the same full mouth and strong teeth.

How could this be?

Before she can untangle it, a new understanding sweeps over her, like a wave washing over sand, erasing every other thought: Jenna was not a *Lanning*. What must that knowledge have done to her? Jenna's very identity was wrapped up in her role as Daddy's girl. Daddy's number-one daughter.

Sarah tries to put herself in her sister's shoes. So much of Jenna's worth had been derived from her family identity. But given how much her father adored her, could Jenna have ever really doubted his love? Surely she knew he would cherish her for who she was, no matter what.

Wouldn't she?

Blood is blood. A lifetime of hearing that might have made her believe otherwise.

Sarah closes her eyes. Jenna was born only seven-and-a-half months after their parents' wedding. Mom always told of conceiving Jenna on their wedding night, but of course, once she and Jenna were old enough to know better, they'd suspected a shotgun wedding. But Sarah certainly never thought to question paternity. She doubted Jenna did, either. Why would she?

Sarah flips through the papers to look again at the birth certificate. Though Harrison Lanning is listed as the father, the evidence of the locket and the lab report weigh heavily against that statement. Once Jenna started putting these puzzle pieces together, the truth must have terrified her. Was that why she had done the DNA test? Hoping to prove herself wrong? To prove the Lanning birthright did, after all, belong to her?

Only it didn't. Of the two of them, Sarah alone has Lanning blood running through her veins.

Could this, then, explain why Jenna had distanced herself from Sarah? Could it be the real reason she had left home? Each new question swirls around inside Sarah's head like an explosion of shrapnel, while she holds the evidence in her hands. The locket. The birth certificate. The DNA report. But when the bits of shrapnel settle, she believes she holds the answer to the question that has plagued her from the day Jonas revealed the cause of her accident. Of TJ's death.

Jenna was afraid.

That was why she lied, and continued to lie. Knowing she had no legitimate claim as Dad's daughter, she must have feared any lapse on her part might sever her hold on him. Or his tenuous love for her.

Sarah lifts her face to the window. It's a beautiful morning, the sun strong and clear, the lightest of breezes swaying the uppermost limbs of the trees. Exactly the kind of morning that, once upon a time, would have inspired her and Mom to throw saddles on the horses and go exploring.

The memory stirs an awakening. Without pausing to think further, she pulls on boots, jeans, a thick sweater. Tugging her hair into a ponytail, she heads for the stairs.

Cork meets her at the front door. Together they emerge into the cold, where frosted air bites at her cheeks. Snow dots the ground, remnants of the storm that passed through two days ago. She makes her way across the courtyard to the stables.

Stepping though the wide double doors, it's immediately warmer. Sarah is warmed further when Sassy greets her with a soft nicker of recognition. She lifts a saddle blanket from its storage place on the wall, her movements swift and sure. "Okay, girl." She enters Sassy's stall. "Here I am."

Five minutes later, they are on their way, Cork trotting joyfully beside the horse. Her initial fear at finding herself high atop Sassy fades quickly as everything she knew about riding before the accident comes flooding back. Plus, Sassy has mellowed with age. When Sarah was young, she could never have handled her. Now it's like they were destined to share this moment.

Leaving the vineyard property behind, Sarah urges Sassy into a canter. The wind tears at her hair and scrubs her cheeks. She throws back her head and laughs aloud, feeling she has rediscovered the girl she once was, a girl eager to meet any new challenge.

A girl not unlike Jenna.

Turning toward home again, she rides into the sun until she comes to the place where Jenna's empty urn is buried alongside their mother's. In the summer months, a mature maple casts its shade over the spot. Today, the tree's branches are bare. She dismounts and approaches the site.

The sun brushes the pair of gravestones in numinous light. Mom's marker is starting to show signs of age, with lichen growing around the edges. *Monica Ridgely Lanning, beloved wife and mother.* And the epitaph Dad chose: *The air of heaven is that which blows between a horse's ears.*

Jenna's marker, also chosen by Dad, is rustic, a chunk of rough-hewn boulder, in keeping with Jenna's life in her last years. *Jenna Lanning Jackson, beloved wife, daughter, sister, friend.* And the line of poetry Samantha had quoted, the one Jenna had posted in her college dorm room. *But one life you are given—just one precious, golden gift. How then will you give it before it is gone?*

Sarah sinks to her knees over Jenna's grave, cold moisture seeping through her jeans, numbing her knees. Touching her fingers to the marker, she traces her sister's name, remembering its meaning. Fair spirit. She presses her palms over the letters until she feels each groove etched into her skin.

And in that moment, she thinks she understands. Why Jenna brought her to Bolivia. Why she bestowed her inheritance on her. And how she wished her to spend it.

CHAPTER 48

JENNA
Age 28
Magdalena, Bolivia

The other women filed from the porch until only Matilde and I remained. Minutes before, we'd finished our weekly women's co-op meeting, followed by an hour of literacy lessons, ending, finally, with fellowship over tea and cookies—the latter made with the gourmet chocolate chips delivered in Vina's latest care package. These dear, hard-working ladies ensured that not a crumb of the rare sweet treat remained.

At the bend in the dusty lane, Luz turned to offer one last wave, which I returned with a smile as she resumed her waddling gait. Her baby would arrive any day. I sent up a silent prayer for a swift and safe delivery as I moved past Matilde, who had remained behind to finish nursing her own baby girl. I lowered myself into the hammock suspended between the house and a pillar, grateful, as always, for this housewarming gift from Jonas. It had become my happy place, a favored spot to spend a lazy hour with a book, rocked by the breeze, riversong as my soundtrack.

I closed my eyes, my heart drifting toward thankfulness, still hardly daring to believe this life belonged to me. This place. This work. These people. And my man. *Jonas*. My lips curled upward at the mere thought of his name.

A contented slurp from Matilde's baby made me open my eyes to find my friend's warm gaze alight on mine. "You are happy here, sí?" Matilde's hand, worn rough by work, softly cupped the downy head of her newest child. The baby-on-the-way formed the merest bump beneath the thick swath of her skirts.

I closed my eyes again, making no effort to hide my smile. "You know I am. I love it here."

"That makes me so happy. Sometimes people come here from far away but do not stay. I think, perhaps, our life is too hard." I heard the hurt behind her words, the rejection of her lifestyle—and of herself. The unspoken verdict that she is not enough. Not enough to stay for.

The very opposite of what I wanted these women to know about themselves, the message I prayed they never heard from me. "It is hard, but it is good. So good. I don't even want to think about leaving for a very long time. It hurts my heart too much." My gaze settled on the black-fuzzed head outlined against the generous curve of Matilde's breast. I loved watching her nurse. It filled me with a longing still indefinable, yet not one I cared to quench.

Following my gaze, a sparkle came into Matilde's eyes. "Why are you not pregnant, my friend? You do not like sex?"

I laughed, allowing the shift in subject. "I like sex just fine."

"Then how is it you and Jonas are not making babies? So that you also may have this." Glancing down, she smiled into the black eyes gazing so trustingly into her own.

I laughed again. "I've told you why. It's the little pill I take every day. Precisely to make sure this doesn't happen."

"But this I do not understand. Jonas does not want it to happen? Or you?"

"We do, someday. But not yet." And not here, I added silently but did not say. Childbirth in this region, even with the medical care La Fuente brought to the community, remained too risky. Two babies born in Magdalena last year died, and one mom in Cortadera didn't survive childbirth. "We want to wait until we can be closer to our families."

"Ah yes, that is good." This, at least, Matilde understood. "Women need their families. But what will you do without your mother? Your sister—Sarah?—will be there for you, sí?"

Unwittingly, I flinched. Matilde couldn't know she'd touched a wound—a wound entirely of my own making but now so deep I had no idea how to heal it. Matilde didn't know. No one did. Not even Jonas. Oh, he knew there was something. When my defenses were down, after an emotionally tough day, guilt would creep into my sleep, making me a restive bed partner and robbing us both of slumber. And just last week, he'd caught me trying to write *something*—a plea for understanding? a begging for forgiveness? But whereas words had always provided me a way through, now they only mocked me. How could words possibly mean anything to Sarah?

Matilde peered at me quizzically, making me realize I'd not answered her question. "I would like her to be. But I'm not sure she would."

"Why not? Sisters take care of each other, no?"

Her words—so close an echo of Dad's mantra, and such an unwelcome reminder of how badly I had failed—made my breath catch. "They should, yes."

"Then … ?"

I shook my head, knowing I could never untangle the complicated mess I'd made of my relationship with Sarah. How, after that terrible discovery among Mom's things, I'd allowed jealousy and insecurity to trump love and loyalty. And then made it worse by leaving. Running away, really, even as I was running toward something good. But for reasons I couldn't fathom, God hadn't allowed that to be the end of my story. In fact, undeservedly, I'd found myself in a place and among people who allowed me to be someone more like He wanted me to be. Loved without condition by Him and, therefore, able to unconditionally love the people around me.

Someone, in fact, a lot more like Sarah.

Matilde's child finished her feeding and slumbered, content, in her mother's arms, milk still shiny on her rosebud mouth. Matilde spoke into the silence. "Whatever it is that troubles you, *mi amiga*, nunca digas nunca, sí? Perhaps Jesus would like to resurrect whatever you believe is dead between you and your sister, just as He resurrected Lazarus from the grave."

Never say never. I stared at her, amazed as much by her uncanny perception as by her transformation. Only six months earlier, Matilde would never have had the confidence nor the faith to claim these words for herself, much less speak them aloud as encouragement to another. I let the warmth of this wrap itself around me as her words unspooled inside my head, conjuring the picture of a shroud-wrapped Lazarus emerging from the tomb to the joy of his sisters.

His sisters …

Yes.

I swung out of the hammock, almost landing on my knees in my hurry, and darted into the darkened house for a pencil and the nearest scrap of paper before returning to the sunlit porch. In answer to Matilde's bemused expression, I jotted notes as I explained the idea her words had sparked—a vision not only for the community but also for the role Sarah might play in creating it.

Matilde was nodding before I even finished. "Sí, amiga, this is what I mean. *Exactamente.*"

As I looked down at the paper scrap holding my nascent idea, a feeling stirred. Hope, welcome and warm. At this first step toward showing my sister how much she meant to me—still and always. And to perhaps speak to her heart in a way my words alone could not.

CHAPTER 49

SARAH
Selah, Washington
Present day

Tomaso emerges from his workshop as Sarah returns from her ride, her mind still swirling with new revelation and what it spells for her future. At the clatter of hooves on the courtyard tiles, Tomaso turns, surprise chasing his thick eyebrows upward. He grins, and she smiles back as she swings Sassy in his direction. Until another figure catches her eye. Dad, standing near the stables, a mug of steaming beverage in one hand, the other stuffed into the pocket of his fleece-lined jacket. Why is he here? He never comes to the stables. Ever. Too many memories of Mom.

Though the sun is behind him, casting his face in shadow, obscuring his expression, something in his stance makes her think he's been there a while. Has he been waiting for her?

Sarah glances between the two men. Harrison, realizing Tomaso has caught her attention, turns away, a slash of disappointment crossing his face. Her brow pinches as he walks toward the house. Unbidden, a thought spools out: Has she played a role in the distance between them? He favored Jenna, always. But did he have room for her as well? Perhaps she closed herself off to that possibility to avoid rejection. In holding herself away, has she chosen to look for the worst?

Is that what she's doing with Shane, too?

A band twists around her heart and tugs.

Harrison's almost reached the house when she veers Sassy in his direction. "Dad!"

He pivots. She catches a flash of surprise before he wipes it from his face. She slows Sassy to a walk and dismounts a few yards from him. His steaming coffee adds a caramel-earthy fragrance to the clean scent of the morning. She chances a glance over her shoulder at Tomaso, who offers a quick wave before continuing toward the fields, pulling on work gloves as he goes. Then she turns and faces her father.

"You've been riding." Wonder laces Dad's voice, his breath puffing into the wintry air.

"Yes."

"How did it feel?"

She pauses. "Magical."

He places his mug on a nearby barrel. "You are so much your mother's daughter."

The band around her heart tightens. "Yours, too, Dad. At least, I hope so."

"Of course you're mine, too. Didn't mean it like that."

"Then what did you mean?"

"Only that—" He strokes Sassy's glistening flank. "Well, it gives me hope to see you ride again."

"Hope?" She doesn't expect that. "Why?"

"I was watching you out there, flying across the fields. You were beautiful. And it made me hope that maybe this part of you hasn't been lost after all." He exhales. "You slept in Jenna's room last night. Why?"

"You knew?"

"You didn't think I could sleep without knowing you were safe, did you?" He shakes his head.

She looks down as she peels off her leather gloves. Truth is, she didn't give any thought to whether he might be worried. When she glances up again, he is gazing out over the vines, his expression pinched. But then he looks at her, and the light in his eyes sparks a new courage inside her. "Dad, there's something I need to tell you. About Jenna."

"Yes?" A shadow flickers in his eyes. "What is it?"

"I finally figured out how she wanted me to spend her money. Why she left it to me like that." She sucks in a breath, chilled air stinging her lungs. "I want to finish my degree. And hopefully get into a study program in Europe."

"She wanted you to go back to school." She can't read his tone. He seems neither surprised nor disappointed. For some reason, this throws her off balance.

"After my accident, I lost my way, as you know. I let it derail my dreams. But I believe Jenna wanted something more for me. She saw I'd taken a wrong turn. I'm sure now that's why she was coming home. To—to talk to me. To help me get back on course." The grooves have not disappeared from between Dad's eyes. How can she put into words what she witnessed in Bolivia, how it connects to her own future?

"In Bolivia, a woman is invisible, Dad. Just another piece of her husband's property. Though she works in the field all day, she gets no credit for it. She certainly has no say in how her income is spent.

Even though Bolivia has laws that protect her rights, the fact is centuries' worth of traditions keeps her in the shadows.

"But Jenna had a vision for these women, to bring them out of the shadows and into the light. So they can be seen ... counted ... valued. Teaching them to read and write was Jenna's starting point. She wanted them literate, educated, so they could in turn offer their families a better life."

"So you're saying Jenna wanted that for you, too? To continue your education?"

"I believe that's exactly what she wanted."

Dad lifts his gaze to the horizon and squints. "I didn't have the privilege of seeing what you saw in Bolivia. If you recall, I wasn't invited." Though he speaks lightly, she picks up the undercurrent of hurt. Then his gaze settles on her once more. "But I trust you, Sarah. You girls ... I know something got lost between you those last few years." She blinks, and he smiles. "You think I didn't notice? I'm your father. Fathers see these things. But I also saw something else, something I'm not sure you could. That deep down, you two were still as devoted to each other as when you were kids. Blood is blood, Sarah. Don't you ever forget that."

Blood is blood. Coming from Dad, she knows she could ask for nothing more by way of blessing.

But he's not through yet. "It's actually been obvious for some time that Silverwood isn't your future." His words carry an unanticipated jab. She must have flinched because he hurries on. "Now, Sarah, don't think I don't appreciate all you've done these last few years. Honestly, I don't know how I would have managed without you, especially with your sister gone. What I mean is, I know this is not how you once envisioned spending your life. I am more than grateful for what you've done. What you're doing. But I know you have other things you want to do."

"How do you know?"

"Your sister told me, the last time she was home."

She swallows down the lump that rises whenever she thinks of Jenna during that particular summer.

"I saw her watching you once, when you were entertaining a couple of kids whose parents had come for a tasting. Before you took charge, the boys had been running around, generally making a nuisance of themselves, the parents with no clue how to control them. Instead of getting mad, you took the boys out on a little field trip into the vineyard. You gave them each a pad of paper and a pencil and taught them how to sketch some of the things they found there. You managed to keep them entertained until the parents were ready to leave.

"Jenna watched it all with a smile on her face. When she realized I'd seen her, she told me I should encourage you to return to your art. To go back to school and finish your degree, and maybe one in education. I think she always regretted not getting her degree and wanted more for you."

Sarah fidgets with her gloves, smoothing out the creases between her fingers. She remembers those boys, that afternoon, though she's not thought of it since. She had no idea anyone was watching. She certainly had no idea it planted any kind of a seed.

"I didn't say anything to you about what Jenna told me because—well, because I didn't want to lose you, too," he says. "Your sister was gone and unlikely to come back. I accepted that much. Truth is, I had come to rely on you. But more than that, I simply liked having you around. My Girl Friday." His hand rests a moment on her head, a benediction, and she has to fight a prickle of tears. "When Shane came along, I began to see a way out. A way to let you go. I knew Jenna was right. This isn't your dream. It's mine. It was unfair of me to ever expect otherwise."

She stares at him, riveted in amazement as more puzzle pieces fall into place. This explains, then, why Dad has been giving Shane greater responsibilities. Trusting him to do more. Not to cut her out, but to provide her a way out.

Too often we see only what we expect to see and become blind to everything else. Tomaso said that once, and he was right. The truth has been here for some time, waiting for her to see.

And Jenna. Thickness closes her throat. Her sister did this for her. Even as Sarah navigates new territory, unsure of Dad's reaction to her news that she's leaving the vineyard, she finds herself pushing on a door that's been unlocked all along.

Sassy blows out a breath and stomps, reminding Sarah she still needs to groom her. Across the courtyard, the lights inside the dining room blink on. The vineyard is springing to life for another day.

Sarah draws a deep breath, reaching for Sassy's reins. Dad startles her by pulling her to him, wrapping her in a hug. She leans into him, her arms around his middle. "Yes, Sarah." The words reverberate inside his chest and vibrate reassuringly beneath her cheek. "Though you didn't ask, my answer is yes. I think going back to school is a good idea for you."

She smiles, but he sets her away from him and levels her a stern look. "What about Shane?"

Her euphoric bubble pops. "What about him?" Turning again toward Sassy, she gathers up the reins, but Dad stills further movement by laying a hand over hers.

"Don't you think you're being a little hard on him?"

"I don't think so, Dad." Tension returns to her arms and neck. "He's been using me. Or, at the very least, he hasn't been completely honest."

"I can understand why you'd think that, given what happened yesterday. But it may be more complicated. Shouldn't you at least listen to what he has to say? He's committed to this vineyard, to our family. I'm not convinced it's as bad as you think. And I believe he cares for you, Sarah." He rubs a hand over his chin, silvery with a day's growth of beard. "It's not just about the money."

She puffs out a breath. He could be right. She understands better now her tendency to see the worst in people instead of looking for the best. Especially, perhaps, those who are closest to her. "Okay, Dad, I'll talk to him. But no promises, okay? First I have to hear what he says. Do you know where he is?"

"Headed to town early on some errands. Should be back soon, I imagine."

"Tell you what. I've got something to do in town myself. I'll look for him there. If I don't see him, I'll talk to him this afternoon." She gives Sassy's reins a tug. As she heads for the warmth of the stables, she calls back over her shoulder, "Don't worry, Dad. I'll figure it out. I promise."

CHAPTER 50

Sarah angles Dad's Chevy truck into a slot in front of the long, low row of main street office buildings. As she steps from the cab, she eyes the mural across the street, one she's seen a thousand times but seldom paid much attention to.

It's one of Mom's. Even if Sarah didn't know it, she'd be able to guess, given the similarities between this one and the one above the Silverwood Cellars tasting counter. She's amazed, in fact, that she's never heard a visitor ask about or make the connection.

She waits for an RV to lumber by before crossing the street for a closer look. Through a series of vignettes, the mural depicts the progression of Washington agricultural history—from the maize fields of the Plateau Indians, to the wheat farms and apple orchards of the mid-twentieth century, to the vineyards of the present day. And there, in the lower right hand corner, she finds what she's looking for: her mother's signature, Monica Ridgely.

And the date, which erases any lingering doubt about the truth of Jenna's secret.

Too often we see only what we expect to see and become blind to everything else. Clues to the truth have been right in front of her all along, but not expecting to see their significance, she hasn't.

It's just past eight o'clock. Most businesses are still closed, but as she anticipated, the lights are on in Beck's office, the outer door unlocked. Although Estela, his receptionist-paralegal, hasn't yet arrived, the fragrance of fresh coffee emanates from a nearly full carafe on the credenza. The door to Beck's private office stands open, and classical music lilts from invisible speakers. Beck sits behind his desk, a half-eaten bagel resting beside a steaming mug of coffee, his attention on the open laptop in front of him.

His face lights in a smile as she pauses in the doorway. "Sarah! What a nice surprise. You should have told me you were coming to town. We could have done breakfast." He comes around his desk to hug her. She returns his embrace. When he sits again, she takes one of the two leather chairs parked in front of his desk. "I imagine you're here to talk about your money."

"Actually, no."

"Okay then." He smiles again. "What's on your mind?"

She pulls an object from her pocket and sets it on his desk beside his bagel.

He stares at the locket, the blood draining from his face, leaving his complexion chalky and gray. "Where did you get that?"

"I found it."

"Where?"

"Among Jenna's things."

"Among … Jenna's?"

"Along with some papers. A DNA report that indicates Dad isn't Jenna's biological father." She pauses. "I believe you are."

He stands abruptly and crosses to the window, his back to her. For a long moment, she hears only the faint strains of violins coming from the speakers. "How much did she know?"

"Everything, I think. Or pretty much, anyway."

With a twist of his fingers, he opens the blinds, revealing the view. Mom's mural.

"That's how it all started, you know." His eyes train on the work of art. "Nearly thirty years ago. Another lifetime."

"Will you tell me what happened? I mean, I can probably guess. But I'd like to hear it from you."

He runs a hand across his eyes and sighs. Then he begins to speak.

⁓ ⊃ ⌐ ⁓

"Your mother was in college but home for the summer." Beck speaks slowly. Lawyer that he is, he measures words carefully. "I'd been practicing in this office about five years, already a respected member of the community. I was a member of the city council who voted to commission Monica to paint that wall. I remember how impressed we were with her vision, excited to be able to offer a fresh, young talent an opportunity to shine. As if we were the ones to discover her." He smiles a little. "That summer, she came every day to paint, first outlining the scene, then filling it in, bit by bit. I found myself watching her, getting distracted from my work. The vibrant colors she chose seemed so much a reflection of her personality.

"Susan and I were going through a rough patch, her health failing along with—other issues. She was taking her frustrations out on me, getting angry about the least little wrong, giving me the silent treatment for days on end.

"My relationship with Monica began innocently enough, though I guess these things usually do. I bumped into Monica at the coffee shop one afternoon. She invited me to join her. We talked. She was so easy to relate to, so passionate about her art. And funny. I couldn't remember the last time I laughed so much. I left her company feeling more enthusiastic about my own work. A few days passed, then I invited her to lunch. And then dinner after work. It was a mistake, I know that. Given how attractive I found her and the fact that she was dating your dad, I should never have—"

He shakes his head. "Anyway, neither of us intended things between us to be anything other than platonic, until they weren't. And then it was like a runaway horse. We couldn't stop.

"I'm still not entirely sure what she saw in me. I was older, and she had a strained relationship with her dad. Maybe that had something to do with it. I don't know. Harrison had long before declared his intentions, and I know she felt pressured into accepting his proposal. Her parents liked him. *She* liked him. But I got the sense she felt smothered by all the expectations. Maybe I was her way to rebel without consequences. We thought we were getting away with it."

He breathes out, the weight of his words falling like the debris from an exploded bomb. "She went back to school in the fall. Once she was gone, it was like a drug had left my system and I could think clearly again. I knew our affair was wrong, even found myself praying that would be the end of it. I made sure Susan and I were in Europe that next Christmas, so there would be no chance of running into Monica by accident when she came home for winter break.

"While we were in London we got the call from Susan's doctor. A diagnosis, finally, for her health issues. Multiple sclerosis. It was a terrible time for us both. Even before the onset of her symptoms, we'd been unhappy together. I think we'd both toyed with the idea of divorce. But now that she was sick, that became an impossible choice. Miserable as I was, I couldn't leave her. Not then, when she needed me the most.

"Months went by, but the diagnosis still felt very new. God knew I hadn't yet come to any kind of peace about it when the school year was over and your mother came home for summer break. But I never saw her. In a small town like this, she couldn't have avoided hearing what was happening to Susan. I think she deliberately stayed away from me. And I from her. I was trying to honor my marriage. And that probably would have been the end of our affair—if it hadn't been for the art show."

He returns to his desk and lowers himself into the leather chair. Sarah remains as still as stone, too stunned to do anything more than breathe. While she had hoped for his story, she hadn't expected this ... outpouring. It's as if seeing the locket again has breached a dam, and in releasing this torrent of details, he's found relief.

"There weren't many art galleries in town in those days," he continues, "but there was one that offered local artists the chance to display their work in a summer art festival. Susan was a big supporter of the arts. She insisted we attend the festival. She had some good days, some bad, and this was one of the good ones. That night we lingered, longer than we should have. Until suddenly Susan was too tired to stay. She saw I was enjoying myself, though, so she offered to get a lift from some friends who were leaving, encouraging me to stay.

"When I finally left, it was quite late. About three miles out of town, I saw a car pulled off the road. It was Monica. Her tire had gone flat. Obviously, I couldn't leave her there, so I gave her a ride home. We talked about her show, her last school year, even Susan. It was as if the year in between had never happened. All the old attraction was there, and, well, you can imagine what happened next.

"About a month later, she came to my office to tell me she was pregnant. I remember how calm she seemed, which amazed me, because I was terrified. I couldn't do anything about it, you see. I couldn't—wouldn't—divorce Susan now.

"I asked Monica what she wanted. Did she want an abortion? To put the baby up for adoption? I'd support her financially any way she needed, but beyond that—" He shook his head, the pain of that day still clear on his face. "She said she didn't want to give me a guilt trip, only wanted me to know because she thought it was my right.

Then she said she was going to marry Harrison Lanning. I asked if he knew about the baby. She told me when she realized she was pregnant she took action to make sure Harrison would assume it was his. *That* was a hard pill to swallow." He rubbed a hand over his face as if to erase the memory. "As Jenna got older, though, I had to wonder if he guessed the truth. Surely I wasn't the only one who saw that Jenna—well, that she looked like me. It seemed so obvious. But maybe it was wishful thinking on my part. Maybe we see what we want to see. Maybe Harrison did the same. I guess I'll never know for sure."

She remembers the shadow in Dad's eyes when she mentioned Jenna this morning. "It's possible he might have known."

"You think so?" He angles her an odd look. "There is one thing that sometimes made me think so, too."

"What's that?"

"The fact that he retained me as his legal counsel. He could have chosen any one of a dozen local attorneys, half of them far more experienced than I. But he insisted on me. Why? I can't help but think it was a point of pride."

"To rub your nose in it?" The idea makes her queasy.

He shrugs. "More to prove to himself he had won, I think. In the end, I gave in. Your father can be very persuasive, you know, and your mom was busy with her own life by then. I hardly saw her. A deliberate choice on her part, I'm sure. But signing on as Harrison's counsel gave me the chance to see Jenna. I realized I did want that, at least." He picks up the locket and opens it to the miniature photograph. "I can't believe she kept this."

"I think Jenna must have found it among Mom's things after she died. And then she put two and two together."

"Well. That explains a few things."

"Like what?"

"Like why Jenna suddenly started giving me the cold shoulder whenever I was around. She had always treated me as something like a favorite uncle. When that changed, I wondered if she had found out." He folds his hands on top of his desk and looks at her. "So. What are you going to do about this?"

She shrugs. "Nothing."

"Nothing?"

"Of course not. I just wanted you to know that I know. I thought it might help, somehow. I was thinking it must have been lonely for you, all these years, to know that Jenna was yours but not to be able to love her like your daughter. And then when Jenna died, for you to know the truth and not be able to grieve for her—publicly, anyway." She considers the awful irony of the La Fuente people delivering the news of Jenna's death to Beck, one whom they assumed to be an impartial observer, so as to soften the blow to Jenna's family. No wonder Beck had waited hours before bringing Dad the news.

"Thank you, Sarah. It does help."

The outer door opens, and Estela calls a *buenos días*. She pauses in the doorway, her round face going blank. "Ai, Sarah, I did not see your name on the calendar."

"No." She stands. "I just barged in."

Estela *tsk*s. "Beck does not mind. After all these years, you are like family to him."

"True, Estela." Sarah meets Beck's glance and smiles.

CHAPTER 51

Sarah's so engrossed in replaying Beck's story that she's halfway down Main Street before remembering she meant to search out Shane while in town. Doubling back, she scans the side streets for a glimpse of his truck, then reaches for her cell to try a text, only to discover she's left her phone at home. Giving up, she heads for the vineyard and finds Shane's Ford parked in front of his cabin.

Her heart skips a beat as she knocks on his office door and enters. But Shane isn't inside, though his still-fragrant, half-empty coffee mug tells her he left quite recently, probably intending to return.

Slightly relieved to have a few more minutes before facing him, she settles in the padded, leather swivel chair behind his desk. Pivoting back and forth while trying to decide how to begin their conversation, the screensaver on his laptop catches her eye. It's a photo of the two of them the night they went out with Tyler and Mia. Before parting ways, Mia had asked Sarah to snap a picture of her and Tyler, then offered to return the favor. Sarah hasn't seen the photo until now. Shane looks happy enough, if a bit uncertain, no doubt caused by her ambivalent behavior. He had put his arm around her for the photo, and she leaned toward him, smiling obligingly. Looking at this image, no one would ever imagine they were anything but a carefree couple. She remembers thinking that night that even with the moments of awkwardness, it did feel good to be doing something as normal as going out with a guy, sharing a meal with friends.

Is that the feeling she needs to recapture now, in order to move forward?

Something he said recently comes back to her. *I'd like to involve you in more of my life. If you'll let me.* What's holding her back? It's more than his working on expansion plans behind her back. Even if there's an explanation for that, it troubles her she was so quick to suspect his motives.

What am I missing?

She glances at her watch. Ten minutes have passed. She's on duty with Vina in the restaurant in an hour, and after her early morning ride on Sassy, she needs to shower first.

She reaches for the pen on Shane's desk, but not finding any sticky notes at hand, she slides open first one drawer, then another in search of a slip of paper.

In the fourth drawer she finally discovers a notepad.

Shane ~ Let's talk. Are you free for dinner? Call me ~ Sarah.

She tears off the top sheet and returns the pad to the drawer. As she does, she spies the corner of a photograph peeking from beneath a stack of envelopes. She pulls it out. It's a date-stamped selfie of Jenna and Shane in ski suits. The day of the accident. A small shock trembles through her. Even already knowing it, seeing proof of Shane's presence that day has a disquieting effect.

In the photo, Jenna is laughing into the camera. But Shane, even as he's holding his phone to snap the shot, is looking at Jenna. And the expression on his face is— *Oh my.*

Samantha's comment rushes back: *He was so crushed when Jenna dumped him, I would never have expected him to want to hang out here of all places.*

Given his and Jenna's past, why has she never thought to wonder why Shane chose Silverwood? Perhaps because he never indulged that line of questioning, always diverting her away from the connection.

She stares at their faces, Shane's and Jenna's, and knows he's never looked at her that way.

Shane insisted that both he and Jenna had moved on after their breakup. But now she sees the truth: Shane's feelings for Jenna ran far deeper than he claimed.

He lied to me, or at least shaded the truth.

Just as with his interest in her inheritance.

What else has he been less than honest about?

The back of her neck prickles as she rummages in the drawer, unsure what she's looking for, understanding only that she'll know it when she sees it. A sheet of paper with the Silverwood emblem rests at the bottom. Dad keeps a notepad like this at his desk for writing personal notes to buyers and clients. She pulls it out. Written in Shane's own hand, it's Jenna's P.O. box in Cortadera.

Sarah goes cold. Jonas said the notes threatening Jenna were posted from different towns in Washington. Towns Shane could have easily visited as he met with buyers for their wine. Like Chelan.

Did Shane send the notes?

She turns to his computer. Considering his meticulous record-keeping, is it possible he's kept account of even something like this?

She goes into his Word documents and clicks on a file folder labeled JENNA. With a shaking hand, she mouses over the most recent document and clicks. The document opens, and the words glare from the screen.

I'm waiting.

The door scrapes open. Shane saunters in on a drift of crisp air and breaks into a grin when he sees her. "Hey, you. Harrison said you were looking for me. Glad we found each—" His smile freezes. "Sarah? What's going on?"

She drills into his gaze, plunging straight to the point. "It was you," she states. "You wrote the notes."

"Notes?" A mask slips over his face, smoothing his features. "What notes?"

"The ones Jenna received. Threatening her. Terrifying her."

His eyes widen almost imperceptibly.

"Don't bother lying, Shane." She taps his laptop screen. "I found your documents."

He stares at her for one heart-stopping moment before turning and carefully shutting the door behind him.

"Why'd you do it?" she says to his back. "For the money?"

He shakes his head.

"Then why, Shane? Why would you do such a thing? To someone you cared about."

He says something she cannot hear.

"What?"

"I said I didn't just care about her." She strains to make out his words. He turns and shuffles to the hardback chair positioned in front of the desk. "I was crazy about her." He sinks his head into his hands. His voice when he speaks sounds as if he's swallowed cotton. "The weeks we dated, they were the best days of my life. She was everything I wanted in a girl."

Sarah tries not to notice the stab his words send through her heart.

"And then she broke up with me. I begged her to tell me why, what I'd done wrong, but she wouldn't. She wouldn't tell me anything! Refused my calls, didn't answer my texts. I hated what she was putting me through. Made worse because I had to see her every day at school. A couple of months went by. It helped to go home for Christmas break. Even though it still hurt, at least I didn't have to see her anymore. I convinced myself I was getting better. Getting over her." He stops and spears Sarah with a look. "And then I saw her again."

She swallows. "On the slopes."

"Yes." He barely utters the acknowledgment, his blue eyes begging her to understand. "She actually seemed glad to see me that day. She let me talk to her. I thought things might work out between us. She seemed, I don't know, willing to listen. I went home hoping we stood a chance. And then—"

She leans forward in her chair. "What?"

He sighs. "The next day, I heard about the avalanche. What happened to you and TJ out there. The whole town was devastated. I figured Jenna would be a wreck. Everyone was talking about what a hero she was, that she'd saved you, but I knew it must have been terrible for her. TJ—" He clears his throat, shaking his head. "So I waited another day to, you know, give her some space. Then I went to see her. I—we—" He stops.

"Tell me."

Still he hesitates. "You'll hate me."

"I doubt anything you say will do much more to damage my opinion at this point."

He winces. "So I came here."

"Here?"

"To the house," he clarifies. "Your house. It was afternoon, no one here but Jenna. Your Dad, Vina, Tomaso, they were all at the hospital. With you. You were still in a coma. Jenna probably shouldn't have been left alone, but there she was. She let me in. She'd been crying. I remember thinking, 'Wow, this woman really loves her sister.' She was that upset. It was only later I realized she wasn't just upset about what had happened to you and TJ."

"It was guilt."

His head jerks slightly, then his eyes narrow. "You know?"

"Jonas told me. Before I left Bolivia. That's why Jenna was coming home. To tell me the truth."

He nods, as if this doesn't surprise him. "That night, we opened a bottle of wine. Or two. It was totally the wrong thing to do. In the state we were in, we shouldn't have gone near alcohol, either of us. Anyway, I let her talk and talk. With you in a coma and TJ dead, she was completely freaking out. She told me how much family meant to your dad. Lannings take care of their own, she said. I'll never forget the way she said it. Like it was a curse instead of a promise. She said she would never forgive herself if something happened to you. I kept telling her it wasn't her fault, it was an accident. She said, 'You don't know the half of it.' I thought she was just drunk and rambling.

"We talked and drank, then drank some more, and the next thing I knew, we ended up—" He shrugs.

"In bed."

He nods. "After she fell asleep, I lay there just looking at her. I was so happy. I was sure things were good between us again. Eventually, I fell asleep too. A few hours later, I woke up. Jenna was talking in her sleep, really agitated."

He pauses for so long Sarah's afraid he might stop if she doesn't say something to keep him going. "She often talked in her sleep. Since we were little. I remember."

His forehead furrows, as if he's reluctant to share any part of Jenna with someone else, but her comment seems enough to spur him on. "She was getting frantic," he continues. "Panicked, like. Thrashing around. So much that I was afraid she might hurt herself. I woke her up. Her eyes were all wild, unfocused. Then she started crying. Deep, horrible sounds. I'd never heard anyone cry like that before, like a wounded animal. I held her, and that's when she told me—" He stopped.

"That she'd skied down first, and TJ and I were coming after her, trying to stop her."

"Yes." He shakes his head. "'My fault, my fault.' She kept saying that, over and over. After a while, she calmed down again and fell back asleep. But in the morning, she was in bad shape. We both were. I told her I was glad that after all we'd been through, she still trusted me. Hinting, you know. Trying to get her to open up again. But she just stared at me. I figured it was part of the hangover. Even when we said goodbye, I thought things were solid between us. But then, when we got back to university, she wouldn't have anything to do with me. It was like that night had never happened. And I realized that, for her, it hadn't. She'd been so drunk, she didn't remember. Any of it. I couldn't believe it."

"Why didn't you tell anyone? About what she told you?"

"Because I still thought she might come around. A few weeks later, she dropped out of school and left the country, and I knew, finally it was over."

"Is that why you took this job—to see if four years later she'd changed her mind? You hoped to hook up again?"

"*No*. It wasn't like that. When I heard about the opening, I did think it would be. . . ironic if I got the job. Then I did. Harrison talked about Jenna all the time, and it kept me kind of hoping, you know? But then, about a year ago, I overheard Tomaso on the phone with her, and I figured out she'd gotten married. I knew it was never going to happen for us. For real."

"Okay." She turns this over for a moment. "But why threaten her?"

"Harrison and I started talking about expansion, but I knew it wasn't possible given the revenues." He stretches out a pleading hand. "It wasn't for me, Sarah. It was for you. It was for your family, and this place. I remembered what she'd told me about her inheritance, how she came into it when she got married. And I thought, this is where that money belongs. Here. At the vineyard. Not in some foreign country where it would be gone like so much water down the drain."

Sarah sits back, stunned as the full truth of what he has done, what he has known, washes over her. "And all this time, you knew. You knew it wasn't my fault TJ died, yet you said nothing. You held Jenna's guilt over her head while never freeing me from mine." He looks away as she stands. "I think you'd better leave now."

"Leave?" He stands, a surprised shadow passing over his face. "You can't fire me. Only Harrison can do that."

She shakes her head, floored by his audacity. He thinks he has the right to demand anything? What's the use in even talking to him? She steps toward the door, wanting now only to be out of his presence. "Harrison certainly will fire you when he learns what you did. Of course, you could always quit, and save him that heartache." She pauses at the threshold. "You don't deserve a choice, but for his sake, I'm willing to give you one." She watches his face long enough to see her words hit. They both know now what his decision will be. She nods and shuts the door behind her.

CHAPTER 52

Six months later

Sarah's cell phone pings, announcing a new email. It's mid-afternoon, in a lull between tour buses. She's retreated to her office to catch up on invoicing, leaving Kellie to operate the tasting counter. Even with the windows open to catch a cross-breeze, her office simmers like a hothouse. She finishes inputting the current column of numbers before picking up her phone, her heart lifting when she sees the display. *Abby*.

Since Christmas, Abby's communications have become more and more sporadic. Sarah fears each new message may be the last. Not that she has had much time to dwell on this lately. When Shane quit, it left them all scrambling to fill the void, everyone shouldering a bigger piece of the load to compensate. Sarah will say this for Shane: he knew how to hire good people. Kellie has made herself indispensable, rising to meet every new challenge and then some.

Last month she took on their languishing Wine Club, introducing innovations that have already brought in dozens of new members.

And just last week, Dad hired a new winemaker, Ricardo, who is coming from Virginia with his wife and three kids. He won't start for another month, though. Just in time to gear up for harvest.

Sarah's own workload has been made even heavier by her return to school. She's shifted her focus from art history to art education. She told Abby this in her last email, including her excitement over the recent news that she's been accepted into the same study program in Florence she abandoned years before. She will leave for the year-long program within a week of Ricardo's arrival.

The last time Abby wrote, she told Sarah that after a months-long search, Rand finally found the right couple to take Jonas and Jenna's place in Magdalena. She also said Dolores and Matilde continued to be at the forefront of an effort to construct a literacy center in Cortadera. They plan to name it after Jenna, having already secured Sarah's promise to paint her envisioned murals as soon as the building is complete. Abby mentions nothing about Chase, but Sarah's resigned to that.

Abby's big news was of Rand's decision to launch a new, networked community in Romania, which, years after the fall of communism, remains one of the most impoverished nations in Europe. Her husband, Luca, has been instrumental in getting that started. They plan to have people on the ground there within months.

Sarah rises from her chair, stretches, and goes to the window to catch the breeze while she reads.

"Sorry it's taken so long to get back to you," Abby writes, "but lots of drama here and very busy. The excitement started about a month ago, soon after your last note. Normally, Sofia's father, Carlos, comes around every few weeks just to remind us that Sofia is his daughter, not ours. But when we hadn't seen him in over a month, Luca thought he should investigate. Sofia hadn't been home to her mother for weeks, so it wasn't until then that we discovered Carlos had been arrested and jailed for killing her. Sadly, by the time we learned of his situation, it was too late for us to help him. The man was dead, murdered in a jail-yard brawl before he could be arraigned.

"Sofia herself took the news with admirable perspective, though she still cries for her mother. Once we understood this new reality, Luca went to the authorities and explained the situation, expressing our wish to adopt her. I am happy to say that ball is now rolling, and we expect to officially call her our own by year's end. Equally exciting, last week Luca was finally free to correct Sofia's cleft palate. I've enclosed a snapshot for you to see the transformation. The tissue is still swollen, but she is healing rapidly. She is very excited to start speech therapy. I have a feeling that once this girl finds her voice, there will be no stopping her."

Sarah's heart rises into her throat as she clicks on the attached image. Sofia's face smiles back at her, her small nose straight, the terrible gap repaired, with only the smallest scarring to show what once was.

The rev of an engine catches Sarah's ear. Through the open window she sees a motorcycle with a single rider winding up the lane toward the house. A new customer. It reminds her of the invoicing she needs to finish before she can get back to the tasting counter. Still savoring Abby's news, she reluctantly returns to her desk.

Thirty minutes later, she crosses the courtyard. Only the motorcycle, a midnight-blue Kawasaki, is parked in front of the restaurant. The bike reminds her of Jenna, of her love-hate relationship with her motorbike. Sarah smiles as she heads for the porch.

The door to the tasting counter stands open. From inside, Kellie's pleasant contralto floats out, followed by another voice, a man's. Remembering she promised Kellie she'd replenish the syrah on her return, Sarah ducks inside the barrel room to grab a case before proceeding. As she crosses the threshold, she observes Cork, blissed out at the feet of the single customer perched on a barstool.

"Oh, hey, there you are." Kellie smiles a welcome, her crimson lipstick matching the headband holding back her dark curls. "I was just coming to fetch you."

"You were? Why—?"

The customer turns.

Sarah freezes.

Chase Maddox, more tanned than she remembers, stands up from the stool. Before she can fully register what's happening, he moves toward her. "Here, let me help you with that," he says as calmly as if they just saw each other yesterday, and lifts the box effortlessly from her arms. Up close, she notices how his aqua t-shirt accentuates his eyes, and her mouth goes dry.

"So," Chase asks, smiling, when she remains rooted mutely to the floor, "where would you like this?"

"Oh!" The long skein of unspoken words inside her head have knit themselves into a tight wad that defies untangling in this moment. She's dazzled and confused at the sight of Chase, for so many months missed and now, suddenly, *here*. "Just on the counter, please."

He sets it down and turns to her expectantly. A silence stretches out.

"Sarah?" Kellie looks at her quizzically, and Sarah finally gets ahold of herself with a laugh.

"Sorry, I'm just surprised! Kellie, in case you didn't know, this is Chase Maddox, but it looks like you've met. He's the pilot who works with Jenna's group in Bolivia. Chase, it's so good to see you." She hugs him quickly, trying not to notice his muscled shoulders, before stepping back. "What are you doing here?"

He grins. "Isn't this where you come for a tasting? I swore that's what the sign said."

"You've come here for a tasting?"

"Well—" He winks. "To start." Her pulse flutters at the look he gives her.

"How long have you been here?" His easy smile loosens her limbs, and she smiles back, discovering she can move naturally again.

"At the vineyard?" As his lips again tug up in a smile, she senses he's laughing at her.

"No, in the States."

"About a week."

"Oh." A whole week? And no one told her? "Why did you come back?"

"Furlough. Fundraising. A little R&R."

"Oh." She feels Kellie's curious stare and realizes her conversation so far has been less than sparkling. "Did you know about what's been happening with Sofia? Abby just emailed me."

"I do know about Sofia. In fact, I told Sofia before I left that I planned to see you. She asked me to give you this." From his back pocket he pulls a sheet of paper folded into a square. She unfolds it and finds a self-portrait of Sofia, her face whole and beautiful.

Sarah feels the burn of tears. "She's going to be all right, isn't she?"

He squeezes her arm softly. "More than all right, I'd say."

"Sarah." She swivels her head in Kellie's direction, having half-forgotten she is here, too. "Why don't you show Chase around? That is—" she turns to him— "if you're interested?"

He looks at Sarah. "I'm interested."

"Good!" Kellie claps her hands. "Off you go, then."

And before she realizes quite how it's happened, Sarah finds herself standing with Chase in the courtyard. She turns to him with a smile. "Where would you like to start?"

"You tell me. You're the vintner's daughter."

She takes him to the stables first, introduces him to Sassy, then they work their way around the property. In the barrel room, she asks him if he hears from Jonas.

"Every day."

"How's he doing?"

His teeth tug at his lower lip. "Struggling." Sadness flashes in his eyes.

"What about the absence seizures?" Last she knew, he was still awaiting his appointment with a neurologist for testing.

"Gone, thank God. His brain apparently healed itself. One thing he no longer has to worry about anyway."

"I'm so glad." She pauses. "He stopped answering my texts months ago, won't take my calls." She regrets letting her feelings show so much the last time they spoke, wishes she'd never begrudged him a phone call.

"I'm seeing him next week." His arm brushes her shoulder. "Is there something I can tell him for you?"

"I want him to know I understand things better now, and he was right. Jenna didn't hate me."

"It might help him to hear that."

"And you were right too, Chase." As they step outside again, into the sunshine, she looks up at him. His unwavering gaze makes her stomach flutter. "There was a reason for why she did what she did."

He runs a hand down her arm, leaving a tingling trail in its wake. "Tell me."

"I think I was a part of her vision for helping women. Helping women help themselves." She tucks her hair behind her ear. "It seems selfish on the surface, maybe, but I think it's kind of like … well, how flight attendants tell parents in an emergency to put on their own oxygen masks before helping their children. That's what I saw Jenna doing in Magdalena, helping women put on their oxygen masks so they could then help everyone else." She mentions, too, her inspiration for the murals for the literary center walls. But she stops short of telling him the secret of Jenna's conception and her role in the accident that took TJ's life, because those are secrets between sisters.

Chase listens without interrupting. When she is done, he nods. "That sounds like Jenna. I think you've found it. You knew each other better than you thought."

"I think I always thought that, deep down. She never really left me, you know. It was only her shadow that obscured the light for a time, for me. But the light never stopped shining. Not really."

They leave the buildings and head for the vineyard, the land's rugged terrain a panorama before them. As he dons his aviator shades against the brightness of the sun, his gaze sweeps the landscape. "Do you remember what you once told me, about your land?" His arm bumps against hers as they fall into step together. "It was when we flew from La Paz to Santa Cruz. I asked how your dad got started with all this. You told me about the great flood millennia before, which set into motion the events that led to the point of your dad being able to grow grapes. A disaster that set the stage for victory."

"I can't believe you remember that."

He looks down at her, his gaze holding hers for a long moment. "I think this place is more yours than you like to admit." They move into the vineyard, the soil hard beneath their feet.

She glances at him. "What do you mean?"

"You once said this vineyard belonged to your father, that you were 'just' his daughter. But you love it, too."

"I suppose I do." She smiles. "It's in my blood. Maybe the difference is I feel I'm here by choice now. And I have the hope of making my own way, which may or may not include staying on."

He searches her eyes, and she senses him taking her measure, assessing, trying to discern her thoughts. She wonders why it matters so much to him.

Deep among the vines, she spies movement, catches a flash of denim, and touches Chase's arm. "This way." She plunges into a row with countless clusters of grapes growing thick on each side. "I want you to meet someone."

As they near, her dad straightens, swiping a forearm across his perspiring forehead. "Hello. Who have we here?"

"Someone you need to meet. Chase, this is my father, Harrison Lanning. Dad, Chase Maddox. He worked with Jenna in Bolivia."

"The pilot, aren't you?" The two men shake hands.

"That's right. And I've not had the chance to tell you, sir, but I am very sorry for your loss. We all are. At La Fuente, we still feel the hole Jenna left. All the time. She's not forgotten."

"Kind of you to say, son. We miss her, too."

"I've heard a lot about you, from both your daughters."

"Well, thanks. Nice to know the old man wasn't far from their thoughts while they were so far away from me." Dad's glance travels between them, a smile toying with the corner of his mouth. "What brings you to our part of the world?"

"Well, I hear you grow good grapes."

Harrison laughs. "That we do. Among the best in the world, I believe."

The two of them fall into conversation about agriculture in general and grapes in particular. She can't help but smile at the ease with which they range over such details as pest control and market fluctuation. When Dad's cell vibrates in the holder clamped to his belt, he slips the device free and squints at its message. "Tomaso needs me in Area Four. You met Tomaso already, Chase?"

"Not yet, sir."

"He's out in the far lot, worried about the cabernets. That cool patch we had in the spring slowed things down too much for comfort. I'll go talk to him now, let him know you're here. Can you stick around for dinner?"

"Absolutely. Thank you."

"Good. I'll have Vina set an extra place."

As Dad disappears among the vines, Sarah turns to Chase. "Would you like to visit Jenna's memorial site? It's a nice walk."

They pick up Cork back at the house and set off. The dog trots ahead, seeming to know where they're heading. The sun nears the horizon, its heat unabated. Their elongated shadow-selves move before them as a breeze swooping from the Cascades ripples the hem of Sarah's white cotton sundress against her calves.

In time, they reach the place where Jenna's urn resides beneath the topsoil, the maple tree casting its shade over the grassy knoll. Fresh flowers rest atop both Jenna's grave and her mother's. *Dad*, Sarah thinks, and her heart warms knowing he was here, and recently.

Sunlight glimmers and birds twitter invisibly, hidden by the verdant limbs overhead, as Chase and Sarah gaze down at the place where Jenna's urn is interred. "I'm going back, you know." She breaks the silence. "To Magdalena. Next summer. To paint the murals on the walls of Jenna's literacy center."

"I heard. Wish I could be there to see them. Jenna always had such confidence in your talent. Maybe you'll send me pictures?"

"Won't—won't you be there to see them yourself?"

He shakes his head. "Unlikely."

"Why?" Trying to ignore the sinking of her heart, which tells her more than she cares to know.

"I've been reassigned."

"Reassigned? Where?"

"A little place called Taut, Romania. Doubt you know of it. Barely a dot on the map."

"Romania. You mean the new network Rand and Luca started?"

"You've heard." He tilts his head and his mouth curves upward in a way that makes her feel melted inside.

"Abby told me. What will you do there?"

"Construction, working with the Roma people, some piloting. They've already found me a plane. I've committed a year to them.

Beyond that—" His gaze captures hers and holds it, as if plumbing its depths for answers to questions she doesn't understand. "I told them we'll have to see."

She gazes out over the land, dismayed to find her vision blurred with tears. "I'm happy for that, Chase. I know they can use you there."

He angles himself so he's standing in front of her. His brow furrows as he brushes a strand of hair from her cheek. "This doesn't look like happiness to me."

"I—no. Sorry, it's—" Feeling the heat of his touch, she wants to lean into it. With effort, she resists. What difference does it make whether he's in Bolivia or at the North Pole? Except that picturing him in his Technicolor world helps her feel grounded somehow. As if she knows where to find him. "I'm glad for you, really." She puts on a smile, trying to convince him.

"I don't think so." He moves forward a step then pauses long, searching her face. For what, she doesn't know. "There was one little detail that tipped the Romania deal for me. Want to know what it was?"

She looks away, unable to bear the light in his eyes.

"I discovered Taut is only two-and-a-half hours from Florence by plane. Less when you catch a tail wind."

"Two-and-a-half—?" Wait, what? He knows about Italy? She raises her eyes to his, hope flying up inside her chest like a wild bird. "You're moving to Europe—for me?"

"Well, not just for you," he says gently, teasing. Then his face grows serious. "I thought—" He stops, his self-assurance faltering for the first time, and her heart softens. He must see it in her expression because now he moves a step nearer, only inches separating them. "I like you, Sarah—I have from the very start. It's not just me, is it? Sometimes I thought you felt it, too."

"I did, and it scared me." Her admission barely a breath.

He closes the distance between them, his hands reaching to cup her face and kisses her, the taste of her father's wine still on his lips. When she twines her arms around his neck, he pulls her closer still.

When they break apart, she draws back, looks him in the eyes. Those cyan eyes. "You'd take that kind of chance, leaving a place you love?" She leaves unspoken the rest: the scant week they spent together, the almost-year they've spent apart, the silence between them. How could he know? But he seems to understand what she's asking.

"Rand needed an answer. I had to commit, one way or the other. And as I told you, Bolivia has a way of revealing what's counterfeit. I knew you were the real deal first by the way you loved Sofia, then watching you struggle to honor your sister's memory when nothing about that came easily. And when it fell apart at the end ... " He shakes his head. "I tried to forget you, after you left. I knew there was another guy in the picture and that you were in such a hurting place, needing time and space to heal. That's why I didn't keep in touch. Not because I didn't care, but because I was afraid I cared too much. When Abby told me things didn't work out with that guy—well, it seemed like a sign. That I should come see you, find out if I stood a chance." He tips her chin, his mouth curving in a way that turns her insides liquid. "I do, don't I?"

She smiles her answer, linking her fingers with his as she pulls him out of the maple's guardian shadow into the sunlight. And it strikes her as appropriate that she and Chase should be marking a new beginning with each other here, in this place that memorializes Jenna. It was, after all, her life and death that brought them together. As Sarah looks back over the last year, especially those first weeks after Jenna's passing, she sees her sister's prescience, her uncanny knack to anticipate what would come. Not that Sarah believes Jenna could have foreseen this, a future between her and this man, but even so ...

The sun wraps warm arms around them, its sweet, golden light flooding the land like spilled chardonnay. And she swears she can feel her sister's pleasure.

ACKNOWLEDGEMENTS

And now for the fun part (for me anyway), in which the book is done and I get to thank all those who helped to make it so.

Many thanks to all the folks at Redemption Press for making it happen, and especially to Hannah McKenzie for your precise and gentle guidance.

Anne Mateer, editor extraordinaire. I marvel at your savvy instincts, which enable you to draw from my words the very best while knocking off the rough edges of all the rest.

Editor Nancy, whose keen eye dots my i's and crosses my t's. Thank you.

Mariela Tarner, for ensuring that my Spanish i's and t's are properly dotted and crossed. ¡Muchas gracias!

My critique partner, Sherri Sand, who understands the beauty of being loved by Jesus and loving Him back, and whose razor-sharp insights make my stories shine.

Early readers Paula Bicknell, Kim Galgano, and Linda Hren. I greatly appreciate your helpful feedback, and your friendship even more.

Scott, my steadfast and romantic husband. You keep me grounded. Without your encouragement and support, I wouldn't still be writing stories.

Jack and Madeline, whom I love beyond measure.

My Jesus, for whom nothing is impossible, as this finished book attests. I love that You love stories. Thank you for telling the best ones and for loving Your people so beautifully.

CPSIA information can be obtained
at www.ICGtesting.com
Printed in the USA
JSHW020053290423
41030JS00002B/102